Top Technique
& Special Stitch
Afghans™

the Needlecraft Shop

Editor DEBORAH LEVY-HAMBURG
Technical Editor DONNA JONES
Copy Editor SHIRLEY PATRICK
Book Design GREG SMITH
Production Artist JOANNE GONZALEZ
Production Supervisor MINETTE SMITH
Photography Supervisor SCOTT CAMPBELL
Photographer ANDY J. BURNFIELD
Photo Assistant MARTHA COQUAT

Chief Executive Officer JOHN ROBINSON
Publishing Director DAVID J. MCKEE
Book Marketing Director CRAIG SCOTT
Editorial Director VIVIAN ROTHE
Publishing Services Manager ANGE VAN ARMAN

Customer Service 1-800-449-0440
Pattern Services (903) 636-5140

ISBN: 1-57367-129-0
First Printing: 2004
Library of Congress Catalog Card Number:
2002112900

Printed in the United States of America.

Visit us at
NeedlecraftShop.com

Every effort has been made to ensure the accuracy
and completeness of the instructions in this book.
However, we cannot be responsible for human error or for
the results when using materials other than those specified
in the instructions, or for variations in individual work.

CONTENTS

INTRODUCTION

Dear Friends,

Ask anyone who knows me and they'll quickly tell you I'm not the world's most organized person. Keeping things together has never been my forté, but that doesn't mean I don't enjoy the thought of having everything right at my fingertips whenever I want it. So, with that thought in mind, this book was born!

Top Technique & Special Stitch Afghans is my idea of a truly organized crochet technique and stitch library. All in one book, you'll find everything from the basic stitches to wonderful ages-old techniques that will elevate your skills to a new level, or simply help you tune-up the skills you already have. And to help keep your memory sharp, you'll find pattern after pattern with which to practice these techniques and stitches.

Handcrafted accessories are truly a personal gift or addition to your home, but we all enjoy putting forth a little extra effort to make our crocheted items even more special. For this reason, you'll also find instructions for adding edgings, trims and other embellishments that will give your needlecraft project a look and feel of its very own.

If you've been longing to have all your favorite crochet techniques and special stitches in one handy book, then look no further. *Top Technique & Special Stitch Afghans* is the book you'll turn to again and again!

Happy stitching,

Deborah

SPECIAL-TOOL
TECHNIQUES

From its humble origins centuries ago to the modern technology of today, crochet still relies on just a few simple tools to fashion the most exquisite designs. Whether you use a plain, simple hook or a lowly broomstick, these techniques are sure to enhance your skills and strengthen your love for the art of crochet.

AMAZING NEEDLE

Spurred by the desire to create a knit-like fabric with the ease of crochet, one talented designer put on her thinking cap and set to work. From the efforts of a small group of designers came a tool that affords crocheters a completely new stitching avenue; a tool like no other—the Amazing Needle. If you have never mastered the art of knitting because two needles were one too many, then this is your chance to shine! With the Amazing Needle, new horizons in needlecraft are just waiting to be explored. Never before has one simple tool allowed the crocheter such flexibility, such freedom. Set your sights on a new adventure in crochet when you experience the Amazing Needle!

SUPPLIES AND TOOLS

For this technique, you will need an Amazing Needle Kit and the yarn of your choice, plus scissors and a yarn needle for hiding ends.

An Amazing Needle looks like a crochet hook with a cord threaded through a hole in the end of the handle. The clip keeps the stitches from falling off the end.

Amazing Needles are sized the same as standard crochet hooks and knitting needles and are available in the following sizes: 3.5mm (E or 4) to 6.5mm (K or 10.5).

(See Supplier Listing on page 174 for purchase information.)

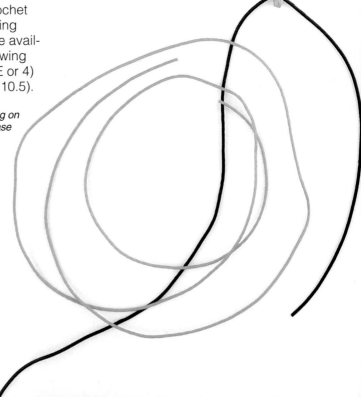

BASIC TECHNIQUE

KNITTING

Thread about 4 inches of one holding cord into the Amazing Needle; place the clip on the other end. Hold the needle like a knife with hook down.

To **cast on,** make designated number of crochet chain stitches, then, with yarn at back, skip first chain and pull up a loop in each chain across, keeping all loops on the needle *(photo A).* At the end, slide all loops onto the cord and remove the needle. Thread the second cord into the needle and place the clip on the loose end in the same manner.

To **transfer cords,** after **each following row,** slide all loops onto the cord and remove needle. Pull the cord from the previous row, thread one end into the needle and clip the other end. Alternate the two cords in this manner for the entire piece.

Knit Stitch (K)

With yarn at back, insert needle from front to back, right to left through loop on cord *(above or below the cord),* yarn over and pull through forming a new stitch on the needle *(photo B).*

Purl Stitch (P)

With yarn at front, insert needle from back to front, left to right through loop on cord *(above or below the cord),* with hook down, catch the yarn with the hook *(no yarn over)* and pull through to back forming a new stitch on the needle *(photo C).*

Bind off

Pull up a loop in first st, (pull up a loop in next st, pull through loop on needle) across *(photo D).* At end, cut yarn about 4 inches long, pull cut end through the loop on needle; pull snug.

CROCHET

Make crochet stitches the same as with a standard crochet hook. Holding cords are not needed.

Tips
& helpful hints

When picking up loops in the starting chain, unless your pattern instructs you to work into one specific loop and as long as you are consistent, you can pick up in any of the three loops of the chain stitch.

To work in flat **rows, turn** the work at end of each row; to work in joined **rounds, do not turn.**

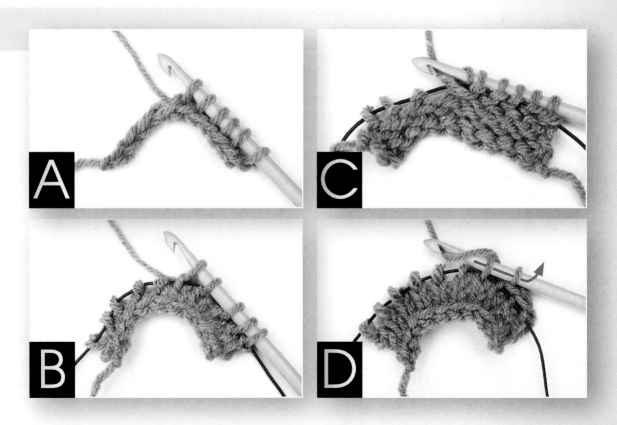

Checks & Chains by Nancy Nehring

TECHNIQUES
Amazing Needle, Color Change, Knit Stitch, Purl Stitch

FINISHED SIZE
About 32 inches square

MATERIALS
❑ Worsted yarn:
    9 oz. light blue
    9 oz. white
❑ 5.0mm (H/8) Amazing Needle

GAUGE
3 knit or crochet sts = 1 inch;
4 knit rows = 1 inch.

BASIC STITCHES
Ch, sl st, sc, dc

INSTRUCTIONS
*NOTE: For **K, P, transfer cords** and **bind off** (shown in **bold type** first time used), see Basic Technique in Amazing Needle Knitting instructions on page 7.*

Row 1: With blue, loosely ch 89, skip first ch, pull up a lp in next 5 chs, ch 12, sl st in **back bar** of first ch of ch-12 *(see illustration)*, (draw up a lp in next 6 chs, ch 12, sl st in back bar of first ch of ch-12) across to last 5 chs, pull up a lp in each ch across, turn. *(89 lps on needle, 14 ch-12 loops)*

Back Bar of Ch

*NOTES: Front of row 1 is **right side** of work; drop all ch-12 loops to right side of work.*

*When changing colors, **do not fasten off** unless otherwise stated. Carry dropped color loosely along ends of rows; pick up again when needed.*

Row 2: With white, **P** across, turn. **Transfer cords** at end of each row.

Row 3: K across, turn.

Row 4: P across, turn.

Row 5: (K 6, ch 12, sl st in back bar of first ch of ch-12) across to last 5 sts, K 5, turn. Drop white *(see Notes)*.

Row 6: With blue, P across, turn.

Row 7: K across, turn.

Row 8: P across, turn.

Row 9: (K 6, ch 12, sl st in back bar of first ch of ch-12) across to last 5 sts, K 5, turn. Drop blue.

Next rows: Repeat rows 2–9 consecutively until there are 15 white stripes, ending with a repeat of row 8.

To **weave ch-12 loops,** pull first row-1 loop through first row-5 loop, (pull next loop through last loop) up to last row; repeat for each column of loops.

Last row: Bind off first 5 sts, (insert needle through next ch-12 loop and through next st, yo, pull through both lps as one, bind off 5) across. **Do not fasten off.**

BORDER
Rnd 1: With right side facing you, working around outer edge, work 3 sc evenly spaced across every 4 rows and sc in each st around with 3 sc in each corner, join with sl st in first sc changing to white *(see illustration)*.

Color Change

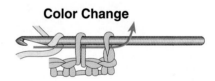

Rnd 2: With white, ch 3, dc in each st around with 3 dc in each center corner st, join with sl st in top of ch-3 changing to blue. Fasten off white.

Rnd 3: Ch 1, sc in each st around with 3 sc in each center corner st, join with sl st in first sc. Fasten off.❧

BROOMSTICK LACE

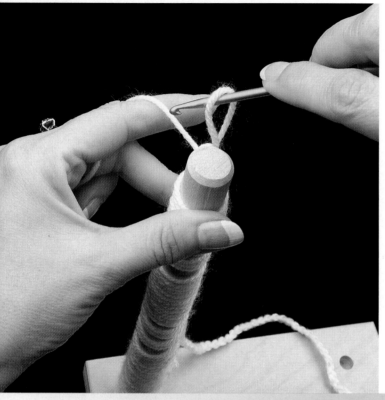

Needlecraft historians tend to believe the origin of crochet lies with fishermen who used wooden bobbins and twine to fashion nets. Through the ages, the art evolved and took on a more civilized form. Chunky string and large pieces of wood gave way to delicate threads and gracefully shaped hooks. Yet somewhere along the line, a curious crafter looked upon a lowly broomstick and wondered, "Could something as simple as an old wooden handle create elegant lace?" There was probably some experimentation at first, but in the end the result was amazing. From a humble beginning comes an elegant end—broomstick lace.

SUPPLIES AND TOOLS

For **broomstick lace,** you'll need a "broomstick" or rod, called a **pin,** to hold loops. This can be a large knitting needle *(up to size 35 or size 50),* a dowel, or even a true broomstick; just so the shaft is the desired size. You'll also need a crochet hook, yarn, scissors, and a yarn needle for hiding ends.

The **Loop Crochet Work Station** is a handy tool consisting of a flat base which rests in your lap to hold the pin as you work. It removes some of the difficulty involved in holding a crocheted piece, crochet hook, yarn and a broomstick all at the same time.

The Work Station has four different-size pins with complete instructions included.

(See Supplier Listing on page 174 for purchase information.)

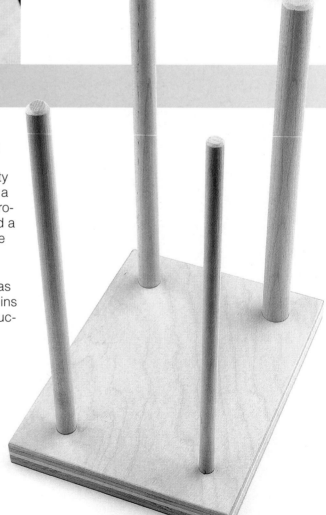

BASIC TECHNIQUE

Begin with a crocheted foundation chain or row of stitches; do not turn the work. Hold the broomstick pin in your left hand and the crochet hook in your right hand like a knife.

For each **loop,** working from left to right, insert the hook in the stitch on the previous row, pull up a long loop and place it over the pin *(photo A),* pull the loop snug but not tight. Repeat until the designated number of loops are on the pin.

To **single crochet (sc) in loops,** at beginning of the row, pull loop up to height of row or make a chain to match height of row; insert hook through center of designated number of loops at same time *(usually about five—photo B)* and remove pin, yarn over and pull through loops, then complete as sc stitch; make the designated number of sc stitches in each group of loops in this manner.

Increases can be made by going through fewer loops as you work the single crochet row, or by working extra single crochet stitches into the group of loops *(photo C).*

Decreases can be made by going through more loops as you work the single crochet row, or by working fewer single crochet stitches into the group of loops *(photo D).*

Tips & helpful hints

You will normally work the same number of single crochet stitches in each group of loops as there are loops in the group.

Corners will lay square if you work half the single crochet stitches through the group of loops, then chain about four or so chains and work the remainder of the single crochet stitches through the same loops. On the next row, pull up a loop in each chain and in each single crochet stitch.

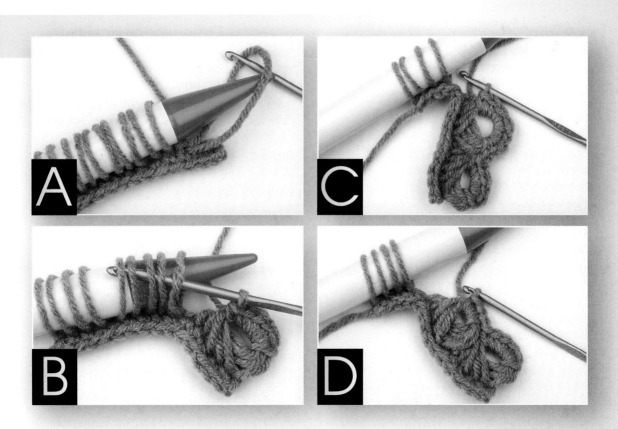

Victorian Lace by Maggie Weldon

TECHNIQUES
Broomstick Lace, Color Change,
Fringe Embellishment

SPECIAL STITCH
Back Loops

FINISHED SIZE
About 49 inches x 63½ inches,
not including Fringe

MATERIALS
❑ Worsted yarn:
   18 oz. white
   12 oz. blue
   12 oz. pink
   12 oz. green
❑ No. 35 broomstick lace pin or similar
   ¾-inch-diameter rod
❑ J crochet hook or size hook needed to
   obtain gauge

GAUGE
9 sc and chs = 2 inches; 8 rows in pattern =
3¼ inches.

BASIC STITCHES
Ch, sc

INSTRUCTIONS

Row 1: With J hook and blue, leaving an 8-inch
end, ch 286, sc in second ch from hook, sc in
each ch across, **do not turn.** *(285 sc made)*

NOTES: *Refer to Broomstick Lace Basic
Technique on page 11.*

*When joining new yarn or fastening off,
always leave an 8-inch end to be
incorporated into Fringe.*

*When **changing colors** (see Stitch Guide on
page 175), work across row until last 2 lps of
last sc are on hook; yo with new color and complete sc. Cut off last color leaving 8-inch end.*

Row 2: Slip last lp onto broomstick pin; working this row from left to right in **back lps** *(see
Stitch Guide),* (pull up lp in next st and place
on pin—*see Notes above)* across; **do not
turn.** *(285 lps on pin)*

Row 3: Pull lp on hook up to 1 inch long,
insert hook through center of first 5 lps at
same time and remove from pin, yo, pull

through, complete as sc, work 4 more sc
in same 5 loops; (work 5 sc in next 5 lps)
across; **do not turn.** Fasten off.

Row 4: Working this row in **back lps,** join
white with sc in first sc, (ch 1, skip next sc,
sc in next sc) across, turn.

Row 5: Ch 1, sc in first sc, sc in next ch sp,
(ch 1, skip next sc, sc in next ch sp) across
with sc in last sc, turn.

Row 6: Ch 1, sc in first sc, (ch 1, skip next
sc, sc in next ch sp) across to last 2 sc, ch 1,
skip next sc, sc in last sc, turn.

Row 7: Ch 1, sc in first sc, sc in next ch sp,
(ch 1, skip next sc, sc in next ch sp) across
to last sc, sc in last sc changing to pink *(see
Notes);* **do not turn.** Fasten off white.

Row 8: With pink, slip last lp onto broomstick
pin; working this row from left to right, (pull up
a lp in **back lp** of next st or ch and place on
pin) across; **do not turn.**

Row 9: Pull lp on hook up to 1 inch long;
insert hook through center of first 5 lps and
remove from pin, yo, pull through, complete
as sc, work 4 more sc in same 5 loops, (work
5 sc in next 5 lps) across; **do not turn.**

Row 10: Slip last lp onto broomstick pin, (pull
up a lp in **back lp** of next st and place on pin)
across; **do not turn.**

Row 11: Pull lp on hook up to 1 inch long;
(work 5 sc in next 5 lps) across; **do not turn.**
Fasten off.

Rows 12–15: Repeat rows 4–7, changing to
green in last st of last row.

Rows 16–19: With green, repeat rows 8–11.

Rows 20–23: Repeat rows 4–7, changing to
blue in last st of last row.

Rows 24–27: With blue, repeat rows 8–11.

Rows 28–121: Working in color sequence
of 4 rows each white, pink, white, green,
white, blue as established, repeat rows 4–11
consecutively, ending with row 9 and blue. At
end of last row, fasten off.

FRINGE
1: For each **Fringe,** cut two 14-inch-long

Continued on page 21

Flower Broomstick by Alice Hyche

TECHNIQUES
Broomstick Lace, Fringe and Appliqué Embellishments

SPECIAL STITCHES
Cross Stitch Variation, Post Stitch

FINISHED SIZE
About 39 inches x 60 inches, not including Fringe

MATERIALS
❑ Worsted yarn:
    32 oz. off-white
    16 oz. blue
    Small amount pink
❑ 7-inch square of cardboard
❑ Loop Crochet Work Station with rod 4 or size 17 knitting needle (broomstick pin)
❑ H crochet hook or size hook needed to obtain gauge

GAUGE
H hook and rod 4 or size 17 needle, 5 sc = 1 inch; 2 rows in lace pattern = 1 inch.

H hook, 4 sts or chs in Border pattern = 1 inch; 2 rows in Border pattern = 1¼ inch.

BASIC STITCHES
Ch, sl st, sc, hdc, dc

INSTRUCTIONS

CENTER
Row 1: With crochet hook and off-white, ch 166, sc in second ch from hook, sc in each ch across, **do not turn.** *(165 sc made)*

NOTE: *Refer to General Instructions in Broomstick Lace Basic Technique on page 11.*

Row 2: Slip last lp onto broomstick pin; working this row from left to right, skip first st; inserting hook from back to front to back around **posts of sts** *(see **back post** in Stitch Guide on page 175),* (pull up lp around next st and place on pin—*see Note above*) across; **do not turn.** *(165 lps on pin)*

Sc sts form ridges on front side of work.

Row 3: Pull lp on hook up to 1 inch long, insert hook through center of first 5 lps and remove from pin, yo, pull through,

complete as sc, work 4 more sc in same 5 loops, (work 5 sc in next 5 lps) across; **do not turn.**

Rows 4–107: Repeat rows 2 and 3 alternately.

Rnd 108: Work around outer edge as follows:
A: Ch 1, sc in first 5 sts, (skip next st, sc in next 4 sts) 32 times *(133 sc made);*
B: Working in ends of rows, 3 sc in first row for corner, (evenly space 2 sc across next lp row, sc in next sc row) across; work 2 more sc in end of last row for corner *(164 sc in ends of rows);*
C: Working on opposite side of starting ch on row 1, sc in first 5 chs, (skip next ch, sc in next 4 chs) 32 times *(133 sc on row 1);*
D: Repeat step B, join with sl st in first sc. Fasten off. *(594 sc made)*

Border
NOTES: *Second st of 3 sts worked at corner is **center corner st.***

*For **cross stitch variation (cross st),** ch 1, skip next 2 chs or sts, dc in next 2 sts, dc back around last 2 dc into second skipped st, leave first skipped st or ch unworked.*

Rnd 1: With H hook, join blue with sl st in center corner st at beginning of either long edge *(see Notes above); complete rnd as follows:*
A: Ch 4, 2 dc in same st as sl st *(ch-4 counts as dc and corner ch-1 sp);*
B: Cross st *(see Notes above)* 40 times ending at next corner, ch 1, (2 dc, ch 1 for corner, 2 dc) in center corner st;
C: Skip next 2 sts, cross st 33 times ending one st before next center corner st, skip next st, ch 1, (2 dc, ch 1 for corner, 2 dc) in center corner st;
D: Repeat step B;
E: Skip next 2 sts, cross st 33 times, skip last st, dc in same st as first ch-4, join with sl st in third ch of ch-4. *(146 cross sts, 16 dc, 4 corner ch sps made)*

Rnd 2: (Sl st, ch 4, 2 dc) in next corner ch sp; *complete rnd as follows:*
A: Skip next dc of 2-dc group, dc in next space between dc, skip next dc of same 2-dc group;

Continued on page 21

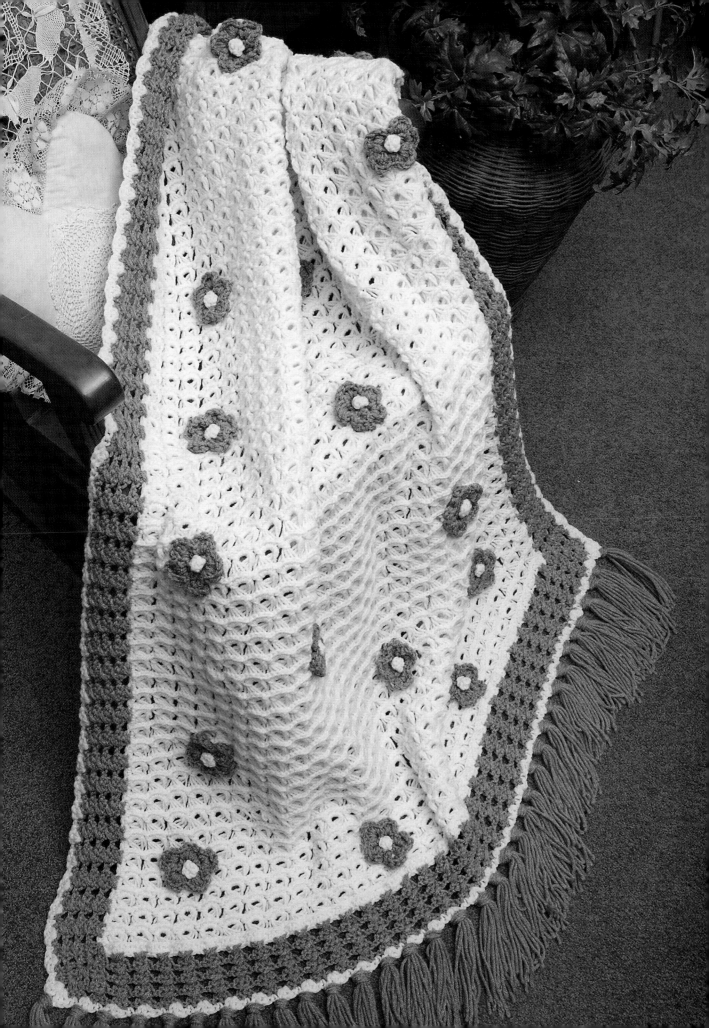

CRO-TATTING

Shrouded in the mists of time, the genteel art of shuttle tatting tells a story of days gone by when all refined ladies were taught the needle arts. Almost as if enchanted by the fairies of the netherworld, beautiful shuttles danced back and forth between dainty fingers to form exquisite lace. As the years passed, another tool made its mark in the tatter's realm—the lowly needle. Never as beautiful as a shuttle, but just as deft, a long, plain needle was found to create lace to rival any lady's shuttle. Today, tatters have choices galore, but only Cro-Tatting easily blends the best of crochet with tatting. With the ease of crochet and the beauty of tatting, Cro-Tatting is a technique you are sure to love.

SUPPLIES AND TOOLS

For **Crochet Tatting (Cro-Tat),** you'll need the special hooks described below, along with yarn, scissors, ruler, etc. and a yarn needle for hiding ends.

The **Cro-Tat Master Hook** is available in standard hook sizes G and H. These hooks have ¼-inch increments marked on the shaft for ease in measuring picots.

(See Supplier Listing on page 174 for purchase information.)

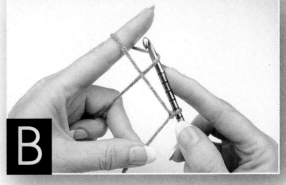

BASIC TECHNIQUE

Each **double stitch (ds)** is made in two sections as follows: For **first half,** hold the yarn with left hand and wrap clockwise around left index finger; scoop hook under yarn from front to back toward the fingertip *(photo A)* and lift yarn off finger to form a loop on the hook, pull yarn slightly snug. Move right index finger over loop just made to hold it in place. For **second half,** wrap yarn counter-clockwise around left index finger; scoop hook under the yarn from back toward the fingertip *(photo B)* and lift yarn off finger to form loop on the hook. Pull yarn to slightly tighten this loop against the last loop; hold in place with right index finger.

For **picot (p),** hold the yarn against the hook with right index finger and make the next ds ½ inch from the last ds *(photo C),* slide the ds just made back to the previous ds forming a loop; the loop is the picot. Make picots ½ inch long unless instructed otherwise.

For **joined picot (jp),** pull up lp in designated place leaving lp on hook *(this lp is not counted as a st);* continue making ds as instructed.

To **close ring (close),** make a loop a little longer than stitches on hook *(photo D),* taking care not to lose loop, yo above loop and pull through all stitches on hook forming second loop *(photo E),* still keeping second loop on hook; insert hook into first loop *(photo F),* pull second loop to tighten first loop, then pull end of yarn to tighten second loop; continue until both loops are snug around hook, yo, pull through both loops on hook forming a ring.

Tips
& helpful hints

Always work loosely as you make double stitches; it is more difficult to pull the hook through tight stitches.

While learning the technique, you may need to pull the hook through the double stitches one at a time. However, with a little practice, you will soon become adept at pulling the hook through all stitches on the hook at once.

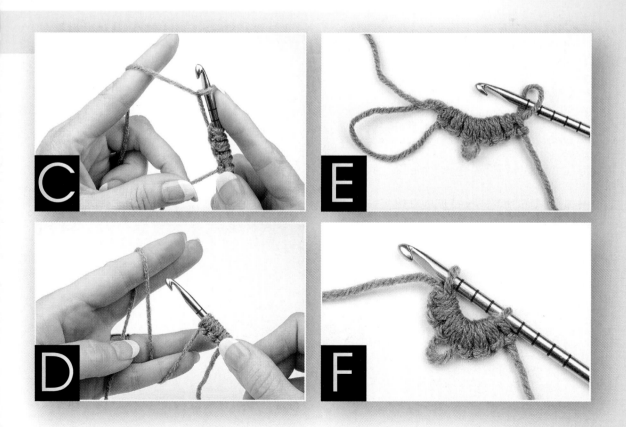

Autumn Fields by Tammy McInroe

TECHNIQUES
Cro-Tatting, Join As You Go

FINISHED SIZE
About 63 inches x 63 inches

MATERIALS
❏ Worsted yarn:
  35 oz. beige
  10 oz. grey
  10 oz. gold
  10 oz. green
  5 oz. off-white
❏ Size H Cro-Tat Master Hook or size hook
  needed to obtain gauge

GAUGE
Ring = 1⅛ inches across; Flower Motif =
4½ inches across, not including picots;
Connector Motif = 2 inches across.

BASIC STITCHES
Ch, sl st

INSTRUCTIONS

FLOWER MOTIF (make 140)
*NOTE: For ds, p, jp and **close** (shown in **bold type** first time used), see Cro-Tatting Basic Technique on page 17.*

Rnd 1: For **petals,** with beige, place slip knot on hook, ch 1; *complete rnd as follows:*
A: Make ring of 4 **ds, p,** 4 ds, p, 4 ds, p, 4 ds, **close;** ch 4;
B: Make ring of 4 ds, **jp** in last p made *(in previous ring),* 4 ds, p, 4 ds, p, 4 ds, close; ch 4;
C: Repeat step B five more times for a total of seven rings;
D: Make ring of 4 ds, jp in last p made, 4 ds, p, 4 ds, jp in first p of first ring, 4 ds, close;

ch 4, join with sl st in first ch-1. Fasten off.

Rnd 2: For **center,** with grey, place slip knot on hook, ch 1; make ring of 4 ds, jp in any ch-4 sp on rnd 1, (4 ds, skip next ch-4 sp on rnd 1, jp in next ch-4 sp) 3 times, close, skip last ch-4 sp on rnd 1, join with sl st in first ch-1. Fasten off.

STRIP (make 14)
Each Strip uses 10 Flower Motifs. Assemble Strips with fronts of all Motifs facing you.

First Connector Motif
Rnd 1: With gold, place slip knot on hook, ch 1; *complete rnd as follows:*
A: Make ring of 3 ds, jp in any p on one Flower Motif *(see A on Motif Assembly illustration),* 3 ds, close; ch 1;
B: Make ring of 3 ds, jp in next p on same Flower Motif *(B on illustration),* 3 ds, close; ch 1;
C: Make ring of 3 ds, jp in any p on another Flower Motif *(C on illustration),* 3 ds, close; ch 1;
D: Make ring of 3 ds, jp in next p on same Flower Motif *(D on illustration),* 3 ds, close; join with sl st in first ch-1. Fasten off.

Rnd 2: With off-white, place slip knot on hook; make ring of ch 1, jp at base of any ring on rnd 1, 3 ds, (jp at base of next ring on rnd 1, 3 ds) 3 times, close, join with sl st in first ch-1. Fasten off.

Next Connector Motif (make 8)
Rnd 1: With gold, place slip knot on hook, ch 1; *complete rnd as follows:*
A: Make ring of 3 ds, jp in **third free p** from last worked p on **last** Flower Motif connected to Strip *(see E on Motif Assembly illustration),* 3 ds, close; ch 1;
B: Make ring of 3 ds, jp in next p on same

Motif Assembly

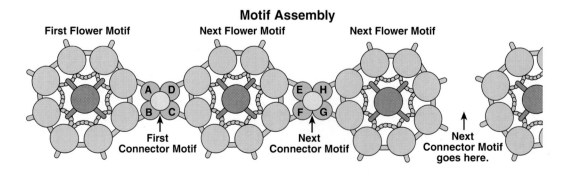

First Flower Motif   Next Flower Motif   Next Flower Motif

First Connector Motif

Next Connector Motif

Next Connector Motif goes here.

Autumn Fields

Continued from page 18

Flower Motif *(F on illustration),* 3 ds, close; ch 1;
C: Make ring of 3 ds, jp in any p on another
Flower Motif *(G on illustration),* 3 ds, close; ch 1;
D: Make ring of 3 ds, jp in next p on same
Flower Motif *(H on illustration),* 3 ds, close;
join with sl st in first ch-1. Fasten off.

Rnd 2: Repeat rnd 2 of First Connector Motif.

STRIP JOINING

Hold Strips with fronts of Motifs facing you;
rotate Strips as needed to join rings where
instructed.

First Fill-in Motif: To **join two strips,** working in opening between first and second
Flower Motifs from ends of Strips, with green,

place slip knot on hook, ch 1; *complete rnd
as follows:*
A: Make ring of 3 ds, jp in ch-1 of Connector
Motif on Strip at left *(see A on Strip Assembly
illustration),* 3 ds, close; ch 5;
B: Make ring of 3 ds, jp in next p on Flower
Motifs of both Strips at same time *(B on
illustration),* 3 ds, close; ch 5;
C: Make ring of 3 ds, jp in ch-1 of Connector
Motif on Strip at right *(C on illustration),*
close; ch 5;
D: Make ring of 3 ds, jp in next p on Flower
Motifs of both Strips at same time *(D on
illustration),* 3 ds, close; ch 4, join with sl st in
first ch-1. Fasten off.

Next Fill-In Motif *(make 8):* Working in next
opening between Flower Motifs, repeat First
Fill-In Motif.

Repeat until all Strips are joined.❧

Strip Assembly

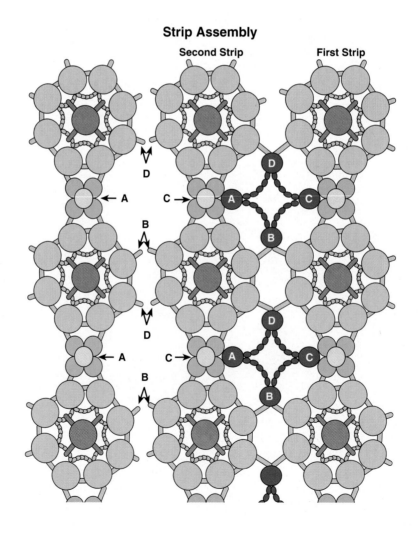

Flower Broomstick

Continued from page 14

B: Skipping ch-1 sps and working into dc, cross st in each cross st across to dc group at next corner, ch 1;

C: Repeat step A, (2 dc, ch 1, 2 dc) in corner ch sp; repeat step A;

D: Repeat steps B, C, B, C, B;

E: Repeat step A, dc in same ch sp as first ch-4, join with sl st in third ch of ch-4. *(146 cross sts, 24 dc, 4 corner ch sps)*

Rnd 3: (Sl st, ch 4, 2 dc) in next corner ch sp, *cross st across to next corner ch sp, (2 dc, ch 1, 2 dc) in corner ch sp; repeat from * 2 more times, cross st across, dc in same ch sp as first ch-4, join with sl st in third ch of ch-4. *(154 cross sts, 16 dc, 4 corner ch sps)*

Rnd 4: Repeat rnd 2. Fasten off. *(154 cross sts, 24 dc, 4 corner ch sps)*

Rnd 5: Join off-white with sc in second dc of 3-dc group before any corner ch sp, skip next dc; *complete rnd as follows:*

A: (3 dc, ch 1, 3 dc) in corner ch sp, skip next dc of 3-dc group, sc in next dc, skip next ch;

B: (3 dc in first dc of next cross st, skip next dc, sc in next dc, skip next ch) across to 3-dc group at next corner;

C: 3 dc in next dc, sc in next dc, skip next dc, (3 dc, ch 1, 3 dc) in corner ch sp, sc in second dc of next 3-dc group;

D: Repeat steps B, C, B, C, B, 3 dc in last dc, join with sl st in first sc. Fasten off.

FLOWER APPLIQUÉ (make 23)

Rnd 1: For **petals,** with H hook and blue, ch 5, sl st in first ch to form ring, ch 4, (sc in ring, ch 3) 4 times, join with sl st in first ch of ch-4. *(5 ch sps made)*

Rnd 2: (Sc, hdc, 3 dc, hdc, sc) in each ch sp around, join with sl st in first sc. Fasten off.

Rnd 3: For **center,** with pink, leaving a 6-inch end, ch 6, sc in first ch to form ring, sc next 2 chs tog, sc in next ch, sc next 2 chs tog; continuing on past beginning of rnd, (sc next 2 sts tog) 3 times. Leaving 6-inch end, fasten off.

With hook, pull last 6-inch end through starting ch-6 to back of center; tie both ends tightly together to form a ball.

Tie 6-inch ends to center of rnd 1.

Sew Flower Appliqués at random to front of Afghan, taking care that stitching does not show on back.

FRINGE

1: For each **Fringe,** cut eight strands of blue yarn each 14 inches long. Hold all strands together as one and fold in half. Insert crochet hook from back to front through st, pull fold through st, pull ends through fold; pull snug. Trim ends even.

2: Fringe in second dc of each 3-dc group across each short edge.

3: Trim ends even. ❧

Victorian Lace

Continued from page 12

strands of yarn of same color as row. Hold both strands together as one and fold in half. Insert crochet hook from back to front through end of row, pull fold through row, pull strand ends *(and any same-color 8-inch end)* through fold; pull snug.

2: Matching row colors, Fringe in each end of each row on Afghan.

3: Trim all ends even. ❧

CROCHENIT

Decades ago when ponchos and purses reigned as the accessory of choice, a crochet form evolved that married the ease of crochet with the look of knit. Called "Crochenit" by the creator, Mary Middleton, this fun-and-easy technique offered stitchers the ability to fashion garments with the look and feel of knit while using a crochet hook. An offshoot of the double-ended hook technique, Crochenit counters the notion all crochet must be thick and bulky. Never before could crocheters create wearables and household items as soft as knit, yet as easy to make as crochet.

SUPPLIES AND TOOLS

For **Crochenit,** you'll need a double-ended Crochenit hook or cable hook with two stoppers and yarns of your choice, along with scissors and a yarn needle for hiding ends.

afghan hook or a circular knitting needle, but it has a crochet hook at both ends.

(See Supplier Listing on page 174 for purchase information.)

A Crochenit hook has a long slender shank that can hold multiple loops *(or stitches),* similar to a standard

BASIC TECHNIQUE

Even if you normally crochet holding your hook like a fork or pencil, hold the Crochenit hook like a knife; this makes your work go much faster and easier.

While you are learning the technique, use two contrasting-color skeins of yarn so you can clearly see your rows and stitches.

Slide lps to opposite end of hook and turn rows only when stated in instructions.

Work **basic stitch** as follows *(Special Stitches for each project are included in the instructions):*

Row 1: Chain (ch) the designated number of ch sts; keeping all loops on hook, skip first ch from hook, pull up a lp in each ch across, **do not turn. To work sts off hook,** yo, pull through one lp on hook *(photo A),* (yo, pull through 2 lps on hook) across *(photo B).*

Row 2: Skip first vertical bar, pull up a lp in each **vertical bar** *(photo C)* across to last vertical bar; for **last stitch,** insert hook under last vertical bar and strand directly behind it *(photo D)* and pull up a lp; work sts off hook.

Next rows: Repeat row 2 for number of rows stated.

Last row: Ch 1, skip first vertical bar, sl st in each vertical bar across. Fasten off.

Tips
& helpful hints

Red means "Stop" and green means "Go"! Lay the green stopper aside while you work. Each time you finish a row of stitches, turn the hook over and transfer the red stopper to the opposite end. When you lay your project aside, place the green stopper on the end where you will begin stitching next time.

To keep yarns from tangling, place one skein on each side of you. Turn your hook counterclockwise after one row, then clockwise after the next row.

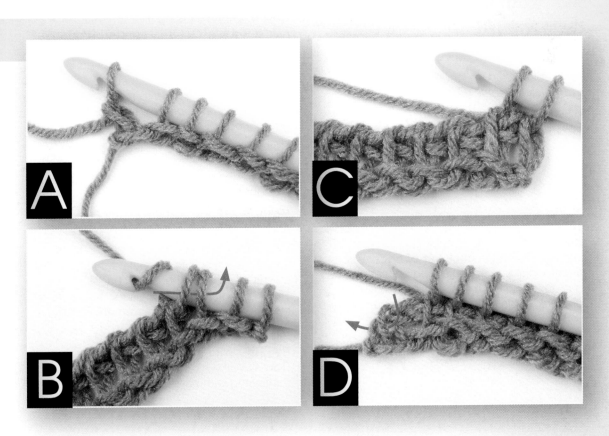

Wildberry Ripple by Darla Fanton

TECHNIQUES
Crochenit, Ripple, Tassel Embellishment

SPECIAL STITCHES
Back Loops, Cluster

FINISHED SIZE
About 46 inches x 64 inches,
not including Tassels

MATERIALS
❑ 26 oz. navy worsted yarn
❑ 24 oz. blue variegated chunky yarn
❑ 7-inch square of cardboard
❑ Yarn needle
❑ K crochet hook (for edgings)
❑ Crochenit™ hook

GAUGE
With crochenit hook, 27 sts of Panel =
about 7½ inches wide before edging;
5 rows =1½ inches.

BASIC STITCHES
Ch, sl st, sc

INSTRUCTIONS

PANEL (make 6)
NOTES: *Read Crochenit Basic Technique on
page 23 before beginning.*

Drop color when no longer needed **(do not
cut),** *pick up again when needed.*

*When picking up a lp in horizontal bar, insert
hook under* **top strand** *only (see illustration).*

Horizontal Bar

Row 1: With crochenit hook and navy, ch 27
loosely; working in **back bar of ch** *(see illustration),* pull up a lp in second ch from hook,
pull up a lp in each ch across, turn. *(27 lps
on hook) Slide all lps to opposite end of hook.*

Back Bar of Ch

Row 2: With variegated, **work lps off hook,
do not turn.** *(One lp on hook)*

Row 3: With variegated, ch 1, skip first 2
horizontal bars, (pull up a lp in next horizontal
bar—*see Note,* yo, pull up a lp in same bar,
skip next horizontal bar) 5 times; *complete
row as follows:*
A: For **center point,** (pull up a lp, yo, pull up
a lp) all under next vertical bar, (pull up a lp,
yo, pull up a lp) all in next horizontal bar, (pull
up a lp, yo, pull up a lp) all under next vertical bar *(center point completed);*
B: (Pull up a lp in next horizontal bar, yo, pull
up a lp in same bar, skip next horizontal bar)
5 times, skip next 2 horizontal bars, pull up a
lp in last horizontal bar, turn. *(41 lps on hook)
Slide all lps to opposite end of hook.*

Row 4: With dropped navy, to **work lps off
hook,** yo, pull through first lp on hook, (ch 1;
to form **cluster,** yo, pull through 4 lps on
hook—*cluster made)* across to last lp, ch 1,
yo, pull through 2 lps, **do not turn.** *(Each
ch-1 forms horizontal bar—14 horizontal bars,
13 clusters, 2 vertical bars)*

Row 5: With navy, skip first vertical bar and
next horizontal bar, (pull up a lp in horizontal
bar at top of next cluster, pull up a lp in
next horizontal bar) 12 times, pull up a lp in
horizontal bar at top of next cluster, skip next
horizontal bar, pull up a lp in last vertical bar,
turn. *(27 lps on hook) Slide all lps to opposite
end of hook.*

Row 6: With dropped variegated, yo, pull
through first lp on hook, (yo, pull through
2 lps on hook) across, **do not turn.** *(One lp
on hook)*

Rows 7–212: Repeat rows 3–6 consecutively,
ending with row 4.

Row 213: With navy, ch 1, sl st in first horizontal bar, (sl st in horizontal bar at top of next
cluster, sl st in next horizontal bar) 12 times, sl
st in horizontal bar at top of next cluster, sl st in
last vertical bar, **do not fasten off.** Transfer lp
on hook to K hook to work Edging.

Edging
Row 1: With variegated side facing you and
continuing with navy, working in ends of rows,
Continued on page 31

CROCHET 'N' WEAVE

Crochet 'n' Weave™ is a simple, fun-and-easy technique that only involves two stitches, double crochet and chain. Even though it is a simple technique, the look and feel of each design is far from simple. From these two stitches, you will learn to crochet a mesh fabric grid that creates the weaving foundation and the weaving technique itself.

SUPPLIES AND TOOLS

For **Crochet 'n' Weave,** you will need a crochet hook, a special weaving needle and the yarn of your choice, along with scissors and a yarn needle for hiding ends.

A weaving needle is a special needle with a large eye to accommodate a crocheted chain *(see photo).* The needles are packaged in a set of two: the needle with the smaller eye is for weaving chains made with a single strand of worsted yarn; the needle with the larger eye is for weaving chains made with two strands of worsted yarn held together.

(See Supplier Listing on page 174 for purchase information.)

A

B

BASIC TECHNIQUE

First, crochet a filet-type grid using double crochet stitches and chain-1 spaces *(photo A)*. For the multi-colored designs, crochet long chains and weave through the grid following a chart and using the following techniques.

To **attach first end,** run first end of Weaving Chain from front through grid opening, pull tail and ¼ inch of Chain to back; thread tail into weaving needle and take a tiny stitch on back of grid *(photo B);* run tail through Chain to hide. Remove needle; thread needle with other end of Chain and weave through grid *(photo C).*

To **lengthen Chain** if Weaving Chain is too short to complete the section, weave to about 6 inches from end of Chain, insert crochet hook through last chain stitch, yarn over with new strand of same yarn, pull through chain stitch *(photo D)* leaving a 6-inch tail, make chain stitches for about 8 inches and remove hook; **do not cut.** Thread needle with new tail, secure by taking a tiny stitch at back of old Chain, then run both tails back through Chains to hide. Return hook to dropped chain stitch, make chain stitches to length needed. Fasten off leaving a 6-inch tail.

To **shorten Chain** if Weaving Chain is too long after section is completed, loosen fasten-off loop, pull tail through loop and unravel chain to desired length leaving ¼ inch of Chain at back of Grid. Fasten off leaving a 6-inch tail.

To **secure last end** of Weaving Chain when finished weaving the section, run end of Chain to back of work. Thread tail into needle and take a tiny stitch on back of grid *(photo E);* run tail back through Chain to hide.

Tips
& helpful hints

Weaving stitches are similar to embroidery or needlepoint stitches, but because of the size and texture of the weaving chains, there are slight variations in some of the stitches. For example, rather than stitching a French knot, the chain is simply tied in a knot at front of the work.

C

D

E

Gold & Jewels by Andy Ashley

TECHNIQUES
Crochet 'n' Weave, Tassel and
Surface Weaving Embellishments

FINISHED SIZE
Before weaving, each Panel is 10¼ inches x
45 inches.

After weaving, Afghan is about 36 inches
wide x 52 inches long, without Tassels.

MATERIALS
❑ Worsted yarn:
  70 oz. black
  20 oz. gold
  12 oz. purple
  12 oz. red
  12 oz. green
❑ 7-inch square of cardboard
❑ Crochet 'n' Weave® needles *(use size best
  suited for individual Chain and Grid)*
❑ G crochet hook or size hook needed to
  obtain gauge

GAUGE
With 2 strands yarn, 4 dc and 4 chs =
2 inches; 4 dc rows = 2 inches.

BASIC STITCHES
Ch, dc

INSTRUCTIONS

PANEL (make 3)
Row 1: With two strands black yarn held
together, ch 44, dc in sixth ch from hook,
(ch 1, skip next ch, dc in next ch) across,
turn. *(Ch sp at beginning of row counts as first
dc and ch-1 sp; 21 dc and 20 ch-1 sps made.)*

Rows 2–90: Ch 4, skip first ch sp, dc in next
dc, (ch 1, skip next ch sp, dc in next dc)
across to last ch sp, ch 1, skip next ch, dc in
next ch, turn. At end of last row, fasten off.

WEAVING CHAINS
For **each Chain,** using two strands yarn
held together of color stated below, leaving
a 6-inch end, ch until piece measures 60
inches long *(extra length will be added to
each Chain as needed).* Leaving a 6-inch
end, fasten off.

  With **purple,** make seven.
  With **red,** make seven.

With **green,** make seven.
With **gold,** make 18.
With **black,** make two.

GRID WEAVING
Center Panel
NOTES: *Read Crochet 'n' Weave Basic
Technique on page 27 before beginning.*

*To weave each Chain (see Gold & Jewels
Panel chart on page 30), use either **Weave
Backstitch Variation, Double Running
Weave Stitch Variation, Weave Chain Stitch
or Weave Cross Stitch** (see illustrations
below and on page 30), or **Knot Stitch.***

*For **Knot Stitch,** bring yarn to front of work
through one opening of grid, tie knot in chain
close to grid, run chain back through opening to back of grid.*

Weave Cross Stitch
1: Working in direction of arrows, going **over**
grid where stitches are shown and **under**
grid at red arrows, weave according to
orange stitches.
2: Turn grid and weave according to green
stitches and arrows.

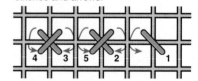

Double Running Weave Stitch Variation
1: Working in direction of arrows, going **over** grid where
stitches are shown and **under** grid at red arrows,
weave according to orange stitches.
2: Turn grid and weave according to green stitches
and arrows.

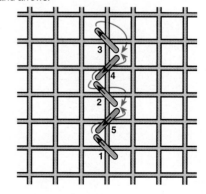

Gold & Jewels

Continued from page 28

1: To weave each Weaving Chain, **attach first end** of Chain at back of row 2 on Panel grid *(see green X on Gold & Jewels Panel chart)*.

2: Weave vertical row of stitches according to Gold & Jewels Panel chart **(lengthen Chain as needed)** to row 89 of Panel; **(shorten Chain** if needed), then fasten off leaving a 6-inch end. **Secure last end.**

3: Repeat steps 1–3 for each vertical row of stitches on Center Panel.

Left Panel
Using purple instead of red, weave same as Center Panel.

Right Panel
Using green instead of red, weave same as Center Panel.

Weave Backstitch Variation
1: Working in direction of arrows, go **over** grid at stitch No. 1 and **under** grid at red arrow No. 2.
2: Go **over** grid in at stitch No. 3 and **under** grid again at green arrow No. 4.
3: Repeat steps 1 and 2 alternately as needed.

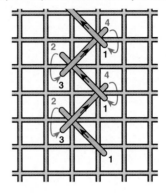

Weave Chain Stitch

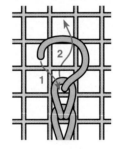

Gold & Jewels Assembly

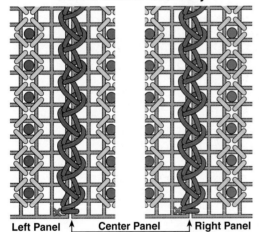

Left Panel ↑   Center Panel   ↑ Right Panel

Gold & Jewels Panel

Weave entire Panel.

Row 90

Row 1

Gold & Jewels Key:
- ■ Red
- ■ Red (Separate Chain)
- ▢ Gold
- ▢ Gold (Separate Chain)
- ✕ Attach Chain

ASSEMBLY

Lay Panels flat with right sides up and ends of rows matching.

For each **seam,** using Weave Chain Stitch, weave ends of rows together as follows *(see Gold & Jewels Assembly illustration):*
A: Secure first end at back of opening on Panel at **left** *(at green X on illustration)* and take a stitch through first opening on row 1 of both Panels; work Chain Stitch in opening at end of row 2 on Panel at **right;**
B: Skip next row on Panel at **left,** work Chain Stitch in opening at end of next row; skip next row on Panel at **right,** work Chain Stitch in opening at end of next row;
C: Repeat step B across seam; stitch top of last Chain Stitch to row 90 on Panel at right, then take a stitch through first opening on row 90 of both Panels. Secure last end.

TASSELS

1: For each **Tassel** *(make eight),* cut a 16-inch strand and a 12-inch strand of black yarn; lay aside. Wrap black 26 times around 7-inch cardboard. Remove loops from cardboard, run 16-inch strand through all loops and pull to center of strand; tightly tie 16-inch strand around center of loops. Holding 16-inch strand ends apart, fold loops at knot and tightly wrap 12-inch strand several times around loops 1 inch below first knot; tie tightly and run ends back through Tassel to hide. Cut loops.

2: Using 16-inch strand ends, tie one Tassel to each corner of afghan and one to each end of each seam; run ends back through Tassel to hide.

3: Trim all ends even. ❧

Wildberry Ripple

Continued from page 24

evenly spacing sts so edge lays flat, ch 1, sc in ends of rows across. Fasten off.

Row 2: With variegated side facing you, working in ends of rows on opposite edge of Panel, join navy with sc in end of row 1; evenly spacing sts so edge lays flat, ch 1, sc in ends of rows across; **do not turn or fasten off.**

Rnd 3: Working around entire piece in sts and in chs on opposite side of row 1 on each Panel, ch 1, sc in each st around with 3 sc at each corner, join with sl st in first sc. Fasten off.

ASSEMBLY AND FINISHING

1: With variegated side up, lay all Panels flat with first row at bottom and last row at top.

2: Using tapestry needle and navy, working in **back lps** *(see Stitch Guide on page 175)* of Edgings, sew Panels together.

3: For each **Tassel** *(make 13),* cut 18-inch strand navy, fold in half; cut 12-inch strand navy. Lay both aside. Hold one strand each navy and variegated together and loosely wrap 24 times around 7-inch cardboard. Remove loops from cardboard, run folded 18-inch navy strand through all loops and pull to center of folded strand; tie very tightly around loops. Keeping ends of 18-inch strand apart, hold all other loops together as one and tightly wrap 12-inch strand several times around loops 1¼ inches below knot of 18-inch strand; tie securely. Run 12-inch ends inside tassel to hide.

4: Cut other end of loops to 6 inches past 12-inch wraps.

5: Using ends of 18-inch strand, tie one Tassel to each point along first and last rows of afghan; run ends back through inside of Tassel to hide.

6: Trim all ends even. ❧

CROCHET ON THE DOUBLE

Loop upon loop, stitch upon stitch, a foundation is laid then deftly built upon, creating a look like no other, a look with twice the appeal—Crochet On the Double. Almost as if woven, the fabric this interesting technique produces is a unique blend of the best of knit and crochet. Whether bold and chunky or delicately lace-like, the magic of the double-ended hook lets you fashion two looks at once using a single color or an artist's pallet, all with the ease of a single hook. Set your spirit of adventure free with Crochet On the Double and you are sure to find this needlecraft technique twice as much fun!

SUPPLIES AND TOOLS

For **Crochet on the Double,** you'll need a standard double-ended hook or swivel hook; both have long slender shanks that can hold multiple loops *(or stitches)* similar to crochet hooks or circular knitting needles, but they have a crochet hook at both ends. You'll also need yarn, scissors and a yarn needle for hiding ends.

(See Supplier Listing on page 174 for purchase information.)

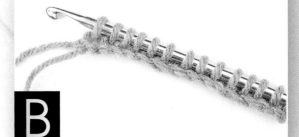

A

B

BASIC TECHNIQUE

To **draw up a lp,** insert hook in designated lp, bar or st, yo, draw lp through *(photo A),* leaving lp on hook.

When picking up lps, leave all lps on hook *(photo B)* unless otherwise stated.

To **turn,** rotate hook 180 degrees and slide all lps to opposite end of hook. **Do not turn** unless otherwise stated.

To **work lps off hook when adding a new color,** with new color, place slip knot on hook, draw slip knot through one lp on hook *(photo C),* (yo, pull through 2 lps on hook) across.

Last lp remaining on hook at end of row is **first vertical bar** of next row *(photo D).*

To **work lps off hook with color already in use,** yo with color from row below, draw through one lp on hook *(photo E),* (yo, pull through 2 lps on hook) across.

To **end a color that is no longer needed,** work across a row and cut yarn leaving a long end; secure the end temporarily by tying to an adjacent yarn end, or permanently by weaving back through an inch or so on the row before.

When **working through the horizontal bar,** insert hook under only the top strand of the horizontal bar unless otherwise stated *(photo F).*

For **last stitch,** insert hook under last vertical bar and strand directly behind it and pull up a lp.

Tips
& helpful hints

While learning the technique, use two contrasting-color skeins of yarn so you can clearly see your rows and stitches. Just be sure all yarns for a project have the same care and cleaning requirements.

To keep yarns from tangling, place one skein on each side of you; turn your hook counterclockwise after one row, then clockwise after the next row.

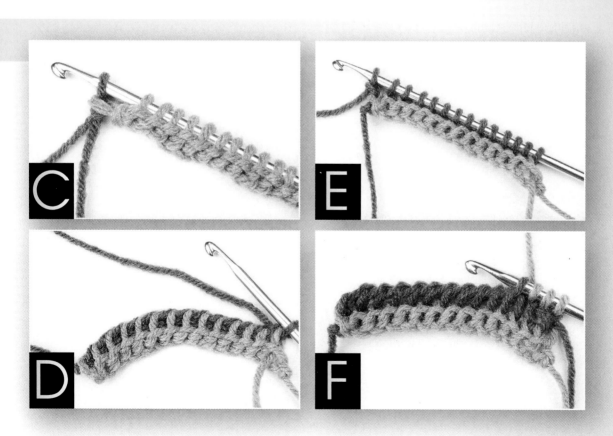

Spring Fling by Christine Grazioso Moody

TECHNIQUE
Crochet on the Double

SPECIAL STITCHES
Front Post, Double Crochet Loop,
Treble Crochet Loop

FINISHED SIZE
48 inches x 55 inches

MATERIALS
❑ Red Heart Super Saver Art. E300 or Art.
E301 by Coats & Clark or worsted yarn:
16 oz. Soft White #316
8 oz. Frosty Green #661
3 oz. Light Blue #381
3 oz. Light Coral #246
3 oz. Cornmeal #220
❑ Size J double-ended swivel hook or size
hook needed to obtain gauge

GAUGE
In pattern: 7 sts = 2 inches; 4 rows = 2 inches.

SPECIAL STITCHES
For **dc lp,** yo, insert hook in ch or horizontal
bar, yo, pull lp through, yo, pull through 2 lps
on hook; leave remaining lps on hook.

For **treble lp (tr lp),** yo 2 times, insert hook in
st, yo, pull lp through, (yo, pull through 2 lps
on hook) 2 times; leave remaining lps on hook.

For **front post (fp),** see Stitch Guide on
page 175.

NOTE
Refer to Basic Crochet on the Double Technique on page 33 for additional information.

INSTRUCTIONS
Row 1: With white, ch 166, **dc lp** *(see Special
Stitches)* in third ch from hook, (skip next 2
chs, 5 dc lps in next ch, skip 2 chs, dc lp
in next ch) across to last ch, dc lp in last
ch, **turn.** Drop white; pick up again when
needed. *(165 lps on hook)*

Row 2: With green, place slip knot on hook; to
work lps off hook, draw through
one loop on hook, (yo, draw through
2 loops on hook) across.

*NOTE: When working in horizontal
bar, insert hook through bar under*

**Horizontal
Bar**

top two strands only (see illustration).

Row 3: Ch 2, skip first dc lp, **fp tr lp** *(see
Special Stitches)* around next dc lp, *skip
next 2 horizontal bars, 5 dc lps in next horizontal bar *(see Note),* skip next 3 horizontal
bars, fp tr lp around next dc lp; repeat from *
across with dc lp in last horizontal bar, **turn.**
Cut green; tie ends together to secure.

Row 4: With white, work lps off hook.

Row 5: To **work in pattern,** ch 2, skip first dc
lp, fp tr lp around next tr lp, (skip next 2 horizontal bars, 5 dc lp in next horizontal bar, skip
next 3 horizontal bars, fp tr lp around next tr lp)
across with dc lp in last horizontal bar, **turn.**

Row 6: With blue, place slip knot on hook,
work lps off hook.

Row 7: Work in pattern. Cut blue, tie ends.

Row 8: With white, work lps off hook.

Row 9: Work in pattern.

Row 10: With green, place slip knot on hook,
work lps off hook.

Row 11: Work in pattern. Cut green, tie ends.

Row 12: With white, work lps off hook.

Row 13: Work in pattern.

Row 14: With coral, place slip knot on hook,
work lps off hook.

Row 15: Work in pattern. Cut coral, tie ends.

Row 16: With white, work lps off hook.

Row 17: Work in pattern.

Row 18: With green, place slip knot on hook,
work lps off hook.

Row 19: Work in pattern. Cut green, tie ends.

Row 20: With white, work lps off hook.

Row 21: Work in pattern.

Row 22: With yellow, place slip knot on hook,
work lps off hook

Row 23: Work in pattern. Cut yellow, tie ends.

Row 24: With white, work lps off hook.

Row 25: Work in pattern.

Row 26: With green, place slip knot on hook,
work lps off hook.

Continued on page 53

Heavenly Blue Star by Sandra Jean Smith

TECHNIQUES
Crochet on the Double, Cro-Tatting

SPECIAL STITCHES
Back Loops, Bobble, Bobble Cluster, Bobble Knit, Bobble Knit Cluster, Knit Stitch, Reverse Single Crochet

FINISHED SIZE
About 64 inches across

MATERIALS
❑ Worsted yarn:
  15 oz. dk. blue
  12 oz. med. blue
  10 oz. lt. blue
  8 oz. white
❑ Crochet stitch markers
❑ J crochet hook
❑ K double-ended hook
❑ K swivel hook

GAUGE
Rnds 1–9 of Star Center = 5½ inches across.

BASIC STITCHES
Ch, sl st, sc, hdc, dc

SPECIAL STITCHES
NOTE: Crochet on the Double (see Basic Technique in Crochet on the Double on page 33)

For **knit st (K st),** insert hook under vertical bar and horizontal bar *(see illustration),* yo, pull up lp.

For **bobble,** pull up lp in st or bar, ch 2.

For **bobble cluster (b-cl),** make 3 bobbles in same st or bar leaving all lps on hook *(these will be worked together on next row).*

For **bobble knit (bk),** insert hook under vertical bar and horizontal bar *(see K st illustration above),* yo, pull up lp, ch 2.

For **bobble knit cluster (bk-cl),** (insert hook under vertical bar and horizontal bar, yo, pull up lp, ch 2) 3 times in same st or bar leaving all lps on hook *(these will be worked together on next row).*

NOTES: Cro-Tat (see Basic Technique in Cro-Tatting on page 17)

*For **ds, p, jp** and **close** (shown in **bold type** first time used), see Cro-Tatting Basic Technique on page 17.*

For **ring,** (3 ds, p) 3 times, 3 ds, close ring.

For **joined picot (jp),** pull up a lp in adjacent picot; leave lp on hook *(not counted as a st).*

For **joined ring,** make ring of 3 ds, **jp** in previous ring *(see above),* 3 ds, p, 3 ds, p, 3 ds, close ring.

For **last joined ring,** make ring of 3 ds, jp in previous ring, 3 ds, p, 3 ds, jp in first ring, 3 ds, close ring.

INSTRUCTIONS

STAR
Center
*Helpful Hint: On each rnd, when work becomes stretched so it's **hard to pick up sts,** slide lps on hook onto center of cable; if needed to provide more flexibility, divide sts and pull excess cable length out into a loop between the sts, then slide last sts made back onto shaft of hook and continue working.*

Rnd 1: With J crochet hook and dk. blue, ch 5, sl st in first ch to form ring, ch 3 *(counts as first dc),* 2 dc in ring, ch 2, (3 dc in ring, ch 2) 5 times, join with sl st in top of ch-3. *(18 dc, 6 ch-2 sps)*

NOTES: *Front of rnd 1 is right side of work.*

Do not join or turn *unless otherwise stated.*

*Work under **vertical bars of row before last** and under **horizontal bars of last row** unless otherwise stated.*

Rnd 2: With K swivel hook, sl st back into last ch made *(counts as first lp on hook),* pull up lp in next 3 sts, (pull up lp in next 2 chs, pull up lp in next 3 sts) 5 times, pull up lp in last ch; **do not join or turn** *(see Notes).* (30 lps on hook)

Rnd 3: Working from left to right, yo, pull through first lp on hook *(first st made),* (yo, pull through 2 lps on hook) 4 times, ch 2, *(yo, pull through 2 lps on hook) 5 times, ch 2; repeat from * around, join with sl st in first st. *(One lp on hook)*

Rnd 4: Working from right to left, sl st in first 2 chs *(one lp on hook),* **K st** *(see Special*

Heavenly Blue Star

Continued from page 36

Stitches) in each of first 5 vertical bars *(see Notes)*, (pull up lp in next 2 chs, K st in next 5 vertical bars) around; working over sl st, pull up lp in first ch. *(42 lps on hook)*

Rnd 5: Working from left to right, yo, pull through first lp on hook, (yo, pull through 2 lps on hook) 6 times, ch 2, *(yo, pull through 2 lps on hook) 7 times, ch 2; repeat from * around, join with sl st in first st. *(One lp on hook)*

Rnd 6: Working from right to left, sl st in first 2 chs *(one lp on hook),* K st in next 3 vertical bars, skip next vertical bar, K st in next 3 vertical bars, (pull up lp in next 2 chs, K st in next 3 vertical bars, skip next vertical bar, K st in next 3 vertical bars) around; working over sl st, pull up lp in first ch. Drop yarn; **do not** cut. *(48 lps on hook)*

Rnd 7: Working from left to right, with white, place slip knot on hook, pull through first lp on hook, (yo, pull through 2 lps on hook) 7 times, ch 2, *(yo, pull through 2 lps on hook) 8 times, ch 2; repeat from * around, join with sl st in first st. *(60 sts and chs made; one lp left on hook)*

Rnd 8: Working from right to left, sl st in first 2 chs *(lp on hook counts as first lp of first b-cl),* *b-cl (see Special Stitches)* in same ch as last sl st *(see Rnd 8 illustration);* skipping each vertical bar, (skip next horizontal bar, b-cl in next horizontal bar) 3 times, skip next horizontal bar, b-cl in next ch; repeat from * around. Fasten off white. *(90 lps on hook)*

Rnd 8

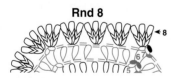

Rnd 9: Working from right to left, pick up dropped dk. blue, yo, pull through first 3 lps on hook, (yo, pull through 4 lps on hook) 4 times, *ch 4, (yo, pull through 4 lps on hook) 5 times; repeat from * around, ch 2, join with hdc in first st. *(Ch-2 and hdc count as joining ch sp—54 sts and chs made; one lp left on hook)*

Rnd 10: Working from right to left, ch 2 *(counts as first bobble),* **bobble** *(see Special Stitches)* in side of hdc; working into horizon-

tal strands at top of b-cls, bobble in each of next 5 b-cls, (bobble in next 4 chs, bobble in next 5 b-cls) around, bobble in 2 chs of joining ch sp. *(54 lps on hook)*

Rnd 11: Working from left to right, yo, pull through first lp on hook, (yo, pull through 2 lps on hook) 8 times, ch 2, *(yo, pull through 2 lps on hook) 9 times, ch 2; repeat from * around, join with sl st in first st. *(66 sts and chs made; one lp left on hook)*

Rnd 12: Using K double-ended hook, sl st in last ch made, sl st in same ch sp; working from left to right; *complete rnd as follows:*
A: Ring *(see Special Stitches),* sl st in same sp as last sl st, **mark center p** in ring just made for corner, **reverse sc** *(see Stitch Guide on page 175)* in each of next 2 horizontal bars on last rnd;
B: Working on last rnd in spaces between vertical bars, *(sl st, **joined ring**—*see Special Stitches,* sl st) in next horizontal bar; reverse sc in each of next 2 horizontal bars; repeat from *;
C: (Sl st, joined ring, sl st) in next ch-2 sp, **mark center p** in joined ring just made for corner; working between vertical bars, reverse sc in each of next 2 horizontal bars on last rnd;
D: Repeat B and C alternately until you have 16 rings, ending at last 6 vertical bars;
E: (Sl st, joined ring, sl st) in next horizontal bar; reverse sc in each of next 2 horizontal bars;
F: Working from left to right, (sl st, **last joined ring**—*see Special Stitches,* sl st) in next horizontal bar, reverse sc in each of next 2 horizontal bars on last rnd, join with sl st in ch at base of first ring. Fasten off. *(18 rings)*

First Point
Row 1: With wrong side facing, join dk. blue with sl st in marked center p at any corner; working from right to left, *complete as follows (do not remove markers until instructed to do so):*
A: Ch 2, sl st in next jp, **turn,** ring, sl st in same jp as last sl st, **turn,** ch 2, sl st in free p of next ring.
B: Ch 2, sl st in next jp, **turn,** joined ring, sl st in same jp as last sl st, **turn,** ch 2, sl st in free p of next ring.
C: Repeat B, ending with last sl st in next marked center p. Fasten off.

Row 2: With wrong side of Star Center facing, join dk. blue with sl st in center p of first

Heavenly Blue Star Key

Crochet:

0 or ○ **Ch**

● or ● **Sl st**

⊗ **Reverse Sc**

┬ **Dc**

◁ **Join**

◄ **Fasten off**

Cro-Tat:

 **Ring or Joined Ring**

On-The-Double:

◊ **Bobble Stitch**

◊ **Bobble Cluster**

○ **Knit Stitch**

(**Basic Stitch (Vertical Bar or Loop on hook)**

= **Pull Through 2 Lps On Hook**

First Point
Rows are shown in different colors for easier working.
Previously worked rnds of Star Center are shown as gray.

↓ or ↓ or ↓ = Sl sts go here.

Star Center
Rnds are shown in different colors for easier working.

Rnd Direction Key

ring on row 1, complete as follows:
A: Ch 2, sl st in next jp, **turn,** ring, sl st in same jp as last sl st, **turn,** ch 2, sl st in free p of next ring.
B: Ch 2, sl st in next jp, **turn,** joined ring, sl st in same jp as last sl st, **turn,** ch 2, sl st in free p of next ring. Fasten off.

Row 3: With wrong side of Star Center facing, join dk. blue with sl st in free center p of first ring on row 2, ch 2, sl st in next jp, **turn,** ring, sl st in same jp as last sl st, **turn,** ch 2, sl st in free p of next ring. Fasten off. Hide all yarn ends.

Second–Sixth Points
Rows 1–3: Joining row 1 in same marked center p as **last** sl st in row 1 of previous Point, repeat rows 1–3 of First Point *(in row 1 of Sixth Point, last sl st will be in same marked center p as first sl st of First Point).*

BORDER
NOTE: *Do not join or turn unless otherwise stated.*

Rnd 1: With right side of Star Center facing

you, using J crochet hook, join dk. blue with sl st in center p at tip of any point; working in free p's and in worked p's beside sl st already made, (ch 2, sl st in next p) 4 times, ch 2; for **decrease (dec),** pull up lp in next p, pull up lp in next marked p on rnd 12, pull up lp in next p on next point, yo, pull through all 4 lps on hook *(dec made; this forms **bottom of V**);* *(ch 2, sl st in next p) 9 times, ch 2,

Heavenly Blue Star

Continued from page 39

dec; repeat from * 4 more times, (ch 2, sl st in next p) 4 times, ch 2, join with sl st in first sl st. Drop yarn; **do not cut.** *(180 sts and chs made)* Remove all markers.

Rnd 2: Working this rnd in **back lps** *(see Stitch Guide),* join white with sc in first sl st, (ch 2, sc) in same sl st as joining sc, sc in next 14 chs and sl sts, skip next dec, sc in next 14 chs and sl sts, *(sc, ch 2, sc) in next sl st at tip of point, sc in next 14 chs and sl sts, skip next dec, sc in next 14 chs and sl sts; repeat from * around, join with sl st in first sc. *(192 sts and chs)*

Rnd 3: Working from right to left, using K swivel hook, keeping all lps on hook, skip first sc, sl st in next ch, *b-cl in same ch-2 sp, (skip next st, b-cl in next st) 7 times, skip next 2 sts at bottom of V, (b-cl in next st, skip next st) 7 times, b-cl in ch-2 sp; repeat from * around, **turn.** Cut white, secure end. *(2 b-cls in each ch-2 sp; 96 b-cls total)*

Rnd 4: Working from left to right, pick up dropped dk. blue, yo, pull through first 3 lps on hook, ch 2, (yo, pull through 4 lps on hook, ch 2) 6 times, pull last ch made through next 6 lps at bottom of V, (ch 2, yo, pull through 4 lps on hook) 7 times, ch 4 at point, *(yo, pull through 4 lps on hook, ch 2) 7 times, pull last ch made through next 6 lps at bottom of V, (ch 2, yo, pull through 4 lps on hook) 7 times, ch 4 at point,; repeat from * around, join with sl st in first st, **turn.** *(282 sts and chs made; one lp left on hook)*

Rnd 5: Working from right to left, (sl st in first 3 chs, ch 2 *(counts as first bobble),* bobble in same ch sp; work bobble in each ch-2 sp and in top strand of each b-cl and work 4 bobbles in each ch-4 sp around to first ch-sp; working over sl sts, work 2 more bobbles in first ch sp. *(198 lps on hook)*

NOTE: *For **dec at bottom of V (V-dec),** yo, pull through designated number of lps on hook.*

Rnd 6: Working from left to right, yo, pull through first lp on hook, (yo, pull through 2 lps on hook) 14 times, work **V-dec** pulling through 4 lps *(see Note),* (yo, pull through 2 lps on hook) 15 times, ch 4 at **point,** *(yo, pull through 2 lps on hook) 15 times, work

V-dec pulling through 4 lps, (yo, pull through 2 lps on hook) 15 times, ch 4 at point; repeat from * around, join. *(210 sts and chs made; one lp left on hook)*

Rnd 7: Working from right to left, (sl st in first 3 chs, ch 2—*counts as first bobble,* bobble) in same ch-4 sp; work **bk** *(see Special Stitches)* in each st and work 4 bobbles in each ch-4 sp around; working over sl sts, work 2 more bobbles in first ch-4 sp. Fasten off. *(210 lps on hook)*

Rnd 8: Working from left to right, with med. blue, place slip knot on hook, pull through first lp on hook, *(yo, pull through 2 lps on hook) across to 3 lps at bottom of V, work V-dec pulling through 4 lps, (yo, pull through 2 lps on hook) across to point ending between second and third sts in ch-4 sp, ch 4; repeat from * around, join. *(216 sts and chs made; one lp left on hook)*

Rnd 9: Working from right to left, (sl st in first 3 chs, ch 2—*counts as first bobble,* bobble) in first ch-4 sp; skipping one st at bottom of each V, work bk in each bobble and 4 bobbles in each ch-4 sp around; working over sl sts, work 2 more bobbles in first ch-4 sp, **turn.** Cut med. blue, secure end. *(210 lps on hook)*

Rnd 10: Working from left to right, with lt. blue, place slip knot on hook, pull through first lp on hook, *(yo, pull through 2 lps on hook) across to two sts at bottom of V; V-dec pulling through 3 lps, (yo, pull through 2 lps on hook) across to point ending between second and third sts in ch-4 sp, ch 4; repeat from * around, join. *(222 sts and chs made; one lp left on hook)*

Rnd 11: With right side facing, using K double-ended hook, sl st in first 2 chs; working from left to right in sps between vertical bars and in ch-4 sps; *complete rnd as follows:*
A: Ring; **mark** center p of ring just made, (sl st, reverse sc) in same ch-4 sp, reverse sc in each of next 2 sps between vertical bars;
B: (Sl st, joined ring, sl st) in next sp; reverse sc in each of next 2 sps;
C: *(Sl st, joined ring, sl st) in next sp, reverse sc in each of next 3 sps; repeat from * across to last 3 sps before ch-4 sp at next point, (sl st, joined ring, sl st) in next sp, reverse sc in each of next 2 sps, (reverse sc, sl st) in ch-4 sp;
D: Repeat steps A–C 5 more times, join with sl st in base of first ring. Fasten off. *(54 rings)*

Rnd 12: With right side facing, working from right to left, using K double-ended hook, join lt. blue with sl st in marked center p of first ring, (ch 5, sl st in free center p of next ring) across to 2 rings at bottom of V, ch 5; for **sl st next 2 p's tog (p-dec),** insert hook through free center p's of next 2 rings at same time, yo, pull through three lps on hook *(p-dec at bottom of V completed)*; *ch 5, (sl st in free center p of next ring, ch 5) across point to 2 rings at bottom of next V, p-dec; repeat from * 4 more times, ch 5, (sl st in free center p of next ring, ch 5) around, join with sl st in first sl st. Fasten off.

Rnd 13: Working this rnd in **back lps,** join med. blue with sc in sl st worked into marked center p on any point, sc in same sl st; skipping p-dec at bottom of V, sc in each ch and in each sl st across to next point, *(2 sc, ch 2, 2 sc) in sl st worked into marked p; skipping p-dec at bottom of V, sc in each ch and in each sl st across to next point; repeat from * 4 more times, 2 sc in same st as joining sc, ch 2, join with sl st in first sc, **turn.**

Rnd 14: Working from right to left, with wrong side facing, sl st in first ch, ch 2 *(counts as first bobble);* bobble in same ch sp, (bobble in each sc across to 3 sc at bottom of V, skip next 3 sc, bobble in each sc across to next ch-2 sp at point, 4 bobbles in ch-2 sp) around, work 2 more bobbles in first ch sp, **turn.** Cut yarn, secure end.

Rnd 15: Working from left to right, with dk. blue, place slip knot on hook, pull through first lp on hook, *(yo, pull through 2 lps on hook) around with (yo, pull through 3 lps on hook) at bottom of each V and ch 4 between second and third lps at each point, join with sl st in first st. *(one lp left on hook)*

Rnd 16: Working from right to left, sl st in first 3 chs, ch 2 *(counts as first bobble)*, bobble in same ch-4 sp; skipping 3 sts at bottom of each V, bk in each st around with 4 bobbles in each ch-4 sp at point. Fasten off.

Rnd 17: With white, repeat rnd 15. Fasten off.

Rnd 18: Working from right to left, join white with sl st in any ch-4 sp, ch 2 *(counts as first bobble)*, work 2 more bobbles in same ch sp *(counts as first b-cl),* *[(inserting hook through vertical bar same as for K st, b-cl in next vertical bar, skip next vertical bar) across to 3 sts at bottom of V, skip 3 sts, (b-cl in next vertical bar, skip next vertical bar) across to ch-4 sp at point], work 6 bobbles in ch-4 sp *(counts as 2 b-cls);* repeat from * 4 more times; repeat between [ ], work 3 more bobbles in first ch-4 sp *(counts as last b-cl).* Fasten off.

Rnd 19: Working from left to right, with dk. blue, place slip knot on hook, pull through first 3 bobbles, ch 2, *(yo, pull through 4 lps on hook, ch 2) across to 6 lps at bottom of V, pull last ch made through next 6 lps at bottom of V, (ch 2, yo, pull through 4 lps on hook) across to point ending between second and third sts worked in point ch sp, ch 4 at point; repeat from * around, join with sl st in first st. *(one lp left on hook)*

Rnd 20: Working from right to left, (sl st in first 3 chs, ch 2—*counts as first bobble*, bobble) in first ch-4 sp; skipping 6 lps worked tog at bottom of each V, bobble in each st and in each ch-2 sp around with 4 bobbles in each ch-4 sp, work 2 more bobbles in first ch-4 sp. Fasten off.

Rnd 21: Working from left to right, with med. blue, place slip knot on hook, pull through first lp on hook, *(yo, pull through 2 lps on hook) around with (yo, pull through 3 lps on hook) at bottom of each V and ch 4 between second and third lps at each point, join with sl st in first st, **turn.** *(one lp left on hook)*

Rnds 22–23: Repeat rnds 9–10.

Rnd 24: Working reverse sc in **6 sps** at bottom of each V, repeat rnd 11. *(78 rings)*

Rnds 25–34: Repeat rnds 12–21.

Rnd 35: Repeat rnd 9.

Rnd 36: Working from left to right, with lt. blue, place slip knot on hook, pull through first lp on hook, *(yo, pull through 2 lps on hook) across to two sts at bottom of V; V-dec pulling through 3 lps, (yo, pull through 2 lps on hook) across to point ending between second and third sts in ch-4 sp, ch 4; repeat from * around, join.

Rnd 37: Working from right to left, sl st in first 3 chs; skipping one st at bottom of each V, K st in each st and pull up lp in each ch around; pull up lp in first 2 sl sts. Cut yarn, secure end.

Rnds 38–39: With med. blue, repeat rnds 36 and 37; at end of rnd 39, **turn.**

Rnds 40–41: With white, repeat rnds 36 and 37.

Rnd 42: With dk. blue, repeat rnd 36. Fasten off.

Rnd 43: With med. blue, repeat rnd 37. Cut yarn, secure end.

Rnd 44: With white, repeat rnd 36. Fasten off. ❧

Faux Monk's Cloth by Eleanor Albano-Miles

TECHNIQUES
Crochet on the Double,
Surface Weaving Embellishment

FINISHED SIZE
About 33 inches x 39 inches

MATERIALS
❑ 25 oz. white sport yarn
❑ Worsted yarn:
   3 oz. variegated blues
   3 oz. variegated browns
❑ 2 tapestry needles
❑ F crochet hook or hook needed to obtain same
   sc gauge as Crochet-on-the-Double gauge
❑ H double-ended swivel hook

GAUGE
H hook and sport yarn, 11 Crochet on the
Double sts = 2 inches; 11 rows = 2 inches.

F hook and sport yarn, 11 sc = 2 inches.

BASIC STITCHES
Ch, sl st, sc, dc

INSTRUCTIONS

AFGHAN
Row 1: With double-ended hook and white,
ch 181 loosely; pull up a lp in second ch from
hook *(see Basic Technique in Crochet on the
Double on page 33),* pull up a lp in each ch
across, turn. *(181 lps on hook) Slide lps to
opposite end of hook.*

Row 2: With separate skein white, to **work
lps off hook,** working from left to right, yo,
pull through first lp on hook, (yo, pull through
2 lps on hook) across, **do not turn.** *(One lp
on hook)*

Row 3: Working from right to left, ch 1, skip
first vertical bar, pull up a loop in each vertical bar across, turn. *Slide lps to opposite end
of hook.*

Row 4: Working from left to right with skein at
this end, work lps off hook, **do not turn.**

NOTE: *As you work, four rows appear to be
one **ridge** and one **valley.***

Next rows: Repeat rows 3 and 4 alternately
until you have 81 ridges on each side, ending
with row 4. At end of last row, fasten off.

WEAVE BLUE SIDE
Weave steps 1–3 for each of seven columns
of diamonds.

1: For first section of weaving in each column
of diamonds *(indicated by lighter shade of
purple on Blues graph on page 53),* cut a
4-yard length of variegated blues and thread
a tapestry needle onto each end of strand.

NOTE: *When weaving, take care that this
color of yarn does not show on opposite side
of work.*

2: To begin, run one end through stitch on
second ridge of Center where indicated on
Blues graph and pull to center of strand.
Weave each end of strand according to
Blues graph; secure ends of strand and
run back through weaving yarn to hide *(If
desired, loose ends can be stitched in place
on weaving yarn using sewing needle and
matching-color sewing thread.).*

3: Using another 4-yard length of variegated
blues, weave remainder of same column
as indicated by darker shade of purple on
Blues graph.

WEAVE BROWN SIDE
1: For each straight line of weaving on narrow
columns only *(pink weaving lines on Browns
graph),* cut a 2-yard length of variegated
browns and thread a tapestry needle onto
one end. Weave strand according to straight
stitching lines on Browns graph; secure both
ends of strand *(see pink dots on graph)* and
run back through weaving yarn to hide *(if
desired, loose ends can be stitched to weaving yarn using sewing needle and matching-
color sewing thread).*

2: For each remaining section of weaving in
wide or narrow columns *(one half of strand
indicated by lt. brown and other half of strand
by dk. brown on Browns graph),* cut a 4-yard
length of variegated browns and thread a
tapestry needle onto each end of strand.
Run one end through stitch on first ridge
of Center *(see graph)* and pull to center of
strand. Weave each half of strand according
to graph; secure and hide ends of strand in
same manner.

Continued on page 53

HAIRPIN LACE

Twisting and turning like a graceful ballerina, the loom of a hairpin lace stitcher spins round and round, dancing an ages-old waltz of hook and thread. Slender rods carry rows of loops later joined in a union of divine elegance. Hairpin lace is one of the more difficult forms of loop-based crochet, yet creates versatility unmatched by other forms. Whether you use soft, fluffy mohair or silky fine thread, you will find the lure of making hairpin lace irresistible. Create striking shawls, throws or simple doilies from this enchanting technique and each will come alive with a spirit of its own.

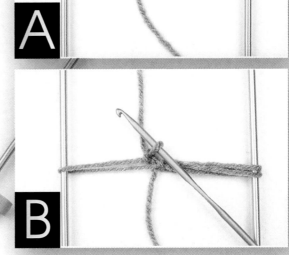

SUPPLIES AND TOOLS

For **hairpin lace** *(sometimes called Maltese crochet),* you will need a crochet hook, a crochet "fork" and the yarn of your choice, along with scissors and a yarn needle for hiding ends.

Crochet forks are about 12 inches long and are adjustable for widths from ½ inch to 4 inches.

(See Supplier Listing on page 174 for purchase information.)

BASIC TECHNIQUE

Adjust the crochet fork to the desired width and work basic **hairpin lace** as follows:

1: Wrap the yarn around both prongs of the fork and tie in a knot at center between the prongs *(photo A).*

2: Bring yarn from ball around right prong of fork from front to back; insert hook between 2 strands of loop on left prong, yo, pull through; ch 1 *(photo B).*

3: Leaving loop on hook, move handle of hook up and over to back through top center of fork; turn fork ½ turn right over left, wrapping yarn around prong of fork *(photo C)* and placing hook at front.

4: Insert hook from bottom through top loop on left prong, yo, pull though *(2 lps now on hook),* yo, pull through both loops on hook *(photo D— single crochet stitch completed)*

5: Repeat steps 3 and 4 alternately until you have the desired number of loops on each prong. Fasten off at end of strip.

If fork is filled before you have enough loops, remove the bottom bar and slide loops off the prongs leaving the top 4 or 5 loops on each prong *(photo E),* then replace the bottom bar.

Tips
& helpful hints

Roll up the completed section of strip, secure with a rubber band or safety pin, etc. and continue working until you have the desired number of loops.

For ease in counting, use crochet stitch markers, small safety pins, or contrasting color yarn to mark every 25 or 50 loops on each prong.

Count loops carefully; it is important to end with the same number of loops on each side of the strip.

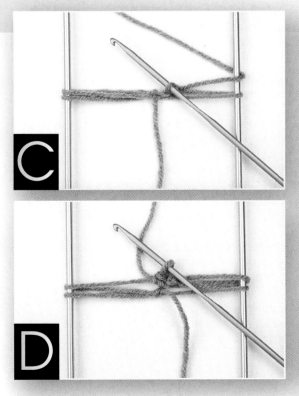

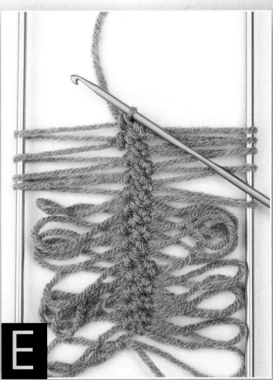

Ripple Hairpin Lace by Darla Fanton

TECHNIQUES
Hairpin Lace, Ripple

SPECIAL STITCH
Shell

FINISHED SIZE
About 47 inches x 67 inches

MATERIALS
❑ Worsted yarn:
    15 oz. white
    11 oz. mulberry solid
    9 oz. mulberry tweed
❑ H crochet hook
❑ Hairpin lace crochet fork set at
    2½ inches wide

GAUGE
Peak to peak of ripple in pattern *(24 hairpin lace loops)* = 5 inches; Each Lace Panel = 3½ inches wide.

BASIC STITCHES
Ch, sl st, sc, hdc, dc

READ BEFORE YOU BEGIN
This pattern uses two colors to make hairpin lace and is a variation of traditional hairpin lace; refer to Basic Technique in Hairpin Lace on page 45 for traditional hairpin lace instructions, as well as Tips and Helpful Hints for working.

INSTRUCTIONS

LACE PANEL (make 18)
Row 1: To work **hairpin lace with two colors,** *complete row as follows:*
A: Wrap solid mulberry yarn around both prongs of crochet fork and tie in a knot at center *(see*

illustration 1). With tweed yarn, place slip knot on hook; keeping yarn ball at back, sl st around knot of solid yarn *(see illustration 2);*
B: Leaving loop on hook, move shaft of hook up and over to back through center of fork; turn fork ½ turn from right to left, wrapping solid yarn around other prong of fork and

bringing hook to front; keep tweed yarn at back;

C: Insert hook from bottom through center of loop on left prong and under loose strand from ball *(see illustration 3);* yo with tweed, pull lp through *(see illustration 4),* complete as sc;
D: Repeat steps B and C alternately until you have 222 loops on each prong. Fasten off both yarns at end of strip.

Row 2: For **border,** with white, place slip knot on hook; working in loops across one long edge of row 1, insert hook through center of first 9 loops at same time, yo, pull through and complete as sc; *complete row as follows:*
A: (Ch 4, insert hook through next 3 loops and complete as sc) 2 times, ch 9, (insert hook through next 3 loops and complete as sc, ch 4) 2 times;
B: Insert hook through next 12 loops and complete as sc;
C: Repeat steps A and B seven more times;
D: Repeat step A;
E: Insert hook through last 9 loops and complete as sc; **do not turn.** Fasten off. *(36 ch-4 sps, 9 ch-9 sps made)*

Row 3: With white, place slip knot on hook; working in loops across remaining long edge of row 1, insert hook through center of first 3 loops, yo, pull through and complete as sc; *complete row as follows:*
A: (Ch 4, insert hook through next 3 loops and complete as sc) 2 times;
B: Ch 4, insert hook through next 12 loops and complete as sc;
C: (Ch 4, insert hook through next 3 loops and complete as sc) 2 times, ch 9, insert hook through next 3 loops and complete as sc, ch 4, insert hook through next 3 loops and complete as sc;
D: Repeat steps B and C seven more times;
E: Repeat steps B and A;
F: Insert hook through last 3 loops and complete as sc. Fasten off. *(38 ch-4 sps, 8 ch-9 sps)*

Continued on page 52

TUNISIAN CROCHET

Sleek and slender like a weaver's shuttle, the Tunisian crochet hook glides effortlessly back and forth, forming row upon row of interlocking loops. Patiently layering stitch within stitch, rich textures and even richer colors seem to evolve before your eyes. Hold a Tunisian crochet hook and you hold the key to a treasure chest filled with myriad patterns and color. A remarkably versatile form of crochet, Tunisian crochet—also called Afghan crochet—lets you produce fabrics for all seasons and all reasons! If you are in the mood for something a little out of the ordinary, you will be pleased with this ageless technique.

SUPPLIES AND TOOLS

For **tunisian crochet** (or **afghan stitch**, *as some prefer to call it*), all you will need is an afghan hook and the yarn of your choice, along with scissors and a yarn needle for hiding ends.

An afghan hook has a long slender shank that can hold multiple loops *(or stitches)* similar to a knitting needle, but it has a crochet hook at the tip rather than a pointed tip like a knitting needle.

Standard afghan hooks are sized in the same manner as crochet hooks and are from 10 inches to 14 inches in length to accommodate multiple stitches.

(See Supplier Listing on page 174 for purchase information.)

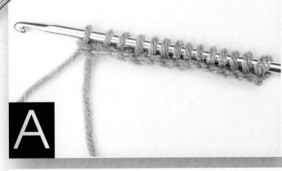

A

B

BASIC TECHNIQUE
Work basic **afghan st** as follows:

Row 1: Ch the designated number of ch sts; keeping all loops on hook, skip first ch from hook, pull up a lp in each ch across, **do not turn.** To **work sts off hook,** yo, pull through one lp on hook *(photo A),* (yo, pull through 2 lps on hook) across *(photo B);* last lp on hook is first st of next row.

Row 2: For basic **afghan stitch,** skip first vertical bar *(lp on hook counts as first st);* pull up a lp in each **vertical bar** *(photo C; some variations will instruct you to pull up a stitch under horizontal bar—photo D);* afghan st across to last vertical bar; for **last stitch,** insert hook under last vertical bar and strand directly behind it *(photo E)* and pull up a lp; work sts off hook.

Next rows: Repeat row 2 for number of rows stated.

Last row: Ch 1, skip first vertical bar, sl st in each vertical bar across. Fasten off.

Tips
& helpful hints

Afghan stitch creates a thick, heavy fabric; the stitches by nature are tight. To avoid a hard, stiff finished project, it's best to work very loosely to retain a soft, plush feel.

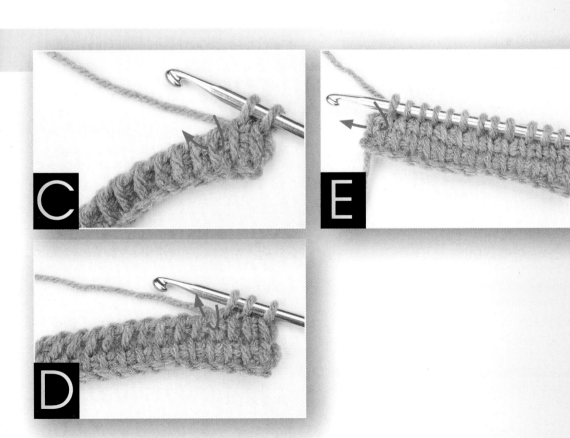

Tweed Stripes by Diane Poellot

TECHNIQUES
Tunisian, Join As You Go

SPECIAL STITCHES
Afghan Stitch, Afghan Twisted Stitch

FINISHED SIZE
About 49½ inches x 67½ inches

MATERIALS
❑ Worsted yarn:
   40 oz. gold
   10 oz. red
   10 oz. blue
   10 oz. green
   10 oz. purple
❑ K afghan hook or size hook needed to
   obtain gauge

GAUGE
16 sts in pattern = 4½ inches; 11 rows
in pattern = 4 inches.

BASIC STITCHES
Ch, sl st, sc, tr

INSTRUCTIONS

FIRST STRIP
NOTES: *Refer to Basic Technique in Tunisian
Crochet on page 49 to work afghan st.*

Drop yarn at end of row; **do not** *cut. Pick up
again when needed.*

For **afghan twisted stitch (twist st),** *insert
hook from left to right under vertical bar
(see arrow on illustration), yo, pull through
vertical bar.*

Row 1: With gold, ch 16 loosely; pull up a lp
in second ch from hook, pull up a lp in each
ch across; (16 lps on hook); drop gold; with
blue, **work sts off hook.**

Row 2: Skip first vertical bar, (afghan st,
twist st—*see Notes*) 7 times, last st; drop
blue; with gold, work sts off hook.

Row 3: Skip first vertical bar, (afghan st, twist
st) 7 times, last st; drop gold; with blue, work
sts off hook.

Row 4: Skip first vertical bar, (twist st, afghan
st) 7 times, last st; drop blue; with gold, work
sts off hook.

Row 5: Skip first vertical bar, (twist st, afghan
st) 7 times, last st; drop gold; with blue, work
sts off hook.

Rows 6–174: Repeat rows 2–5 consecutively,
ending with row 2.

Row 175: Continuing with gold, ch 1, skip
first vertical bar, (inserting hook as for afghan
st, sl st in next vertical bar; inserting hook as
for twist st, sl st in next vertical bar) 7 times,
sl st in last vertical bar. Fasten off.

SECOND STRIP
Row 1: Join gold with sl st in starting ch at
right end of row 1 on previous Strip, ch 16
loosely; pull up a lp in second ch from hook,
pull up a lp in each ch across; (16 lps on
hook); drop gold; with red, work lps off hook.

NOTE: *For* **joined last st,** *pull up lp in last
vertical bar; drop yarn; insert hook through
one corresponding gold strand and one
other-color strand at edge of previous Strip;
with* **opposite color** *for this Strip, yo, pull
through 2 strands and one lp on hook.*

Row 2: Continuing with red, ch 1, skip first
vertical bar, (afghan st, twist st) 7 times;
joined last st *(see Note);* with gold, work
remaining lps off hook.

Row 3: Continuing with gold, skip first vertical bar, (afghan st, twist st) 7 times, joined
last st; with red, work remaining lps off hook.

Row 4: Continuing with red, skip first vertical
bar, (twist st, afghan st) 7 times, joined last st;
with gold, work remaining lps off hook.

Row 5: Continuing with gold, skip first vertical bar, (twist st, afghan st) 7 times, joined
last st; with red, work remaining lps off hook.

Rows 6–174: Repeat rows 2–5 consecutively,
ending with row 2.

Row 175: Continuing with gold, ch 1, skip
first vertical bar, (inserting hook as for afghan
st, sl st in next vertical bar; inserting hook as
for twist st, sl st in next vertical bar) 7 times,
sl st in last vertical bar, sl st in first sl st on
last row of previous Strip. Fasten off.

Tweed Stripes

Continued from page 50

THIRD STRIP
Using purple instead of red, work same as Second Strip.

FOURTH STRIP
Using green instead of red, work same as Second Strip.

FIFTH STRIP
Using blue instead of red, work same as Second Strip.

SIXTH STRIP
Repeat Second Strip.

SEVENTH STRIP
Using purple instead of red, work same as Second Strip.

EIGHTH STRIP
Using green instead of red, work same as Second Strip.

NINTH STRIP
Using blue instead of red, work same as Second Strip.

TENTH STRIP
Repeat Second Strip.

ELEVENTH STRIP
Using purple instead of red, work same as Second Strip.

BORDERS
Row 1: For **first Border,** with wrong side facing you, working across last rows on all Strips, join gold with sc in first sl st at corner, (ch 5, skip next 4 sl sts, sc in next sl st) across all Strips, turn. *(35 ch sps made)*

Row 2: Ch 1; *skipping each sc, sc in next 2 chs, (sc, ch 2, sc) in next ch, sc in next 2 chs; repeat from * across to last sc, sl st in last sc, turn.

Row 3: Ch 7; skipping each sc, sc in next ch-2 sp, (ch 5, sc in next ch-2 sp) across, ch 3, tr in last sc on row 1, turn.

Row 4: Ch 1, (sc, ch 2, sc) in first tr, *skipping each sc, sc in next 2 chs, (sc, ch 2, sc) in next ch, sc in next 2 chs; repeat from * across to last ch-7, sc in next 2 chs, (sc, ch 2, sc) in next ch leaving remaining chs unworked. Fasten off.

Row 5: For **second Border,** working in chs on opposite side of row 1 on all Strips, with wrong side facing you, join gold with sc in first ch at corner, (ch 5, skip next 4 chs, sc in next ch) across all Strips, turn. *(35 ch sps)*

Rows 6–8: Repeat rows 2–4.❦

Ripple Hairpin Lace

Continued from page 46

ASSEMBLY
Lay Lace Panels flat with row 2 on Panel at right corresponding to row 3 on Panel at left; join as follows:
A: Join white with sc in first sc *(worked into 9 lps)* on Panel at right, ch 3, sc in first sc *(worked into 3 lps)* on Panel at left;
B: (Ch 2, sc in next sc on Panel at right, ch 2, sc in next sc on Panel at left) 2 times;
C: Ch 2, sc in fifth ch of next ch-9 on Panel at right, ch 2, sc in next sc on Panel at left *(worked into 12 lps),* ch 2, sc in same ch on Panel at right;
D: (Ch 2, sc in next sc on Panel at left, ch 2, sc in next sc on Panel at right) 2 times;
E: Ch 2, sc in fifth ch of next ch-9 on Panel at left, ch 2, sc in next sc on Panel at right *(worked into 12 lps),* ch 2, sc in same ch on Panel at left;
F: Repeat steps B–E seven more times;
G: Repeat steps B–D;
H: Ch 2, sc in last sc on Panel at left, ch 3, sc in last sc on Panel at right. Fasten off.

BORDER
NOTE: For shell, (sc, hdc, dc, ch 2, dc, hdc, sc) in ch sp or loop indicated.

Join white with sc in first ch-4 sp on either end of assembled Panels, (hdc, dc, ch 2, dc, hdc, sc) in same ch sp *(first shell made);* work **shell** *(see Note)* in each ch-3 sp, in each ch-4 sp and in each solid-color loop at end of each row 1 around with 3 shells in each ch-9 sp, join with sl st in first sc. Fasten off.❦

Faux Monk's Cloth

Continued from page 42

BORDER

Rnd 1: Using crochet hook, join white with sc in last st at any corner, work 2 more sc in same st; spacing sts evenly so edges lay flat, sc in sts and in ends of rows around with 3 sc in each corner st, join with sl st in first sc, **turn.**

Rnd 2: Ch 1, sc in each st around with 3 sc in each center corner st, join, **turn.**

Rnd 3: Ch 3 *(counts as first dc),* dc in each st around with 3 dc in each center corner st, join with sl st in top of ch-3, **turn.**

Rnds 4–5: Ch 1, sc in each st around with 3 sc in each center corner st, join in first sc, **turn.**

Rnds 6–8: Repeat rnds 3–5. At end of last rnd, fasten off. ❦

Blues

Go **over valleys** where weave stitches are shown; go **under two strands on ridges** where weave stitches are not shown.

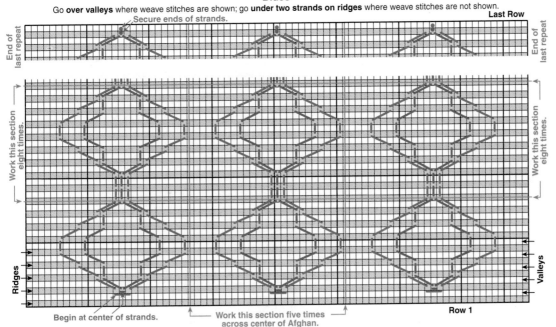

Secure ends of strands.

Last Row

End of last repeat

Work this section eight times.

Ridges

Begin at center of strands.

Work this section five times across center of Afghan.

Row 1

Valleys

Work this section eight times.

End of last repeat

Browns

Go **over valleys** where stitches are shown; go **under two strands on ridges** where stitches are not shown.

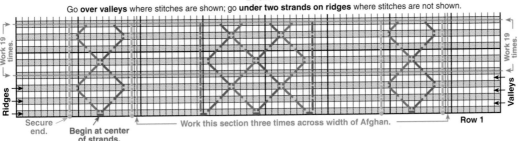

Work 19 times.

Ridges

Secure end.

Begin at center of strands.

Work this section three times across width of Afghan.

Row 1

Work 19 times.

Valleys

Spring Fling

Continued from page 34

Rows 27–109: Repeat rows 3–26 consecutively, ending with row 13. At end of last row, **do not turn.**

Row 110: Yo with white, pull through first 3 lps on hook, *(yo, pull through 2 lps on hook) 3 times, yo, pull through 3 lps on hook; repeat from * across, **turn.**

Row 111: Working in ends of rows, skipping each even-numbered row, (sc, dc, sc) around dc lp at end of each pattern row across. Fasten off.

Row 112: Working in ends of pattern rows on opposite side, join white with sc in row 1, (dc, sc) in same row, (sc, dc, sc) in each pattern row across. Fasten off. ❦

TRADITIONAL-STYLE CLASSICS

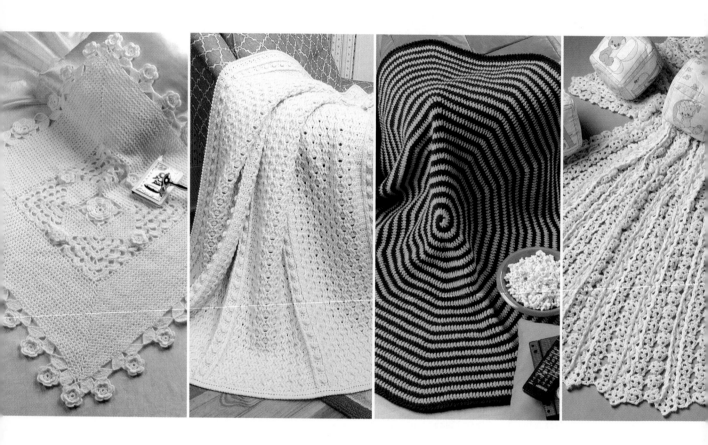

Whether draped elegantly over the pristine duvet in a romantic inn or thrown casually across your favorite chair in the den, nothing says "welcome" like the heartfelt warmth of a handmade afghan. These time-honored designs and classic styles are projects you're sure to turn to time and time again when you want to stitch something from the heart!

Christening Blanket by Ferosa Harold

TECHNIQUES
Irish Crochet, Join As You Go

SPECIAL STITCHES
Joined Double Crochet Stitch, Picot, Scallop

FINISHED SIZE
33 inches x 33 inches

MATERIALS
- ❏ 16 oz. White #1 Red Heart Baby Fingering Pompadour Art. E255 by Coats & Clark or baby yarn
- ❏ Bobby pins or split stitch markers
- ❏ No. 5 steel hook or size hook needed to obtain gauge

GAUGE
Rnds 1–9 = 3½ inches across; 12 jdc = 4 inches; 12 jdc rows = 4 inches.

BASIC STITCHES
Ch, sl st, sc, dc, hdc, tr

SPECIAL STITCHES
For **picot**, ch 3, sl st in third ch from hook.

For **first joined double crochet (first jdc),** (yo, insert hook in **next** ch sp, yo, pull through, yo, pull through 2 lps on hook) 2 times, yo, pull through all 3 lps on hook.

For **joined double crochet (jdc),** yo, insert hook in same ch sp as last dc made, yo, pull through, yo, pull through 2 lps on hook, yo, insert hook in next ch sp, yo, pull through, yo, pull through 2 lps on hook, yo, pull through all 3 lps on hook.

For **6-dc scallop,** (dc, picot) 5 times in next ch sp, dc in same ch sp as last dc made.

For **8-dc scallop,** (dc, picot) 7 times in next ch sp, dc in same ch sp as last dc made.

INSTRUCTIONS
Rnd 1: For **large center rose,** ch 8, sl st in first ch to form ring, ch 1, 16 sc in ring, join with sl st in first sc. *(16 sc made)*

Rnd 2: Ch 1, sc in first st, ch 3, skip next st, (sc in next st, ch 3, skip next st) around, join. *(8 sc, 8 ch sps)*

Rnd 3: For **petals,** (sl st, ch 1, sc, hdc, 3 dc, hdc, sc) in first ch sp, (sc, hdc, 3 dc, hdc, sc) in each ch sp around, join. *(8 petals)*

Rnd 4: Sl st back into sp between first and last sc, ch 1, sc in same sp, ch 4; working behind petals, (sc in next sp between petals, ch 4) around, join. *(8 ch sps)*

Rnd 5: For **petals,** (sl st, ch 1, sc, hdc, 5 dc, hdc, sc) in first ch sp, (sc, hdc, 5 dc, hdc, sc) in each ch sp around, join.

Rnd 6: Sl st back into sp between first and last sc, ch 1, sc in same sp, ch 5; working behind petals, (sc in next sp between petals, ch 5) around, join.

Rnd 7: For **petals,** (sl st, ch 1, sc, hdc, 7 dc, hdc, sc) in first ch sp, (sc, hdc, 7 dc, hdc, sc) in each ch sp around, join.

Rnd 8: Sl st back into sp between first and last sc, ch 1, sc in same sp, (ch 6; working behind petals, sc in next sp between petals) around, ch 3, join with dc in first sc *(ch sp and joining dc counts as joining ch sp).*

Rnd 9: For **petals,** (ch 3, 4 dc, hdc, sc) in joining ch sp, (sc, hdc, 9 dc, hdc, sc) in each ch sp around to joining ch sp, (sc, hdc, 4 dc) in joining ch sp, join with sl st in top of ch-3.

Rnd 10: Ch 15, (sc in fifth dc of next petal, ch 11, tr in fifth dc of next petal, ch 5 at **corner,** tr in same st as last tr, ch 11) 3 times, sc in fifth dc of next petal, ch 11, tr in same dc of first petal as ch-15, ch 2, join with dc in fourth ch of ch-15 at **corner.**

Rnd 11: Ch 8, dc in joining ch sp, *ch 2, dc in next tr, (ch 2, skip next 2 chs, dc in next st or ch) 8 times, ch 2, (dc, ch 5, dc) in next corner ch-5 sp; repeat from * 2 more times, ch 2, dc in next tr, (ch 2, skip next 2 chs, dc in next st or ch) 8 times, ch 2, join with dc in third ch of ch-8.

Rnd 12: Ch 6, sl st in third ch from hook *(first picot made),* (dc, **picot**—see Special Stitches, dc, picot, dc) in joining ch sp, *(ch 2, **jdc**—see Special Stitches) 11 times, ch 2; **6-dc scallop** *(see Special Stitches)* in next corner ch sp; repeat from * 2 more times, (ch 2, jdc) 11 times, ch 2, (dc, picot) 2 times in joining ch sp, join with sl st in third ch of ch-6.

Rnd 13: Sl st into picot, ch 8, skip 2 picots, *dc in last dc of scallop, ch 2; **first jdc** *(see*

Christening Blanket

Continued from page 55

Special Stitches), (ch 2, jdc) 10 times, ch 2, dc in first dc of next scallop, ch 5, skip next 2 picots, (dc, ch 5 at corner, dc) in next picot, ch 5, skip next 2 picots; repeat from * 2 more times, dc in last dc of scallop, ch 2, first jdc, (ch 2, jdc) 10 times, ch 2, dc in first dc of next scallop, ch 5, dc in same picot as first ch-8, ch 2, join with dc in third ch of ch-8.

Rnd 14: Ch 6, sl st in third ch from hook, (dc, picot, dc, picot, dc) in joining ch sp, 6-dc scallop in next ch-5 sp, *first jdc, (ch 2, jdc) 10 times, 6-dc scallop in each of next 3 ch sps; repeat from * 2 more times, first jdc, (ch 2, jdc) 10 times, 6-dc scallop in next ch sp, (dc, picot) 2 times in joining ch sp, join with sl st in third ch of ch-6.

Rnd 15: Sl st into picot, ch 8, skip next 2 picots and next dc, dc in next space between scallops, (ch 5, skip next 2 picots and next dc, dc in next picot or in next jdc) 2 times; *complete the rnd as follows:*
A: First jdc, (ch 2, jdc) 8 times, dc in next jdc;
B: (Ch 5, skip next 2 picots and next dc, dc in next picot or in next space between scallops) 3 times, ch 5 at corner, dc in same picot as last dc made;
C: Ch 5, skip next 2 picots and next dc, dc in next space between scallops, (ch 5, skip next 2 picots and next dc, dc in next picot or in next jdc) 2 times;
D: Repeat steps A, B and C consecutively 2 more times;
E: Repeat step A;
F: (Ch 5, skip next 2 picots and next dc, dc in next picot or in next space between scallops) 2 times, ch 5, dc in same picot as first ch-8, ch 2, join with dc in third ch of ch-8.

Rnd 16: Ch 6, sl st in third ch from hook, (dc, picot, dc, picot, dc) in joining ch sp; *complete the rnd as follows:*
A: 6-dc scallop in next ch sp, (sc, picot, sc) in next ch sp, 6-dc scallop in next ch sp;
B: Skip next dc, dc in next jdc, first jdc, (ch 2, jdc) 6 times, dc in next jdc;
C: 6-dc scallop in next ch sp, (sc, picot, sc) in next ch sp, 6-dc scallop in each of next 3 ch sps, (sc, picot, sc) in next ch sp, 6-dc scallop in next ch sp;
D: Repeat steps B and C alternately 2 more times;

E: Repeat steps B, A;
F: (Dc, picot) 2 times in joining ch sp, join with sl st in third ch of ch-6.

Rnd 17: Sl st in picot, ch 10, skip next 2 picots and next dc, dc in next space between scallops, (ch 6, skip next 2 picots, dc in next picot or in next jdc) 4 times; *complete the rnd as follows:*
A: First jdc, (ch 2, jdc) 4 times, dc in next jdc;
B: (Ch 6, skip next 2 picots, dc in next picot or in next space between scallops) 4 times, ch 6, skip next 2 picots, (tr, ch 5 at corner, tr) in next picot;
C: Ch 6, skip next 2 picots and next dc, dc in next space between scallops, (ch 6, skip next 2 picots, dc in next picot or in next jdc) 4 times;
D: Repeat steps A, B and C consecutively 2 more times;
E: First jdc, (ch 2, jdc) 4 times, dc in next jdc;
F: (Ch 6, skip next 2 picots, dc in next picot or in next space between scallops) 4 times, ch 6, tr in same picot as first ch-10, ch 2, join with dc in fourth ch of ch-10.

Rnd 18: Ch 6, sl st in third ch from hook, (dc, picot, dc, picot, dc) in joining ch sp; *complete the rnd as follows:*
A: 6-dc scallop in next ch sp, *(sc, picot, sc) in next ch sp, work **8-dc scallop** *(see Special Stitches)* in next ch sp; repeat from *; **mark** fourth picot on last scallop made;
B: Skip next dc, dc in next jdc, first jdc; **mark** st just made, (ch 2, jdc) 2 times, **mark** last jdc made, dc in next jdc;
C: 8-dc scallop in next ch sp; **mark** fourth picot on scallop just made, (sc, picot, sc) in next ch sp, 8-dc scallop in next ch sp, (sc, picot, sc) in next ch sp, 6-dc scallop in each of next 3 ch sps, (sc in next ch sp, picot, sc in same ch sp, 8-dc scallop in next ch sp) 2 times; **mark** fourth picot on last scallop made;
D: Repeat steps B, C, B, C, B;
E: 8-dc scallop in next ch sp; **mark** fourth picot on scallop just made, (sc, picot, sc) in next ch sp, 8-dc scallop in next ch sp, (sc, picot, sc) in next ch sp, 6-dc scallop in next ch sp;
F: (Dc, picot) 2 times in joining ch sp, join with sl st in third ch of ch-6.

Rnd 19: Sl st in picot, ch 10, skip next 2 picots, dc in next space between scallops, (ch 7, skip next 2 picots, dc in next picot) 2 times, (ch 7, skip next 3 picots, dc in

Christening Blanket

Continued from page 56

next picot) 3 times, ch 7, skip next 3 picots and next st, dc in next jdc; *complete the rnd as follows:*

A: First jdc, dc in next jdc;

B: (Ch 7, skip next 3 picots, dc in next picot) 4 times, (ch 7, skip next 2 picots, dc in next picot or in next space between scallops) 2 times, ch 7, (tr, ch 5, tr) in next picot;

C: Ch 7, skip next 2 picots, dc in next space between scallops, (ch 7, skip next 2 picots, dc in next picot) 2 times, (ch 7, skip next 3 picots, dc in next picot or in next jdc) 4 times;

D: Repeat steps A, B and C consecutively 2 more times;

E: First jdc, dc in next jdc;

F: (Ch 7, skip next 3 picots, dc in next picot) 4 times, (ch 7, skip next 2 picots, dc in next picot or in space between scallops) 2 times, ch 7, tr in same picot as first ch-10, ch 2, join with dc in fourth ch of ch-10.

Rnd 20: Ch 6, sl st in third ch from hook, (dc, picot, dc, picot, dc) in joining ch sp; *complete the rnd as follows:*

A: 6-dc scallop in next ch sp, *(sc, picot, sc) in next ch sp, 8-dc scallop in next ch sp; repeat from * 2 more times;

B: Skip next dc, sc in next jdc;

C: (8-dc scallop in next ch sp, sc in next ch sp, picot, sc in same ch sp) 3 times, 6-dc scallop in each of next 3 ch sps, (sc in next ch sp, picot, sc in same ch sp, 8-dc scallop in next ch sp) 3 times;

D: Repeat steps B, C, B, C, B;

E: (8-dc scallop in next ch sp, sc in next ch sp, picot, sc in same ch sp) 3 times, 6-dc scallop in next ch sp;

F: (Dc, picot) 2 times in joining ch sp, join with sl st in third ch of ch-6.

Rnd 21: Sl st in picot, ch 8; *complete the rnd as follows:*

A: Skip next 2 picots, dc in next space between scallops, ch 5, skip next 2 picots, sc in next picot, ch 5, skip next 2 picots, dc in next picot;

B: Ch 7, skip next 3 picots, sc in next picot, ch 7, skip next 3 picots, dc in next picot, ch 7, skip next 3 picots, sc in next picot;

C: (Ch 7, skip next 3 picots, tr in next picot) 2 times; **mark** top of last tr made, ch 7, skip next 6 picots, tr in next picot; **mark** top of tr

just made, ch 7, skip next 3 picots, tr in next picot, (ch 7, skip next 3 picots, sc in next picot, ch 7, skip next 3 picots, dc in next picot) 2 times;

D: Ch 5, skip next 2 picots, sc in next picot, ch 5, dc in next space between scallops, ch 5, (dc, ch 5, dc) in next picot, ch 5;

E: Repeat steps A–D consecutively 2 more times;

F: Repeat steps A–C;

G: Ch 5, skip next 2 picots, sc in next picot, ch 5, dc in next space between scallops, ch 5, dc in same picot as first ch-8, ch 2, join with dc in third ch of ch-8.

Rnd 22: Ch 5, *dc in next dc, (ch 2, dc in next ch sp, ch 2, dc in next dc, in next sc or in next tr) across to next corner, ch 2, (dc, ch 5, dc) in corner ch sp, ch 2; repeat from * 2 more times, dc in next dc, (ch 2, dc in next ch sp, ch 2, dc in next dc, in next sc or in next tr) across to next corner, ch 2, dc in same place as first ch-5, ch 2, dc in third ch of first ch-5.

Rnds 23–40: Ch 5, *jdc, (ch 2, jdc) across side with last jdc in next corner ch-5 sp, ch 2, (dc, ch 5, dc) in corner ch sp, ch 2; repeat from * 2 more times, jdc, (ch 2, jdc) across side with last jdc in joining ch sp, ch 2, dc in joining sp, ch 2, join with dc in third ch of first ch-5. At end of last rnd, fasten off. *(72 ch-2 sps and 71 jdc on each side; 4 corner ch sps on last rnd)*

Small Center Roses

Rnd 1: Ch 6, sl st in first ch to form ring, ch 1, 12 sc in ring, join with sl st in first sc. *(12 sc made)*

Rnd 2: Ch 1, sc in first st, ch 3, skip next st, (sc in next st, ch 3, skip next st) around, join. *(6 sc, 6 ch sps)*

Rnd 3: For **petals**, (sl st, ch 1, sc, hdc, 3 dc, hdc, sc) in first ch sp, (sc, hdc, 3 dc, hdc, sc) in each ch sp around, join. *(6 petals)*

Rnd 4: Sl st back into sp between first and last sc, ch 1, sc in same sp, ch 5; working behind petals, (sc in next sp between petals, ch 5) around, join. *(6 ch sps)*

Rnd 5: For **petals**, (sl st, ch 1, sc, hdc, 3 dc) in first ch sp, sl st in any marked st on rnds 18 or 21 of Blanket, (2 dc, hdc, sc) in same ch sp on Rose as last dc, *(sc, hdc, 3 dc) in next ch sp, sl st in next marked st on Blanket, (2 dc, hdc, sc) in same ch sp on Rose as last dc; repeat from * around, join. Fasten off.

Repeat rnds 1–5 in each of three remaining groups of marked sts on rnds 18 and 21.

BORDER (work from right corner to left corner across each side of rnd 40)

First Leaf: Ch 12, sc in second ch from hook, hdc in next ch, dc in next 2 chs, tr in next ch, 2 tr in each of next 2 chs, tr in next ch, dc in next ch, hdc in next ch, 2 sc in last ch; counting right to left on last rnd of Blanket, sl st in third jdc from corner, sc in same ch on Leaf as last sc made; continuing on opposite side of ch, hdc in next ch, dc in next ch, tr in next 2 chs, sl st in last dc at right corner of Blanket, tr in same ch on Leaf as last tr made, 2 tr in next ch, tr in next ch, dc in next 2 chs, hdc in next ch, sc in next ch, join with sl st in first sc. Fasten off.

NOTE: *Inner point of Leaf attached to rnd 40 is* **base,** *outer point is* **tip.**

Second Leaf: Ch 12, sc in second ch from hook, hdc in next ch, dc in next 2 chs, tr in next ch, 2 tr in next ch, tr in next ch; counting toward left on last rnd of Blanket, skip next 2 unworked jdc, sl st in next jdc, tr in same ch on Leaf as last tr made, tr in next ch, dc in next ch, hdc in next ch, 2 sc in last ch, sl st in same jdc as joining of previous Leaf, sc in same st on Leaf as last sc made; continuing on opposite side of ch, hdc in next ch, dc in next ch, tr in next ch, 2 tr in each of next 2 chs, tr in next ch, dc in next 2 chs, hdc in next ch, sc in next ch, join with sl st in first sc on this Leaf. **Do not** fasten off.

Third Leaf: Ch 12, sc in second ch from hook, hdc in next ch, dc in next 2 chs, tr in next ch, 2 tr in each of next 2 chs, tr in next ch, dc in next ch, hdc in next ch, 2 sc in last ch; counting toward left on last rnd of Blanket, skip next 6 unworked jdc, sl st in next jdc, sc in same ch on Leaf as last sc made; continuing on opposite side of ch, hdc in next ch, dc in next ch, tr in next 2 chs; counting toward right, skip next 2 jdc on Blanket, sl st in next jdc, tr in same ch on Leaf as last tr made, 2 tr in next ch, tr in next ch, dc in next 2 chs, hdc in next ch, sc in next ch, sl st in tip of previous Leaf, join with sl st in first sc on this Leaf. Fasten off.

Fourth–Seventh Leaves: Repeat Second and Third Leaves alternately.

Large Side Rose

Rnd 1: Ch 8, sl st in first ch to form ring, ch 1, 16 sc in ring, join with sl st in first sc. *(16 sc made)*

Rnd 2: Ch 1, sc in first st, ch 3, skip next st, (sc in next st, ch 3, skip next st) around, join. *(8 sc, 8 ch sps)*

Rnd 3: For **petals,** (sl st, ch 1, sc, hdc, dc, hdc, sc) in first ch sp, (sc, hdc, dc, hdc, sc) in each ch sp around, join. *(8 petals)*

Rnd 4: Sl st back into sp between first and last sc, ch 1, sc in same sp, ch 4; working behind petals, (sc in next sp between petals, ch 4) around, join. *(8 ch sps)*

Rnd 5: For **petals,** (sl st, ch 1, sc, hdc, 3 dc, hdc, sc) in first ch sp, (sc, hdc, 3 dc, hdc, sc) in each ch sp around, join.

Rnd 6: Sl st back into sp between first and last sc, ch 1, sc in same sp, ch 5; working behind petals, (sc in next sp between petals, ch 5) around, join.

Rnd 7: For **petals,** (sl st, ch 1, sc, hdc, 5 dc, hdc, sc) in first ch sp, (sc, hdc, 5 dc, hdc, sc) in each ch sp around, join.

Rnd 8: Sl st back into sp between first and last sc, ch 1, sc in same sp, (ch 6; working behind petals, sc in next sp between petals) around, ch 6, join.

Rnd 9: For **petals,** (sl st, ch 1, sc, hdc, 7 dc, hdc, sc) in first ch sp, (sc, hdc, 7 dc, hdc, sc) in each of next 4 ch sps; *complete as follows:*
A: (Sc, hdc, 4 dc) in next ch sp, skip next 3 unworked jdc on Blanket, sl st in next jdc, (3 dc, hdc, sc) in same ch sp on Rose as last dc made;
B: (Sc, hdc, 4 dc) in next ch sp; counting toward Leaves, skip next jdc on Blanket, sl st in next jdc, (3 dc, hdc, sc) in same ch sp on Rose as last dc made;
C: (Sc, hdc, 4 dc) in next ch sp, skip next 5 sts on last Leaf made, sl st in next st, (3 dc, hdc, sc) in same ch sp on Rose as last dc made, join. Fasten off.

Eighth Leaf: Ch 12, sc in second ch from hook, hdc in next ch, dc in next 2 chs, tr in next ch, 2 tr in next ch, tr in next ch, skip next 4 unworked jdc on Blanket, sl st in next jdc, tr in same ch on Leaf as last tr made, tr in next ch, dc in next ch, hdc in next ch, 2 sc in last ch; counting toward Large Rose just made, skip next 2 unworked jdc on Blanket, sl st

Christening Blanket

Continued from page 59

in next jdc, sc in same ch on Leaf as last sc made; continuing on opposite side of ch, hdc in next ch, dc in next ch, tr in next 2 chs, sl st in center dc of next free Petal on Rose, tr in same ch on Leaf as last tr made, 2 tr in next ch, tr in next ch, dc in next 2 chs, hdc in next ch, sc in next ch, join with sl st in first sc on this Leaf. **Do not** fasten off.

Ninth Leaf: Repeat Third Leaf.

10th–14th Leaves: Repeat Second and Third Leaves alternately, ending with Second Leaf at left corner of Blanket edge.

15th Leaf: Ch 12, sc in second ch from hook, *hdc in next ch, dc in next 2 chs, tr in next ch, 2 tr in each of next 2 chs, tr in next ch, dc in next ch, hdc in next ch, 2 sc in last ch**, sl st in center dc of next free petal at left on Large Rose, sc in same ch on Leaf as last sc made; continuing on opposite side of ch, repeat from * to **, sl st in next sl st between tips of Leaves, join with sl st in first sc. Fasten off.

16th Leaf: Working at right of Large Rose, repeat 15th Leaf.

SMALL SIDE ROSES

On each side of Border, make six Small Side Roses and join between following pairs of Leaves:

First and Second Leaves
Third and Fourth Leaves
Fifth and Sixth Leaves
Ninth and 10th Leaves
11th and 12th Leaves
13th and 14th Leaves

Rnds 1–4: Work rnds 1–4 of Small Center Rose on page 58.

Rnd 5: For **petals,** (sl st, ch 1, sc, hdc, 5 dc, hdc, sc) in first ch sp, (sc, hdc, 5 dc, hdc, sc) in each of next 2 ch sps; *join to Leaves as follows:*

A: (Sc, hdc, 2 dc) in next ch sp, sl st in fifth st from tip of Leaf at left, (3 dc, hdc, sc) in same ch sp on Rose as last dc made;

B: (Sc, hdc) in next ch sp, skip next 4 sts on same Leaf, sl st in next st, 3 dc in same ch sp on Rose as last hdc made, sl st in fourth st from base of next Leaf at right, (hdc, sc) in same ch sp on Rose as last dc made;

C: (Sc, hdc, 2 dc) in next ch sp, skip next 4 sts on same Leaf, sl st in next st, (3 dc, hdc, sc) in same ch sp on Rose as last dc made, join. Fasten off.

SMALL CORNER ROSE
(make one at each corner)

Rnds 1–4: Work rnds 1–4 of Small Center Rose.

Rnd 5: For **petals,** (sl st, ch 1, sc, hdc, 5 dc, hdc, sc) in first ch sp, (sc, hdc, 5 dc, hdc, sc) in each of next 2 ch sps; *join to Leaves as follows:*

A: (Sc, hdc, 2 dc) in next ch sp, sl st in tip of First Leaf at right, (3 dc, hdc, sc) in same ch sp on Rose as last dc made;

B: (Sc, hdc, 2 dc) in next ch sp, sl st in corner ch sp on rnd 40 of Blanket, (3 dc, hdc, sc) in same ch sp on Rose as last dc made;

C: (Sc, hdc, 2 dc) in next ch sp, sl st in tip of next Leaf at left (3 dc, hdc, sc) in same ch sp on Rose as last dc made, join. Fasten off. ❧

Irish Crochet

The term Irish Crochet refers to a specific design style made popular during the mid-1800s when crocheters in Ireland stitched exquisite masterpieces in order to earn an income. With the economy destroyed by the "potato famine," men, women and children alike learned the art of "poor man's lace" to help get a nation back on its feet. Commonly associated today with the term "Irish Crochet" are the raised rose motifs with their pointed leaves that were so prominent in those designs. While today's threads are much heavier than those used in the Irish lace creations, it is still easy to achieve a small taste of yesteryear by adding these motifs to your projects.

Golden Pineapples An Original by Annie

TECHNIQUE
Mile-A-Minute

SPECIAL STITCHES
Front Loop, Picot

FINISHED SIZE
About 42 inches x 75 inches

MATERIALS
❏ 36 oz. Gold #171 Wool Ease Art. 620 by Lion Brand Yarn or worsted yarn
❏ F hook or size hook needed to obtain gauge

GAUGE
5 sts = 1 inch. Pineapple is 4½ inches wide x 6 inches long.

BASIC STITCHES
Ch, sl st, sc, dc

INSTRUCTIONS

PANEL (make 11)
Row 1: Ch 5, sl st in first ch to form ring, ch 3 *(counts as first dc),* (dc, ch 1, 2 dc) in ring, turn.

Row 2: Ch 5, 2 dc in sp between first 2 dc, (dc, ch 2, dc) in ch-1 sp, 2 dc in sp between last 2 dc, turn.

Row 3: Ch 5, 2 dc in sp between first 2 dc, ch 1, (2 dc, ch 3, 2 dc) in ch-2 sp, ch 1, 2 dc in sp between last 2 dc, turn.

Row 4: Ch 5, 2 dc in sp between first 2 dc, ch 2, (2 dc, ch 3, 2 dc) in ch-3 sp, ch 2, 2 dc in sp between last 2 dc, turn.

Row 5: Ch 5, 2 dc in sp between first 2 dc, ch 2, 8 dc in ch-3 sp, ch 2, 2 dc in sp between last 2 dc, turn. *Front of row 5 is* **right side** *of work.*

Row 6: Ch 5, 2 dc in sp between first 2 dc, ch 3, dc in first dc of 8-dc group, (ch 1, dc in next dc) 7 times, ch 3, 2 dc in sp between last 2 dc, turn.

Row 7: Ch 5, 2 dc in sp between first 2 dc, (ch 3, sc in next ch-1 sp) 7 times, ch 3, 2 dc in sp between last 2 dc, turn.

Rows 8–12: Ch 5, 2 dc in sp between first 2 dc, ch 3, skip next ch-3 sp, (sc in next ch-3 sp, ch 3) across to last ch-3 sp, skip last ch-3 sp, 2 dc in sp between last 2 dc, turn.

Row 13: Ch 5, 2 dc in sp between first 2 dc, ch 3, skip next ch-3 sp, sc in next ch-3 sp, ch 3, skip next ch-3 sp, 2 dc in sp between last 2 dc, turn.

Row 14: Ch 5, 2 dc in sp between first 2 dc, 2 dc in sp between last 2 dc, turn.

Row 15: Ch 5, 2 dc in sp between first 2 dc, ch 1, 2 dc in sp between last 2 dc, turn.

Rows 16–168: Repeat rows 2–15 consecutively, ending with row 14 on last repeat.

Row 169: Sl st in first 3 dc, skip last dc, turn.

Row 170: Ch 5, sc in sp between last 2 dc of row before last, sl st in side of last dc, turn.

Row 171: Ch 1; in ch-5 loop work (3 sc, ch 3; for **picot,** sl st in **front lp** *(see Stitch Guide on page 175)* of last sc made, 3 sc), sl st in same dc on row 169 that last sl st was worked into. Fasten off.

ASSEMBLY
The odd-numbered rows are the right side of the Panel.

The pineapples in all Panels must be facing the same direction before you join.

Seam 1: Hold Panels 1 and 2 side by side with right sides facing you *(see Panel Placement).* Beginning at first end of Panels, join with sc in first ch-5 loop on side of Panel 1 *(see Seam Illustration);* you will skip first 3 ch-5 loops on Panel 2 and complete the seam as follows:

Seam Illustration

A: (Ch 2, sc in next ch-5 loop on Panel 2, ch 2, sc in next ch-5 loop on Panel 1) 2 times, ch 2, (sc in next ch-5 loop on Panel 2, ch 1) 2 times, sc in next ch-5 loop on Panel 2.
B: (Ch 2, sc in next ch-5 loop on Panel 1,

Golden Pineapples

Continued from page 61

ch 2, sc in next ch-5 loop on Panel 2) 2 times, ch 2, (sc in next ch-5 loop on Panel 1, ch 1) 2 times, sc in next ch-5 loop on Panel 1.

C: Repeat A and B alternately 10 more times.

D: (Ch 2, sc in next ch-5 loop on Panel 2, ch 2, sc in next ch-5 loop on Panel 1) 2 times, ch 2, sc in next ch-5 loop on Panel 2. Fasten off.

Seam 2: Hold Panel 3 on opposite side of Panel 2 with right sides facing you *(see Panel Placement)*. Beginning at first end of Panels, join with sc in first ch-5 loop on Panel 3 *(see Seam Illustration)*; you will skip first 3 ch-5 loops on Panel 2 and complete the seam as follows:

A: (Ch 2, sc in next ch-5 loop on Panel 2, ch 2, sc in next ch-5 loop on Panel 3) 2 times, ch 2, (sc in next ch-5 loop on Panel 2, ch 1) 2 times, sc in next ch-5 loop on Panel 2.

B: (Ch 2, sc in next ch-5 loop on Panel 3, ch 2, sc in next ch-5 loop on Panel 2) 2 times, ch 2, (sc in next ch-5 loop on Panel 3, ch 1) 2 times, sc in next ch-5 loop on Panel 3.

C: Repeat A and B alternately 10 more times.

D: (Ch 2, sc in next ch-5 loop on Panel 2, ch 2, sc in next ch-5 loop on Panel 3) 2 times, ch 2, sc in next ch-5 loop on Panel 2. Fasten off. Repeat seams 1 and 2 alternately until all Panels are joined.❦

Panel Placement
Place last rows of Panels at this end.

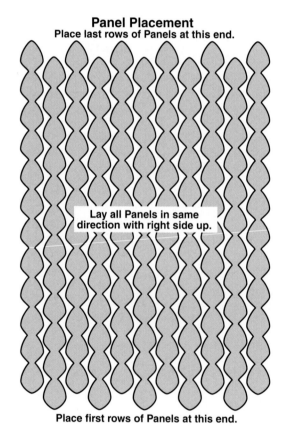

Lay all Panels in same direction with right side up.

Place first rows of Panels at this end.

Mile-A-Minute

Popularized in the '70s as a super quick strip style afghan that was joined as you worked, today the Mile-A-Minute name has come to symbolize any design which is worked in long strips. These strips can be simple or difficult and can be joined in any fashion.

Old-World Fisherman by Melissa Leapman

TECHNIQUE
Aran

SPECIAL STITCHES
Back Posts/Front Posts, Cluster, Popcorn, Reverse Single Crochet, Rope Stitch

FINISHED SIZE
56 inches x 70 inches

MATERIALS
❏ 80 oz. Fisherman #099 Wool-Ease Art. 620 by Lion Brand Yarn or worsted yarn
❏ H hook or size hook needed to obtain gauge

GAUGE
4 hdc = 1 inch; 7 hdc rows = 2 inches.

BASIC STITCHES
Ch, sl st, sc, hdc, dc, tr

SPECIAL STITCHES
For **rope st cluster (rope st),** yo 2 times, insert hook around post of corresponding st on row before last, yo, pull lp through, (yo, pull through 2 lps on hook) 2 times, yo 2 times, insert hook around post of same st on row before last, yo, pull lp through, (yo, pull through 2 lps on hook) 2 times, yo, pull through all 3 lps on hook. *(After row 3, each rope st is worked around rope st on row before last.)*

For **popcorn (pc),** 5 dc in next st; drop lp from hook, insert hook front to back through top of first dc of group, return dropped lp to hook and pull through st.

INSTRUCTIONS
Row 1: Ch 216, hdc in third ch from hook, hdc in each ch across turn. *(2 chs at beginning of row counts as first hdc—215 hdc made)*

Row 2: Ch 2, hdc in each st across, turn.

NOTES: *Treble crochet front post and double crochet back post of previous rows are referred to as **post sts.***

Unless otherwise stated, skip one st on last row behind each rope st or post st worked into a previous row.

Row 3: Ch 2, hdc in next 2 sts; *work the following steps to complete the row:*

A: Rope st *(see Special Stitches and Note),* hdc in next st on last row, **pc** *(see Special Stitches),* hdc in next st, rope st, hdc in next 3 sts on last row;
B: Counting from last rope st made, skip next 5 sts on row before last, **tr front post (trfp—** *see Stitch Guide on page 175)* around each of next 2 sts on row before last;
C: (Skipping st behind each trfp—*see Note,* hdc in next 4 sts on last row; working in front of last 2 hdc made, trfp around each of next 2 unworked sts on row before last, skip next 4 sts on row before last, trfp around each of next 2 sts) 4 times, hdc in next 4 sts on last row; working in front of last 2 hdc made, trfp around each of next 2 unworked sts on row before last, hdc in next 3 sts on last row;
D: Repeat steps A–C 3 more times;
E: Rope st, hdc in next st, pc, hdc in next st, rope st, hdc in last 3 sts, turn.

Front of row 3 is right side of work.

Row 4: Ch 2, hdc in next 10 sts, ***dc back post (dcbp—** *see Stitch Guide)* around each of next 2 **post sts** *(see Note),* hdc in next 4 sts, (dcbp around each of next 4 post sts, hdc in next 4 sts) 4 times, dcbp around each of next 2 post sts, hdc in next 11 sts; repeat from * across, turn.

Row 5: Ch 2, hdc in next 2 sts; *work the following steps to complete the row:*
A: (Rope st, hdc in next 3 sts on last row) 2 times;
B: Hdc in next 2 post sts; working in front of last 2 hdc just made, trfp around same 2 posts sts, skip next 4 hdc on last row, trfp around next 2 post sts; working behind last 2 trfp just made, hdc in tops of same 2 posts;
C: Repeat step B four more times;
D: Hdc in next 3 sts, (rope st, hdc in next 3 sts on last row) 2 times;
E: Repeat steps B–D across, turn.

Row 6: Ch 2, hdc in next 12 sts, *[dcbp around each of next 4 post sts, (hdc in next 4 post sts, dcbp around each of next 4 post sts) 4 times], hdc in next 15 sts; repeat from * 2 more times; repeat between [ ], hdc in last 13 sts, turn.

Row 7: Ch 2, hdc in next 2 sts; *work the following steps to complete the row:*

Continued on page 69

Sunny Chrysanthemums by Rena V. Stevens

TECHNIQUES
Fringe Embellishment, Ripple

SPECIAL STITCHES
Back Loops/Front Loops, Cluster, Post Stitch

FINISHED SIZE
About 60 inches x 66 inches,
not including Tassels

MATERIALS
❑ Red Heart TLC Art E510 by Coats & Clark
 or worsted yarn:
 32 oz. Butterscotch #5263 *(med. yellow)*
 25 oz. White #5001
 13 oz. Lt. Yellow #5257
 11 oz. Natural #5017 *(off-white)*
❑ H hook or size hook needed to
 obtain gauge

GAUGE
16 hdc in ripple pattern = 3½ inches;
8 hdc rows in ripple pattern = 6 inches.

BASIC STITCHES
Ch, sl st, sc, hdc, dtr

INSTRUCTIONS
Row 1: With med. yellow, ch 307, 2 hdc in
third ch from hook, hdc in next 4 chs, (skip
next ch, hdc in next ch) 3 times, skip next ch,
hdc in next 4 chs, *5 hdc in next ch, hdc in
next 4 chs, (skip next ch, hdc in next ch) 3
times, skip next ch, hdc in next 4 chs; repeat
from * across to last ch, 3 hdc in last ch,
turn. *(2 chs at beginning of row counts as first
hdc—305 sts made.)* **Front** of row 1 is **right
side** of work.

Row 2: Working this row in **horizontal bars**
(see illustration), (ch 2, 2 hdc) in first st, hdc
in next 4 sts, (skip next st, hdc in next st) 3
times, skip next st, hdc in next 4 sts, *5 hdc
in next st, hdc in next 4 sts, (skip next st, hdc
in next st) 3 times, skip next st, hdc in next 4
sts; repeat from * across to last st, 3 hdc in
last st, turn. Fasten off.

Row 3: Working this row in **back lps** *(see
Stitch Guide on page 175),* join lt. yellow with
sl st in first st, (ch 2, 2 hdc) in same st as sl
st, hdc in next 4 sts, (skip next st, hdc in next
st) 3 times, skip next st, hdc in next 4 sts,
*5 hdc in next st, hdc in next 4 sts, (skip next
st, hdc in next st) 3 times, skip next st, hdc
in next 4 sts; repeat from * across to last st,
3 hdc in last st, turn.

Row 4: Working this row in **horizontal bars,**
(ch 2, 2 hdc) in first st, hdc in next 4 sts, (skip
next st, hdc in next st) 3 times, skip next st,
hdc in next 4 sts, *5 hdc in next st, hdc in next
4 sts, (skip next st, hdc in next st) 3 times, skip
next st, hdc in next 4 sts; repeat from * across
to last st, 3 hdc in last st, turn. Fasten off.

Rows 5–6: With off-white, repeat rows 3
and 4.

Rows 7–8: With white, repeat rows 3 and 4.

*NOTE: For **dtr-2-tog (cluster) in next st,**
yo 3 times, insert hook in designated st, yo,
pull through, (yo, pull through 2 lps on hook)
3 times leaving 2 lps on hook, yo 3 times,
insert hook in same st, yo, pull through, (yo,
pull through 2 lps on hook) 3 times, yo, pull
through 3 lps on hook.*

Row 9: For **Chrysanthemums (mums)**
panel, for **first half of mums,** join med.
yellow with sc in first st, *ch 5, (skip next
2 sts, **cluster** in next st—*see Note)* 2 times,
skip next 3 sts, (cluster in next st, skip next
2 sts) 2 times, ch 5, sc in next st; repeat from
* across, turn. *(38 ch-5 sps, 76 clusters)*

Row 10: Ch 1, sl st in first st, (ch 5, skip
next ch-5, sc in next cluster, ch 2, skip next
2 clusters, sc in next cluster, ch 5, skip next
ch-5, sl st in next sc) across, turn. *(38 ch-5
sps, 19 ch-2 sps)*

*NOTE: Clusters and ch-5 pairs on rows 10 and
11 are worked into and counted as **petals.***

Row 11: Ch 1, sc in first sl st; *complete the
row as follows:*
A: For **second half of mums,** ch 2, skip next
ch-5 and next sc, (cluster, ch 3) 3 times in
next ch-2 sp, cluster in same ch-2 sp, ch 2,
skip next sc and next ch-5, sc in next sl st
(single mum completed; 10 petals total on
both halves);

Light the Way by Patricia Zihala

TECHNIQUE
Filet

SPECIAL STITCH
Back Loops

FINISHED SIZE
52 inches x 78½ inches

MATERIALS
- ❑ 48 oz. Aran #313 Red Heart Super Saver Art. E300 by Coats & Clark or worsted yarn
- ❑ H hook or size hook needed to obtain gauge

GAUGE
7 sts and chs = 2 inches; 3 dc **back lp** rows = 2 inches.

BASIC STITCHES
Ch, dc

SPECIAL STITCHES
For **block,** dc in next st or ch sp, dc in next st.

For **mesh,** ch 1, skip next st or ch sp, dc in next st.

INSTRUCTIONS
Row 1: Ch 183, dc in fourth ch from hook, dc in each ch across, turn. *(3 chs at beginning of row counts as first dc—181 sts made.)*

Rows 2–59: Ch 3; working in **back lps** *(see Stitch Guide),* work according to corresponding row of Light The Way Graph, turn.

Rows 60–117: Repeat rows 2–59.

Row 118: Ch 3; working in **back lps,** dc in each st across. Fasten off. ❧

Key:
- ■ Block
- ☐ Mesh

Light The Way

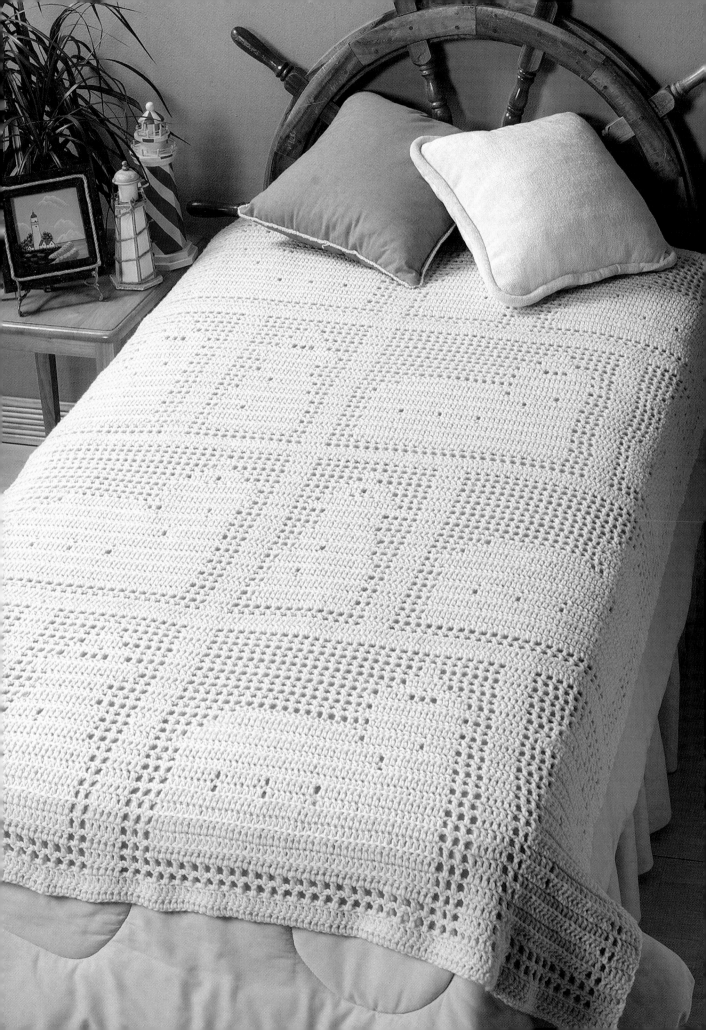

Mosaic Stair-Step by Melissa Leapman

TECHNIQUE
Color Change

SPECIAL STITCHES
Back Loops/Front Loops,
Long Double Crochet

FINISHED SIZE
48 inches x 68 inches

MATERIALS
❏ Wool-Ease Art. 620 by Lion Brand Yarns or
worsted yarn:
30 oz. Purple #147 *(dark)*
30 oz. Lavender #143 *(light)*
❏ H hook or size hook needed to obtain gauge

GAUGE
In pattern, 14 sts = 4 inches, 8 rows =
2 inches.

BASIC STITCHES
Ch, sc, dc

SPECIAL STITCH
For **long dc (ldc),** yo, insert hook in **front
lp** of corresponding same-color stitch three
rows below, complete as dc, pulling st up to
height of this row.

INSTRUCTIONS
Row 1: With dark, ch 171, sc in second ch
from hook, sc in each ch across, turn. *(170
sts made)*

Row 2: Ch 1, sc in each st across changing
to light in last st *(see Stitch Guide on page
175),* turn.

NOTES: *Front of row 1 is* **right side** *of work.*

*Carry dropped color loosely along edge of
work;* **do not cut.**

*Dropped colors will be worked over in first
rnd of Border.*

Row 3: Ch 1, sc in first st; working in **back
lps** *(see Stitch Guide),* sc in each st across to
last st; sc in **both lps** of last st, turn.

Row 4: Ch 1; sc in **both lps** of each st across
changing to dark in last st, turn.

Row 5: Ch 1, sc in **both lps** of first st; *sc
in **back lps** of next 6 sts, **ldc** *(see Special

Stitch) 2 times; repeat from * across to last st;
sc in **both lps** of last st, turn.

Row 6: Ch 1; sc in **both lps** of each st across
changing to light in last st, turn.

Row 7: Ch 1, sc in **both lps** of first st; (ldc 2
times, sc in **back lps** of next 6 sts) across to
last st; sc in **both lps** of last st, turn.

Row 8: Ch 1; sc in **both lps** of each st across
changing to dark in last st, turn.

Row 9: Ch 1, sc in **both lps** of first st, sc
in **back lps** of next 2 sts, ldc 2 times, (sc in
back lps of next 6 sts, ldc 2 times) across to
last 5 sts; sc in **back lps** of next 4 sts, sc in
both lps of last st, turn.

Row 10: Ch 1; sc in **both lps** of each st
across changing to light in last st, turn.

Row 11: Ch 1, sc in **both lps** of first st, sc
in **back lps** of next 4 sts, ldc 2 times, (sc in
back lps of next 6 sts, ldc 2 times) across to
last 3 sts, sc in **back lps** of next 2 sts, sc in
both lps of last st, turn.

Row 12: Ch 1; sc in **both lps** of each st
across changing to dark in last st, turn.

Next rows: Repeat rows 5–12 consecutively
until piece is about 65 inches long, or desired
length, ending with a wrong-side row worked
with dark. Fasten off light; **do not fasten
off dark.**

BORDER
Rnd 1: With right side of work facing, working
around outer edge in sts, in ends of rows and
in chs on opposite side of row 1, spacing
sts evenly across ends of rows so edge lays
flat and covering dropped colors as you go,
ch 1, sc in sts and in ends of rows around with
3 sc at each corner, join with sl st in first sc,
do not turn.

Rnd 2: Ch 1, sc in each st around with 3 sc
in each center corner st, join. Fasten off.

Rnd 3: Join light with sc in first st, sc in each
st around with 3 sc in each center corner
st, join.

Rnd 4: Ch 1, sc in each st around with 3 sc
in each center corner st, join. Fasten off.

Rnds 5–6: With dark, repeat rnds 3 and 4.❦

Interlocking Intrigue by Nancy Nehring

TECHNIQUE
Interlocked Layers

SPECIAL STITCH
Back Loops

FINISHED SIZE
38 inches x 70 inches

MATERIALS
❑ TLC Essentials Art. E514 by Coats & Clark
  or worsted yarn:
  24 oz. Baby Yellow #2222
  24 oz. Light Thyme #2672 *(green)*
❑ H hook or size hook needed to obtain gauge

GAUGE
7 sts and chs of same color = 2 inches;
6 same-color rows = 5 inches.

BASIC STITCHES
Ch, sl st, sc, dc

SPECIAL STITCH
Interlock each green row as follows: With green ch or row held in front of previous row, to work green dc **behind** last yellow row, yo, insert hook from back through ch sp of previous yellow row into designated green ch or dc; to work green dc in **front** of previous yellow row, work dc as normal into designated green ch or st.

Yellow stitches are only worked into other yellow stitches; after row 1, they are always worked behind a green row. **Green** stitches are only worked into other green stitches; they alternate one stitch in front of and one stitch behind the previous yellow row.

INSTRUCTIONS

Row 1: With yellow, ch 134, dc in eighth ch from hook, (ch 2, skip next 2 chs, dc in next ch) across, **do not turn.** Remove loop from hook. *(3 chs at beginning of row count as first dc—44 dc, 43 ch sps made.)*

Row 2: With green, ch 137; holding ch in front of row 1, working **behind** last yellow row into green chs only *(see Special Stitch);* inserting hook through second yellow ch sp, dc in 12th green ch from hook (ch 2, skip next 2 green chs; working in **front** of yellow, dc in next ch, ch 2, skip next 2 green chs; working **behind** yellow, dc in next green ch) across to last

5 chs, ch 4, skip next 4 green chs; working in **front** of yellow, dc in last green ch, **turn.** Remove loop from hook. *(43 dc, 42 ch sps)*

Row 3: Return yellow loop to hook; working **behind** last green row into yellow sts only, ch 5 *(counts as first dc and ch-2 sp),* (dc in next dc, ch 2) across to last ch sp, skip next 2 chs, dc in next ch, **do not turn.** Remove loop from hook.

Row 4: Return green loop to hook, ch 7 *(counts as first dc and ch-4 sp);* working **behind** last yellow row into green sts only, dc in next dc, (ch 2; working in **front** of yellow, dc in next green dc, ch 2; working **behind** yellow, dc in next green dc) across to last green ch sp; working in **front** of yellow, ch 4, skip next 4 green chs, dc in next ch of ch-7, **turn.** Remove loop from hook.

Row 5: Repeat row 3.

Row 6: Return green loop to hook, ch 7; working in **front** of yellow, dc in next green dc, (ch 2; working **behind** yellow, ch 2, dc in next green dc; working in **front** of yellow, dc in next green dc) across to last green ch sp; working **behind** yellow, ch 4, skip next 4 green chs, dc in next ch of ch-7, **turn.** Remove loop from hook.

Rows 7–164: Repeat rows 3–6 consecutively, ending with row 4, or to desired length. At end of last row, fasten off both colors.

BORDER

Rnd 1: Working over both colors as one around all edges, join yellow with sc in corner sp at beginning of last row, work 4 more sc in same corner sp, *sc between first yellow and green sts, (2 sc in next space between yellow and green sts, sc in next space between next yellow and green sts) across to corner sp, 5 sc in corner sp; working across ends of rows, (skip next yellow row, 2 sc in next opening at end of row, skip next green row, sc in next opening at end of row) across to corner ch sp**, 5 sc in corner ch sp; repeat from * to **, join with sl st in first sc. Fasten off.

Rnd 2: Working this rnd in **back lps** *(see Stitch Guide on page 175),* join green with sl st in any st, ch 3, dc in each st around with 5 dc in each center corner st, join with sl st in top of ch-3. Fasten off. ❧

Baby Magic Square by Janet Rehfeldt

TECHNIQUE
Magic Square Folding

FINISHED SIZE
About 28 inches x 28 inches

MATERIALS
❏ 19 oz. Powder Yellow #5322 Red Heart
  TLC Baby Art. 511 by Coats & Clark or
  worsted yarn
❏ J hook or size hook needed to obtain gauge

GAUGE
14 sts = 4 inches; 9 rows = 2 inches.

BASIC STITCHES
Ch, sl st, sc, dc

INSTRUCTIONS
Row 1: Ch 135; working in **back bar of ch**
(see illustration), skip first ch from hook, sl st
in second ch, sl st in each ch across. **Do not
join or turn** unless otherwise stated. *(134 sl
sts made)*

Back Bar of Ch

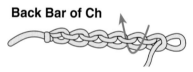

Rnd 2: Working on opposite side of ch, (sc
in next ch, dc in next ch) across to end; sc in
skipped first ch, (dc in next sl st, sc in next sl
st) around, dc in end of starting ch on row 1.
(270 sts)

NOTE: *Mark first st of each rnd.*

Rnd 3: To **work in pattern,** dc in each sc
and sc in each dc around.

Next rnds: Repeat rnd 3 until piece
measures approximately 19 inches from
starting ch when piece is laid flat *(see
Measuring Illustration),* or until last rnd
touches and piece forms a square when
folded in on itself *(see Folding Illustration).*
Mark fold *(see arrow on illustration),* then
continue working in pattern across to mark.
Fasten off, leaving a yarn end long enough
to sew seam.

Fold piece as shown in Folding Illustration;
sew tops of sts on last row together across
to opposite corner.❦

Measuring Illustration

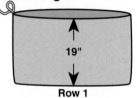

19"

Row 1

Folding Illustration

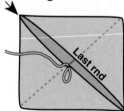

Last rnd

Row 1 is on bottom.

Magic Square Folding

The Magic Square Folding technique is very
versatile and can be adapted to a variety
of uses. You may have seen it used in the
past for hot pads or pillows. This project
adapts the Magic Folding Square to a
child's afghan. The double-thick fabric adds
warmth and softness any youngster will
love. Add tassels at the corners for a little
something extra!

Post Stitch Ripple by Nanette Seale

TECHNIQUE
Ripple

SPECIAL STITCHES
Post Stitch, Post Stitch Cluster

FINISHED SIZE
48 inches x 60 inches

MATERIALS
❑ Red Heart TLC Art. E510 by Coats & Clark
  or worsted yarn:
  26 oz. Polo Ombre #5976 *(gold/green/blue/red)*
  17 oz. Amber #5644 *(gold)*
  17 oz. Dark Sage #5666 *(green)*
  17 oz. Navy #5861 *(blue)*
  17 oz. Claret #5915 *(red)*
❑ I hook or size hook needed to obtain gauge

GAUGE
In pattern, 10 sts = 3 inches, 4 rows =
2 inches.

BASIC STITCHES
Ch, sl st, dc

SPECIAL STITCH
For **front post dc cluster (fp cl),** yo, insert
hook from front to back to front around post
of next st, *(see **front post** in Stitch Guide
on page 175),* yo, pull through st, yo, pull
through 2 lps on hook, yo, insert hook from
front to back to front around post of same st,
yo, pull through st, yo, pull through 2 lps on
hook, yo, pull through all 3 lps on hook.

INSTRUCTIONS

Row 1: With green, ch 204, dc in fourth ch
from hook, skip next ch, (dc in next 15 chs,
3 dc in next ch, dc in next 15 chs, skip next
2 chs) 5 times, dc in next 15 chs, 3 dc in next
ch, dc in next 15 chs, skip next ch, dc in last
2 chs, turn. *(3 chs at beginning of row counts
as first dc—202 sts made.)*

Row 2: Ch 3, **fp cl** around next st *(see Special
Stitch),* skip next st, (dc in next st, fp cl around
next st) 7 times; *complete row as follows:*
A: Dc in next st, 3 dc in next st, fp cl around
next st, (dc in next st, fp cl around next st)
7 times, skip next 2 sts, (dc in next st, fp cl
around next st) 7 times;

B: Repeat step A 4 more times;
C: Dc in next st, 3 dc in next st, fp cl around
next st, (dc in next st, fp cl around next
st) 7 times, skip next st, dc in next st, fp cl
around last st, turn.

Row 3: Ch 3, fp cl around next st, skip next
st, (fp cl around next st, dc in next st) 7 times;
complete row as follows:
A: Fp cl around next st, 3 dc in next st, dc in
next st, (fp cl around next st, dc in next st)
7 times, skip next 2 sts, (fp cl around next st,
dc in next st) 7 times;
B: Repeat step A 4 more times;
C: Fp cl around next st, 3 dc in next st, dc
in next st, (fp cl around next st, dc in next
st) 7 times, skip next st, dc in next st, fp cl
around last st, turn.

Row 4: Repeat row 2. Fasten off.

Row 5: Join blue with sl st in first st, ch 3,
fp cl around next st, skip next st, (fp cl
around next st, dc in next st) 7 times;
complete row as follows:
A: Fp cl around next st, 3 dc in next st, dc
in next st, (fp cl around next st, dc in next st)
7 times, skip next 2 sts, (fp cl around next st,
dc in next st) 7 times;
B: Repeat step A 4 more times;
C: Fp cl around next st, 3 dc in next st, dc
in next st, (fp cl around next st, dc in next
st) 7 times, skip next st, dc in next st, fp cl
around last st, turn.

Rows 6–8: Work rows 2, 3 and 2. At end of
last row, fasten off.

Rows 9–10: With ombre, work rows 5 and 2.
At end of last row, fasten off.

Rows 11–14: With red, work rows 5, 2, 3 and
2. At end of last row, fasten off.

Rows 15–18: With gold, work rows 5, 2, 3
and 2. At end of last row, fasten off.

Rows 19–22: With ombre, work rows 5, 2, 3
and 2. At end of last row, fasten off.

Rows 23–26: With green, work rows 5, 2, 3
and 2. At end of last row, fasten off.

Rows 27–88: Repeat rows 5–26 consecutively, ending with row 22. ❧

Spiral Lapghan by Pauline Turner

TECHNIQUE
Spiral

SPECIAL STITCH
Reverse Single Crochet

FINISHED SIZE
41 inches in diameter

MATERIALS
❑ Worsted yarn in desired colors *(bright green and navy are shown)*:
   8 oz. light color
   8 oz. dark color
❑ 2 crochet stitch markers
❑ H hook or size hook needed to obtain gauge

GAUGE
7 dc = 2 inches; rnd 5A and 5B = 5½ inches across.

BASIC STITCHES
Ch, sl st, sc, hdc, dc

INSTRUCTIONS

Rnd 1: With light, ch 6, sl st in first ch to form ring, (sl st, sc, hdc, 3 dc) in first half of ring; remove hook and **place marker (M)** in lp for beginning of light rnd *(6 light sts made)*; join dark with sl st in ring, (sl st, sc, hdc, 3 dc) in second half of ring; **place M** in lp on hook for beginning of dark rnd *(6 dark sts made)*.

Rnd 2: 2 dc in each of next 6 light sts; remove hook and move M directly below up to lp *(12 dark sts)*; place light lp on hook, 2 dc in each of next 6 sts, move M directly below up to lp on hook *(12 light sts)*.

NOTE: *For* **increase (inc),** *2 dc in same st.*

Rnd 3: (Dc in next st, **inc**—*see Note*—in next st) 6 times; remove lp from hook and move M directly below up to lp *(18 light sts);* place lp from previous rnd on hook; (dc in next st, inc in next st) 6 times, move M directly below up to lp on hook *(18 dark sts).*

Rnd 4: (Dc in next 2 sts, inc) 6 times; remove hook and move M directly below up to lp *(24 dark sts);* place lp from previous rnd on hook; (dc in next 2 sts, inc) 6 times, move M directly below up to lp on hook *(24 light sts).*

Rnd 5: Dc in each st across to next M with inc in second st of each inc; remove hook and move M directly below up to lp *(30 light sts);* place lp from previous rnd on hook; dc in each st across to next M with inc in second st of each inc, move M directly below up to lp on hook *(30 dark sts).*

Next rnds: Repeat rnd 5 until there are 40 sts from one inc to next inc, ending with dark color and 480 sts on last rnd. Remove dark lp from hook.

Next rnd: Place light lp from previous rnd on hook, dc in next st, hdc in next 3 sts, sc in next 3 sts, sl st in next 3 sts. Fasten off light color yarn.

Next rnd: Return dark lp to hook, dc in each st and in each sl st around with inc in second st of each inc.

Next rnd: Hdc in next st, sc in each st around, sl st in first hdc.

Last rnd: Working from left to right, ch 1, **reverse sc** *(see Stitch Guide on page 175)* in each st around, join with sl st in first reverse sc. Fasten off.❧

Pretty Baby Pastels by Dot Drake

TECHNIQUES
Celtic, Join As You Go

SPECIAL STITCHES
Cluster, Shell

FINISHED SIZE
About 36 inches x 47 inches

MATERIALS
❑ Red Heart TLC Baby Art. E511 by Coats & Clark or sport yarn:
14 oz. White #5011
4 oz. each of four desired colors *(shown are Powder Pink #5737, Powder Blue #5881, Powder Lilac #5545, Powder Yellow #5322)*
❑ G hook or size hook needed to obtain gauge

GAUGE
Shell = 1 inch; 3 shell rows = 2 inches. Panel is 4½ inches wide.

BASIC STITCHES
Ch, sl st, sc, dc, tr

SPECIAL STITCHES
For **2-dc cluster (2-dc cl),** (yo, insert hook in ring, yo, pull through ring, yo, pull through 2 lps on hook) 2 times, yo, pull through all 3 lps on hook.

For **3-dc cluster (3-dc cl),** (yo, insert hook in ring, yo, pull through ring, yo, pull through 2 lps on hook) 3 times, yo, pull through all 4 lps on hook.

For **shell,** (3 dc, ch 5, 3 dc) in next ch-5 sp.

INSTRUCTIONS

FIRST PANEL
(use any two desired colors for Layers 1 and 2)

Layer 1
With first desired color, ch 7, *[sl st in seventh ch from hook to form ring, **turn; for flower,** (sc, ch 2, **2-dc cl**—*see Special Stitches,* ch 5, **3-dc cl,** ch 5, 3-dc cl, ch 5, 2-dc cl, ch 2, sc) in ring *(flower made)]*, **turn;** ch 20; repeat from * 32 more times; repeat between [ ]. Fasten off. *(34 flowers, 33 ch-20 sps made)*

Layer 2
With second desired color, repeat Layer 1.

Layer 3
Row 1: With white, ch 5, (2 dc, ch 5, 3 dc) in fifth ch from hook *(counts as first shell),* turn.

Row 2: Ch 4, **shell** *(see Special Stitches),* tr in top of ch-5, turn.

Rows 3–70: Ch 4, shell, tr in top of ch-4, turn.

Rnd 71: Working around entire Panel, (2 sc, ch 3, 2 sc) in end of each row across; working on opposite side of row 1, ch 3, (3 dc, ch 3, 3 dc) in same ch as first shell, ch 3; working in ends of rows, (2 sc, ch 3, 2 sc) in end of each row across; working across row 70, sl st in first 3 sts, (2 sc, ch 3, 2 sc) in next ch sp, sl st in next 3 sts, join with sl st in first sc. Fasten off.

To **assemble layers,** with right sides up and without twisting chs, place Layer 1 on flat surface with flowers on alternate sides to form a zigzag pattern; place Layer 2 over Layer 1 with flowers in reverse zigzag pattern; place Layer 3 over top.

Pull first flowers of Layers 1 and 2 through openings at both ends of row 3 on Layer 3; (skip ends of next row on Layer 3 and pull next flowers through openings at both ends of next row) across, leaving ends of row 70 free.

Rnd 72: Skip first 3 sc on rnd 71, join white with sl st in fourth sc; *complete row as follows:*
A: Working across long edge of flowers, 3 sc in first ch-5 sp of first flower, ch 3, (2 sc, ch 3, 2 sc) in next ch-5 sp, ch 3, 2 sc in last ch-5 sp of this flower;
B: Sc same ch-5 sp of this flower and first ch-5 sp of next flower together, work 2 more sc in first ch-5 sp, ch 3, (2 sc, ch 3, 2 sc) in next ch-5 sp, ch 3, 2 sc in last ch-5 sp of this flower;
C: Repeat step B across all flowers; on last flower, work one more sc in last ch-5 sp;
D: Working across end of Layer 3, *(2 sc, ch 3, 2 sc) in next ch-3 sp, sl st in next 3 sts; repeat from *, (2 sc, ch 3, 2 sc) in next ch-3 sp;
E: Repeat steps A, B and C, sl st in first sc worked into free ch-3 sp of Layer 3. Fasten off.

Continued on page 87

Granny's Flower Garden by Maggie Weldon

TECHNIQUE
Join As You Go

FINISHED SIZE
50 inches x 60 inches

MATERIALS
❑ Jiffy Art. 450 by Lion Brand Yarn or chunky yarn:
  27 oz. White #100
  21 oz. Pistachio #169 *(green)*
  3 oz. Lemon #158 *(yellow)*
  3 oz. each of four flower colors *(shown are Baby Blue #106, Rose #140, Light Pink #101 and Lilac #144)*
❑ H hook or size hook needed to obtain gauge

GAUGE
Motif = 2 inches across.

BASIC STITCHES
Ch, sl st, dc

NOTE
To **join,** drop loop from hook, insert hook in ch-1 sp of previous Ring, return loop to hook and ch 1.

INSTRUCTIONS
Begin at top left corner and use color for each Motif as shown on Quilt Assembly illustration on page 86.

Number at center of each Motif on Quilt Motif Joinings illustration on page 87, indicates which Motif to make.

Motif No. 1
Ch 6, sl st in first ch to form ring, (ch 3—*counts as first dc,* 2 dc) in ring, ch 1 at corner, (3 dc in ring, ch 1 at corner) 5 times, join with sl st in top of ch-3. Fasten off. *(18 dc, 6 corner ch sps made)*

Motif No. 2 (joins on one side)
Ch 6, sl st in first ch to form ring, (ch 3, 2 dc) in ring, **join** *(see Note)* to designated ch-1 sp on previous Motif, 3 dc in ring, join to next ch-1 sp on same previous Motif, (3 dc in ring, ch 1) 4 times, join with sl st in top of ch-3. Fasten off.

Motif No. 3 (joins on two sides)
Ch 6, sl st in first ch to form ring, (ch 3, 2 dc) in ring, join to next free ch-1 sp on previous row, 3 dc in ring on this Motif, join to next joined ch-1 sp on previous row, 3 dc in ring, join to next ch-1 sp on last Motif on this row, (3 dc in ring, ch 1) 3 times, join. Fasten off.

Motif No. 4 (joins on three sides)
Ch 6, sl st in first ch to form ring, (ch 3, 2 dc) in ring, join to next free ch-1 sp on previous row, 3 dc in ring on this Motif, (join to next joined ch-1 sp on previous row, 3 dc in ring) 2 times, join to next ch-1 sp on last Motif on this row, (3 dc in ring, ch 1) 3 times, join. Fasten off.

Motif No. 5 (joins on three sides with unjoined side between)
Ch 6, sl st in first ch to form ring, (ch 3, 2 dc) in ring, join to free ch-1 sp on previous row *(see red dot on Fourth Row of Quilt Motif Joinings illustration on page 87),* 3 dc in ring on this Motif, join to next free ch-1 sp on same Motif on previous row, (3 dc in ring, join to adjacent ch-1 sp on last Motif made on this row) 2 times, (3 dc in ring, ch 1) 2 times, join. Fasten off.❦

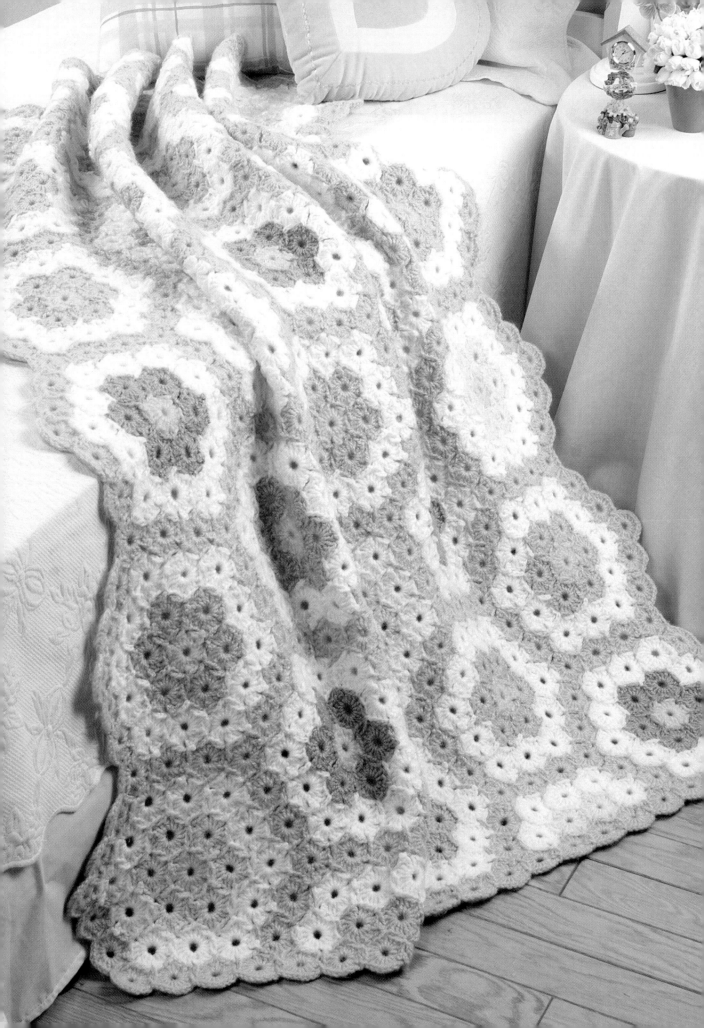

Granny's Flower Garden

Continued from page 84

Quilt Motif Joinings

First Row

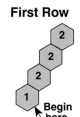

Second Row

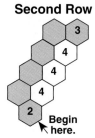

Quilt Assembly

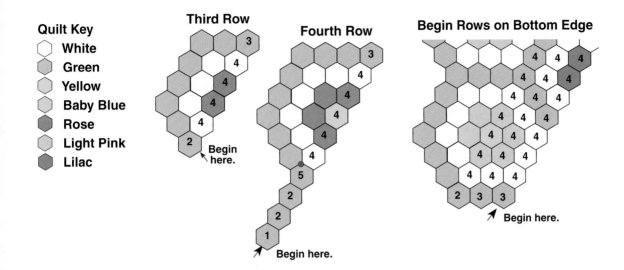

Quilt Key

- ⬡ White
- ⬡ Green
- ⬡ Yellow
- ⬡ Baby Blue
- ⬡ Rose
- ⬡ Light Pink
- ⬡ Lilac

Third Row

Begin here.

Fourth Row

Begin here.

Begin Rows on Bottom Edge

Begin here.

Pretty Baby Pastels

Continued from page 82

NEXT PANEL (make 7)

Layers 1 and 2

Repeat Layers 1 and 2 of First Panel.

Layer 3

Row 1–Rnd 71: Repeat rows 1–70 and rnd 71 of Layer 3 on First Panel.

Assemble Layers same as First Panel.

Rnd 72: Skip first 3 sc on rnd 71, join white with sl st in fourth sc; *complete row as follows:*
A: Repeat steps A, B, C and D of rnd 72 on First Panel;

B: To **join to Previous Panel,** 3 sc in first ch-5 sp of first flower on this Panel, ch 3, 2 sc in next ch-5 sp, ch 1, sc in center ch-3 sp of first flower on last Panel, ch 1, 2 sc in same ch-5 sp on this Panel, ch 3, 2 sc in last ch-5 sp of this flower;
C: Sc same ch-5 sp of this flower and first ch-5 sp of next flower together, work 2 more sc in first ch-5 sp, ch 3, 2 sc in next ch-5 sp, ch 1, sc in center ch-3 sp of next flower on last Panel, ch 1, 2 sc in same ch-5 sp on this Panel, ch 3, 2 sc in last ch-5 sp of this flower;
D: Repeat step C across all flowers; on last flower, work one more sc in last ch-5 sp, sl st in first sc worked into free ch-3 sp of Layer 3. Fasten off.❦

Celtic

Reminiscent of the mysterious, complex Celtic knots used in ancient and modern art, the Celtic method is a special technique of crocheting two or more separate sections, then popping them through open areas to make one beautiful piece. Depending upon the design, the result can produce a different look on each side that is completely reversible.

Guatemalan Tapestry by Carol Ventura

TECHNIQUES
Color Change,
Fringe-As-You-Go Embellishment

FINISHED SIZE
36-inch diameter, without fringe

MATERIALS
❏ Handpaint Originals by Halcyon Yarn or
   worsted homespun yarn:
   14 oz. Forest Floor #HP70 *(variegated green)*
   10½ oz. Cream Puff #HP85 *(cream)*
❏ Crochet stitch markers:
   One dark-color *(for first st)*
   12 light-color *(for increases)*
❏ I hook or size hook needed to obtain gauge

GAUGE
3 sc = 1 inch; 3 sc rows = 1 inch.

BASIC STITCHES
Ch, sl st, sc

SPECIAL STITCH
For **color change** *(see Stitch Guide on page 175),* carry dropped color across back of work covering dropped color with stitches as you go; pick up again when needed.

INSTRUCTIONS
Rnd 1: With green, leaving an 8-inch end, ch 4, sl st in first ch to form ring; working over end, 6 sc in ring; pull end snug. *(6 sc made)*

NOTES: *Work in continuous rnds;* **do not join or turn** *unless otherwise stated.* **Mark** *first st of each rnd with* **dark-color** *stitch marker.*

When working into marked st, remove marker, work st, place marker in st just made.

Rnd 2: Still working over end, 2 sc in each st around *(see Notes).* *(12)* Cut off remainder of end.

Rnd 3: Working over separate strand of cream until otherwise stated, 2 sc in each st around. *(24)*

Rnd 4: (Sc in next st, 2 sc in next st) around. *(36)*

Rnd 5: Sc in each st around.

Rnd 6: (Sc in next 2 sts, 2 sc in next st) around. *(48)*

Rnd 7: Sc in each st around.

Rnd 8: (Sc in next 3 sts, 2 sc in next st) around. *(60)*

Rnd 9: (Sc in next 4 sts, 2 sc in next st) around. *(72)*

Rnd 10: Sc in each st around.

Rnd 11: (Sc in next 5 sts, 2 sc in next st; **mark** last st made with **light-color** stitch marker) around. *(Stitch counts include marked st—7 sts between markers, 84 sts total)*

Rnds 12–13: (Sc in each st across to marker, 2 sc in marked st) around. *(8, 9 sts between markers)*

Rnd 14: Sc in each st around.

Rnds 15–16: (Sc in each st across to marker,
Continued on page 92

Tapestry Afghan

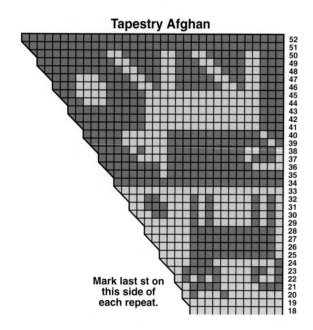

52
51
50
49
48
47
46
45
44
43
42
41
40
39
38
37
36
35
34
33
32
31
30
29
28
27
26
25
24
23
22
21
20
19
18

Mark last st on this side of each repeat.

Tapestry Afghan Key
◻ **Cream Sc**
◥ **Cream—2 sc in next st**
◼ **Green Sc**
◥ **Green—2 sc in next st**

Fair Isle by Karen Whooley

TECHNIQUES
Color Change

SPECIAL STITCH
Back Loop

FINISHED SIZE
51½ inches x 67½ inches

MATERIALS
❑ Wool-Ease Art. 620 by Lion Brand Yarn or worsted yarn:
  30 oz. White #100
  12 oz. Ranch Red #102
  12 oz. Forest Green Heather #180
  3 oz. Denim #114 *(blue)*
❑ Bobby pins for markers
❑ H hook or size hook needed to obtain gauge

GAUGE
7 sc in **back lps** = 2 inches, 3 **back lp** sc rows = 1 inch.

BASIC STITCHES
Ch, sl st, sc, dc, tr

INSTRUCTIONS

CENTER
Row 1: With white, ch 158, sc in second ch from hook, sc in each ch across; **do not turn.** Fasten off. *(157 sc made)*

NOTES: *On color-change rows, carry dropped color along back of work, covering dropped color with sts as you go; on white rows, work over a second strand of white to achieve same texture as color-change rows.*

Hide yarn ends as you go, either by working over them or weaving back through sts with a tapestry needle.

Rows 2–26: Working in **back lps** *(see Stitch Guide on page 175)* and **changing colors** *(see Stitch Guide)* according to corresponding row on graph; working over dropped color *(see Notes)*, join white with sc in first st, sc in each st across; **do not turn.** Fasten off.

Row 27: Working over separate strand white, join white with sc in first st, sc in each st across; **do not turn.** Fasten off.

Rows 28–183: Repeat rows 2–27 consecutively.

BORDER
Rnd 1: Working around outer edge *(in **both lps** of row 183)*, join white with sc in first st; **mark** sc just made, sc in each st across with 2 sc in last st; *complete the rnd as follows:*
A: Working in ends of rows, sc in row 183; **mark** sc just made, sc again in row 183, sc in end of each row with (2 sc in same row) 3 times evenly spaced across and with 2 sc in row 1;
B: Working in ch on opposite side of row 1,

Fair Isle

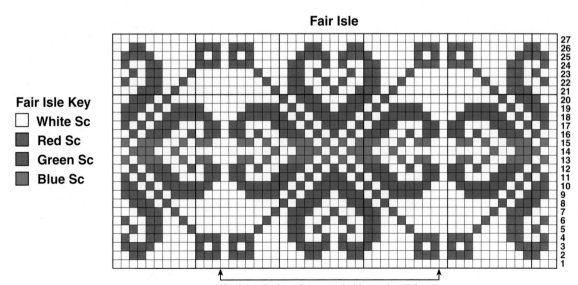

Fair Isle Key
☐ White Sc
▦ Red Sc
▦ Green Sc
▦ Blue Sc

Work beginning of row, work this section 5 times, then work end of row.

Fair Isle

Continued from page 90

sc in first ch; **mark** sc just made, sc in each ch across with 2 sc in last ch;

C: Working in ends of rows, sc in row 1; **mark** sc just made, sc again in row 1, sc in end of each row with (2 sc in same row) 3 times evenly spaced across and with 2 sc in row 183, join with sl st in first sc. *(157 sc between marker sts on each short edge, 187 sc between marked sts on each long edge, 4 marked corner sts)*

NOTE: *When working into marked st, remove marker, work st, mark st just made.*

Rnd 2: Moving markers as you go *(see Note),* ch 1, sc in first st, sc in same st as last sc, (sc in each st across to next marked corner st, 2 sc in marked st, sc in same st as last sc) 3 times, sc in each st across, sc in same st as first sc, join. *(159 sc between markers on each short edge, 189 sc between markers on each long edge, 4 marked corner sts; 700 sts total)*

Rnd 3: Ch 1, sc in marked corner st, (ch 2, skip next st, dc in next st, ch 2, skip next st, tr in next st, ch 3, skip next st, tr in next st, ch 2, skip next st, dc in next st, ch 2, skip next st*, sc in next st) around, ending last repeat at * *(first sc of a repeat is worked into each marked corner st),* join.

Rnd 4: (Ch 5, dc) in first st, work 3 sc in each ch-2 sp and 5 sc in each ch-3 sp around with (dc, ch 2, dc) in each marked corner st, join with sl st in third ch of ch-5.

Rnd 5: (Sl st, ch 5, dc, ch 2, dc) in first corner ch sp; *complete the rnd as follows:*
A: Skip next 3 sts, (dc in next st, ch 2, skip next 2 sts) 2 times;
B: (Dc, ch 3, dc) in next st, ch 2, skip next 2 sts, dc in next st, ch 2, skip next 2 sts; working across next 6 sts and skipping 4 sts between, dc next st and sixth st tog, ch 2, skip next 2 sts, dc in next st, ch 2, skip next 2 sts;
C: Repeat step B across to 9 sts before next corner ch sp;
D: (Dc, ch 3, dc) in next st, (ch 2, skip next 2 sts, dc in next st) 2 times, skip next 2 sts, (dc, ch 2, dc, ch 2, dc) in corner ch sp;
E: Repeat steps A–D 2 more times, then repeat steps A–C;
F: (Dc, ch 3, dc) in next st, (ch 2, skip next 2 sts, dc in next st) 2 times, skip last 2 sts, join with sl st in third ch of ch-5.

Rnd 6: (Sl st, ch 3, dc, ch 2, 2 dc) in first ch sp of corner, sc in next dc, (2 dc, ch 2, 2 dc) in next ch sp of corner, *[sc in next sp between dc; work 3 sc in each ch-2 sp and 5 sc in each ch-3 sp across to last dc before next 3-dc corner group, sc in next sp between dc], (2 dc, ch 2, 2 dc) in first ch sp of corner, sc in next dc, (2 dc, ch 2, 2 dc) in next ch sp of corner; repeat from * 2 more times; repeat between [ ], join with sl st in third ch of ch-5.

Rnd 7: Ch 1; skipping 2 sts at base of each "V", sc in each st around with 3 sc in each ch sp and 3 sc in center st of each 5-sc group, join with sl st in first sc. Fasten off.❦

Guatemalan Tapestry

Continued from page 88

2 sc in marked st) around. *(10, 11)*

Rnd 17: Sc in each st around.

Rnd 18: (Sc in each st across to marker, 2 sc in marked st) around, **changing to cream** in last st made *(see Special Stitch). (12)*

Rnd 19: Working over dropped yarn throughout, (sc in each st across to marker, 2 sc in marked st) around. *(13)*

Rnds 20–52: Changing colors according to corresponding row of graph on page 88 and repeating graph around, working over dropped strand, sc in each st around with 2 sc in each marked st when indicated on graph, changing to cream in last st of last rnd. *(At end of last rnd, 34 sts between markers.)*

Rnd 53: For **fringe,** with cream, (ch 30, sc in next 2 sts on rnd 52 changing to green in last st, ch 30, sc in next 2 sts on rnd 52 changing to cream in last st) around, join with sl st in same st as first ch-30. Fasten off.❦

SCRAP & SAMPLER
SPECIAL STITCHES

Celebrate your love of crochet with fabulous designs that showcase your stitching skills. Brilliant shades and subtle hues blend to create a wonderland of texture and color using classic crochet stitch patterns that are loved by all. Choose stripes or motifs or the basic one-piece to try each and every stitch!

Keep Me in Stitches by Marilyn Mezer

TECHNIQUES
Aran, Joined Rings,
Tassel Embellishment, Tunisian

SPECIAL STITCHES
Afghan Stitch, Back Loops/Front Loops, Back
Posts/Front Posts, Berry, Bow, Dragonfly,
Flower Stitch, Leaf Stitch, Rickrack, Shell
Cluster, Half Shell Cluster

FINISHED SIZE
53 inches x 57 inches, not including Tassels

MATERIALS
❑ Sport yarn:
    44 oz. ivory
    2 oz. burgundy
    2 oz. gray
    2 oz. blue
❑ 7-inch square of cardboard
❑ Tapestry needle
❑ G crochet hook or size hook needed to
obtain gauge
❑ H afghan hook or size hook needed to
obtain gauge

GAUGES
Afghan hook: 9 afghan sts = 2 inches;
8 rows = 2 inches.

Crochet hook: 9 sc = 2 inches;
5 rows = 1 inch.

BASIC STITCHES
Ch, sl st, sc, hdc, dc, tr, dtr

NOTE
Refer to Tunisian Crochet Basic Technique on
page 49 to work afghan st.

INSTRUCTIONS

CENTER
*Special Stitch: For **berry st,** ch 3, pull up
a lp in next vertical bar. Push ch-3 loops to
front of work.*

Row 1: With afghan hook and ivory yarn, ch
60 loosely, pull up a lp in second ch from
hook, pull up a lp in each ch across *(60 lps
on hook);* **work lps off hook** *(see Note—one
lp remains on hook).*

Row 2: To **work in afghan st,** skip first
vertical bar, pull up a lp in each vertical bar
across *(60 lps on hook);* work lps off hook
(one lp remains on hook).

Rows 3–34: Work in afghan st and **berry st**
(see Special Stitch for this Panel) according
to House Graph. At end of last row, fasten off.

Key
☐ **Afghan St**
■ **Berry St**

House Graph

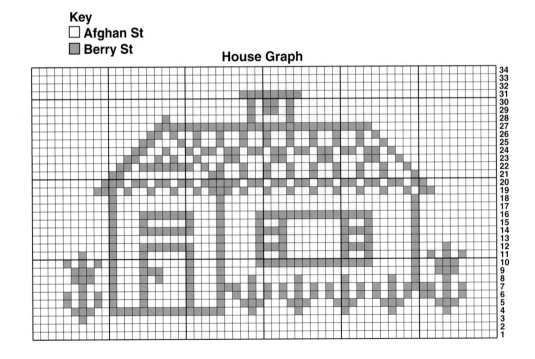

Keep Me in Stitches

Continued from page 94

Rnd 35: For **border,** working around outer edge in **front lps** of sts and chs *(see Stitch Guide on page 175)* and in one strand at ends of rows, with crochet hook, join burgundy with sc in any corner st, sc in same st as joining sc, sc in each st and in end of each row and in each ch on opposite side of row 1 around with 3 sc in each corner st, sc in same st as joining sc, join with sl st in first sc, **turn.** *(192 sc made)*

Rnd 36: Ch 1, 3 sc in first st, sc in each st around with 3 sc in each center corner st, join, **turn.** Fasten off.

Rnd 37: Join gray with sc in any center corner st, sc in same st as joining sc, sc in each st around with 3 sc in each center corner st, sc in same st as joining sc, join with sl st in first sc, **turn.**

Rnd 38: Repeat rnd 36.

Rnd 39: With blue, repeat rnd 37.

Rnd 40: Repeat rnd 36.

RIBBON PANEL (make 2)
Special Stitch: For bow st, work as follows:
A: For **streamers,** yo 3 times; working in fourth row below, pull up a loop in vertical bar 2 sts to the right of st corresponding to next st, (yo, pull through 2 lps on hook) 3 times;
B: Yo 3 times, pull up a loop in next vertical bar on fourth row below, (yo, pull through 2 lps on hook) 3 times;
C: Yo 3 times, skip next vertical bar on fourth row below, pull up a loop in next vertical bar, (yo, pull through 2 lps on hook) 3 times;
D: Repeat step B, yo, pull through 4 lps on hook (lp just made is **top** of streamers); skip next vertical bar on last row;
E: Work lps off hook across to lp at top of streamers; for **bow loops,** ch 5, pull last ch made through lp at top of streamers, ch 5, pull last ch made through next lp on hook; push bow loops to front of work. Streamers and Bow loops are at front of work.

Row 1: With afghan hook and ivory yarn, ch 19 loosely; pull up a lp in second ch from hook, pull up a lp in each ch across *(19 lps on hook);* work lps off hook.

Rows 2–8: Work in afghan st.

Row 9: Skip first vertical bar, pull up a lp in next 3 vertical bars, make **streamers** of **bow st** *(see Special Stitch for this Panel),* pull up a lp in next 9 vertical bars, make streamers of bow st, pull up a loop in last 4 vertical bars; *work lps off hook across to loop at top of streamers, make **bow loops** (see Special Stitch for this Panel) at top of streamers; repeat from *, work lps off hook across.

Rows 10–13: Work in afghan st.

Row 14: Skip first vertical bar, pull up a lp in next 8 vertical bars, make streamers of bow st, pull up a lp in last 9 vertical bars; work lps off hook across to loop at top of streamers, make bow loops at top of streamers, work lps off hook across.

Rows 15–18: Work in afghan st.

Row 19: Skip first vertical bar, pull up a lp in next 3 vertical bars, make streamers of bow st, pull up a lp in next 9 vertical bars, make streamers of bow st, pull up a loop in last 4 vertical bars; *work lps off hook across to loop at top of streamers, make bow loops at top of streamers; repeat from *, work lps off hook across.

Rows 20–79: Repeat rows 10–19 consecutively.

Rows 80–84: Work in afghan st. At end of last row, fasten off.

RINGS PANEL (make 2)
First ring: With crochet hook and ivory yarn, ch 25, sl st in first ch to form ring, ch 3 *(counts as first dc),* 47 dc in ring, join with sl st in top of ch-3. Fasten off. *(48 dc made)*

Second ring: With crochet hook and ivory yarn, ch 25, insert opposite end of ch from back to front through last ring made and sl st in first ch to form ring, ch 3, 47 dc in ring, join with sl st in top of ch-3. Fasten off.

Next rings: Repeat second Ring until you have 14 rings.

Edging row 1: Working across one long edge of Panel, join ivory with sl st in any dc on last ring made; *complete as follows:*
A: Ch 6 *(first 3 chs count as dc),* skip next 3 dc, dc in next dc, ch 3, skip next 3 dc;
B: Tr next dc and any dc on next ring tog, (ch 3, skip next 3 dc, dc in next dc) 2 times, ch 3, skip next 3 dc;
C: Repeat step B 12 more times, dc in next dc; **fasten off;**

D: Working across other long edge of Panel, skip next 15 dc of same ring as last dc made, join with sl st in next dc, repeat step A;
E: Skipping 15 dc from last st made on next ring, tr next dc on this ring and 16th dc on next ring tog; (ch 3, skip next 3 dc, dc in next dc) 2 times, ch 3, skip next 3 dc;
F: Repeat step B 12 more times, dc in next dc, turn. *(28 ch sps on each long edge)*

Edging rnd 2: Ch 1, *3 hdc in each ch sp across long edge to last ch sp, (3 hdc, 3 sc) in last ch sp, evenly space 14 sc across unworked sts of ring, 3 sc around side of next dc*, 3 hdc in same ch sp as sc sts just made; repeat between first and second *, join with sl st in first hdc. Fasten off. *(84 hdc on each long edge)*

FLORAL PANEL (make 2)

Special Stitches: For **flower st,** work as follows:
A: Yo 3 times; working in third row below, pull up a loop in vertical bar 2 sts to the right of st corresponding to next st, (yo, pull through 2 lps on hook) 3 times;
B: Yo 3 times, pull up a loop in next vertical bar on third row below, (yo, pull through 2 lps on hook) 3 times;
C: Repeat step B 3 more times, yo, pull through 5 lps on hook (lp just made is **bottom** of flower st); skip next vertical bar on last row.

For **leaf st,** work as follows:
A: Yo 3 times; working in third row below, pull up a loop in vertical bar 2 sts to the right of st corresponding to next st, (yo, pull through 2 lps on hook) 3 times;
B: Yo 3 times, skip next 3 vertical bars on third row below, pull up a lp in next vertical bar, (yo, pull through 2 lps on hook) 3 times (lp just made is **bottom** of leaf st); skip next vertical bar on last row.
Flowers and leaves are at front of work.

Row 1: With afghan hook and ivory yarn, ch 19 loosely; pull up a lp in second ch from hook, pull up a lp in each ch across *(19 lps on hook)*; work lps off hook *(one lp remains on hook).*

Rows 2–9: Work in afghan st.

Row 10: Skip first vertical bar, pull up a loop in next 3 vertical bars, **flower st** *(see Special Stitches for this Panel),* pull up a loop in next 9 vertical bars, flower st, pull up a loop in last 4 vertical bars; work lps off hook.

Rows 11–12: Work in afghan st.

Row 13: Skip first vertical bar, pull up a loop in next 3 vertical bars, **leaf st** *(see Special Stitches for this Panel),* pull up a loop in next 9 vertical bars, leaf st, pull up a loop in last 4 vertical bars; work lps off hook.

Row 14: Work in afghan st.

Row 15: Skip first vertical bar, pull up a loop in next 8 vertical bars, flower st, pull up a loop in last 9 vertical bars; work lps off hook.

Rows 16–17: Work in afghan st.

Row 18: Skip first vertical bar, pull up a loop in next 8 vertical bars, leaf st, pull up a loop in last 9 vertical bars; work lps off hook.

Rows 19–25: Work in afghan st.

Rows 26–73: Repeat rows 10–25 consecutively.

Rows 74–84: Work in afghan st. At end of last row, fasten off.

CENTER PANELS ASSEMBLY

NOTE: When joining Panels, have last row of Floral Panel and row 1 of all other Panels at same end of work.

1: For **first seam** *(see Note),* with wrong sides together, hold one Ribbon Panel behind one Rings Panel matching 84 hdc sts of Rings Panel to ends of rows on Ribbon Panel; working through both layers as one, join ivory with sc in first hdc past 3 sc at corner, sc in each hdc across to 3 sc at next corner. Fasten off.

2: For **second seam** *(see Note),* with wrong sides together, hold one Flower Panel behind opposite side of same Rings Panel, work same as first seam.

3: Matching corners of first or last rows of the three assembled Panels to center corner sts on rnd 35 of Center Panel, easing to fit, sew assembled Panels to remaining **back lps** of rnd 35 across one long edge of Center Panel.

4: Repeat steps 1 and 2 with remaining Panels; sew to other long edge of Center Panel in same manner as step 3.

CHAIN LINKS PANEL

Special Stitches: For **chain st,** working between dtr sts of previous chain st, dtr into each of two skipped vertical bars on previous chain st row; skip 2 vertical bars on last row behind dtr sts. Dtr sts are at front of work.

Row 1: With afghan hook and ivory yarn, ch 46

Keep Me in Stitches

Continued from page 97

loosely; pull up a lp in second ch from hook, pull up a lp in each ch across *(46 lps on hook);* work lps off hook *(one lp remains on hook).*

Rows 2–6: Work in afghan st.

Row 7: Skip first vertical bar, pull up a lp in next vertical bar; for **first chain st,** (dtr in vertical bar of st on third row below corresponding to next st) 2 times *(first chain st made);* skip 2 vertical bars on last row behind dtr sts *(first chain st made),* (pull up a lp in next 6 vertical bars, first chain st) 5 times, pull up a lp in last 2 vertical bars; work lps off hook.

Rows 8–9: Work in afghan st.

Row 10: Skip first vertical bar, pull up a lp in next vertical bar, **chain st** *(see Special Stitches for this Panel),* (pull up a lp in next 6 vertical bars, chain st) 5 times, pull up a lp in last 2 vertical bars; work lps off hook.

Rows 11–199: Repeat rows 8–10 consecutively.

Rows 200–202: Work in afghan st. At end of last row, fasten off.

RICKRACK PANEL
Special Stitches: *For **first rickrack st:***
A: Yo 3 times, pull up a loop in vertical bar of st on third row below corresponding to third st back, (yo, pull through 2 lps on hook) 3 times;
B: Yo 3 times, skip next 4 vertical bars on third row below, pull up a loop in next vertical bar, (yo, pull through 2 lps on hook) 3 times;
C: Yo, pull through 2 lps on hook (lp just made is **top** of rickrack st); skip next vertical bar on last row.

*For **rickrack st:*** Yo 3 times, pull up a loop in next unworked vertical bar on third row below, (yo, pull through 2 lps on hook) 3 times; work steps B and C of first rickrack st.

*For **shell cluster:***
A: Yo, pull up a loop in second vertical bar on second row below, yo, pull through 2 lps on hook (2 lps on hook);
B: Yo 2 times, pull up a loop in fourth vertical bar one row below, (yo, pull through 2 lps on hook) 2 times (3 lps on hook);
C: Yo 3 times, pull up a loop in sixth vertical bar on this row, (yo, pull through 2 lps on

hook) 3 times (4 lps on hook);
D: Yo 2 times, pull up a loop in fourth vertical bar on next row above, (yo, pull through 2 lps on hook) 2 times (5 lps on hook);
E: Yo, pull up a loop in second vertical bar on second row above, yo, pull through 2 lps on hook (6 lps on hook), pull up a lp in end of next unworked row, yo, pull through all lps on hook.

Rickrack sts and shell clusters are at front of work.

Row 1: With afghan hook and ivory yarn, ch 46 loosely; pull up a lp in second ch from hook, pull up a lp in each ch across *(46 lps on hook);* work lps off hook *(one lp remains on hook).*

Rows 2–6: Work in afghan st.

Row 7: Skip first vertical bar, pull up a lp in next 9 vertical bars, **first rickrack st** *(see Special Stitches for this Panel),* *pull up a lp in next 5 vertical bars, **rickrack st** *(see Special Stitches for this Panel);* repeat from * 4 more times, pull up a lp in last 5 vertical bars; work lps off hook.

Rows 8–12: Work in afghan st.

Rows 13–202: Repeat rows 7–12 consecutively, ending with row 10. At end of last row, fasten off.

Row 203: With right side of work facing you, working in ends of rows, using crochet hook, join ivory with sc in row 1, sc in next 6 rows, **shell cluster** *(see Special Stitches for this Panel),* (sc in next 7 rows, shell cluster) 27 more times, sc in last 6 rows. Fasten off.

DRAGONFLIES PANEL
Special Stitches: *For **dragonfly wing,*** working across 9 lps on hook, (yo, pull through 2 lps on hook) 9 times (wing made); working behind lps just made, pull up a lp in next 8 horizontal bars, pull up lp in same vertical bar as last lp of wing.

*For **dragonfly body,*** inserting hook between fourth and fifth vertical bars of both wings at same time, dtr around center of wings below; skip one vertical bar on last row behind dtr worked into previous row. Dragonflies are at front of work.

Row 1: With afghan hook and ivory yarn, ch 46 loosely; pull up a lp in second ch from hook, pull up a lp in each ch across *(46 lps on hook);* work lps off hook *(one lp remains on hook).*

Rows 2–4: Work in afghan st.

Row 5: Skip first vertical bar, pull up a lp in next 19 vertical bars *(20 lps on hook),* work **dragonfly wing** *(see Special Stitches for this Panel),* pull up a lp in next 15 vertical bars, work dragonfly wing, pull up a lp in last 11 vertical bars; work lps off hook.

Row 6: Repeat row 5.

Rows 7–8: Work in afghan st.

Row 9: Skip first vertical bar, pull up a lp in next 13 vertical bars *(14 lps on hook),* work **dragonfly body** *(see Special Stitches for this Panel),* pull up a lp in next 14 vertical bars, work dragonfly body, pull up a lp in last 16 vertical bars; work lps off hook.

Rows 10–13: Work in afghan st.

Rows 14–15: Skip first vertical bar, pull up a lp in next 13 vertical bars, work dragonfly wing, (pull up a lp in next 14 vertical bars, work dragonfly wing) 2 times, pull up a lp in last 4 vertical bars; work lps off hook.

Rows 16–18: Work in afghan st.

Row 19: Skip first vertical bar, pull up a lp in next 8 vertical bars, work dragonfly body, (pull up a lp in next 13 vertical bars, work dragonfly body) 2 times, pull up a lp in last 8 vertical bars; work lps off hook.

Rows 20–22: Work in afghan st.

Rows 23–202: Repeat rows 5–22 consecutively. At end of last row, fasten off.

ZIGZAG PANEL

*Special Stitches: For **dc in vertical bar on second row below,** yo, pull up a loop in vertical bar on second row below corresponding to next st, (yo, pull through 2 lps on hook) 2 times (dc made); skip next vertical bar on last row.*

*For **dc front post (dcfp,** see Stitch Guide on page 175); skip next vertical bar on last row behind dcfp. Dcfp sts are at front of work.*

*For **half-shell cluster:***
A: Yo 3 times, pull up a loop in fourth vertical bar from end of next row, (yo, pull through 2 lps on hook) 3 times (2 lps on hook);
B: Yo 2 times, pull up a loop in third vertical bar from end of next row to the left, (yo, pull through 2 lps on hook) 2 times (3 lps on hook);
C: Yo, pull up a loop in second vertical bar from end of next row to the left, yo, pull through 2 lps on hook (4 lps on hook);
D: Pull up a lp in end of next unworked row,

yo, pull through all lps on hook.

Row 1: With afghan hook and ivory yarn, ch 46 loosely; pull up a lp in second ch from hook, pull up a lp in each ch across *(46 lps on hook);* work lps off hook *(one lp remains on hook).*

Rows 2–3: Work in afghan st.

Row 4: Skip first vertical bar, pull up a lp in next 5 vertical bars, **(dc lp**—*see Special Stitches for this Panel)* 4 times, (pull up a lp in next 6 vertical bars, dc in next 4 vertical bars on second row below) 3 times, pull up a lp in last 6 vertical bars; work lps off hook.

Row 5: Skip first vertical bar, pull up a lp in next 4 vertical bars, *dc in next vertical bar on second row below, **dcfp** (see Special Stitches for this Panel) around each of next 3 dc, pull up a lp in next 6 vertical bars; repeat from * 3 more times, pull up a lp in last vertical bar; work lps off hook.

Row 6: Skip first vertical bar, pull up a lp in next 3 vertical bars, (dc in next vertical bar on second row below, dcfp around each of next 3 dc, pull up a lp in next 6 vertical bars) 4 times, pull up a lp in last 2 vertical bars; work lps off hook.

Row 7: Skip first vertical bar, pull up a lp in next 2 vertical bars, (dc in next vertical bar on second row below, dcfp around each of next 3 dc, pull up a lp in next 6 vertical bars) 4 times, pull up a lp in last 3 vertical bars; work lps off hook.

Row 8: Skip first vertical bar, pull up a lp in next vertical bar, (dc in next vertical bar on second row below, dcfp around each of next 3 dc, pull up a lp in next 6 vertical bars) 4 times, pull up a lp in last 4 vertical bars; work lps off hook.

Row 9: Skip first vertical bar, pull up a lp in next vertical bar, (dcfp around each of next 4 dc, pull up a lp in next 6 vertical bars) 4 times, pull up a lp in last 4 vertical bars; work lps off hook.

Row 10: Skip first vertical bar, pull up a lp in next 2 vertical bars, (dcfp around each of next 3 dc, dc in next vertical bar on second row below, pull up a lp in next 6 vertical bars) 4 times, pull up a lp in last 3 vertical bars; work lps off hook.

Row 11: Skip first vertical bar, pull up a lp in next 3 vertical bars, (dcfp around each of

Continued on page 114

Classic Sampler by Ann Parnell

TECHNIQUES
Color Change, Filet, Surface Slip Stitches

SPECIAL STITCHES
Back Loops/Front Loops, Back Post/Front Post, Basketweave, Berry, Cluster, Knobby Stitch, Long Double Crochet, Long Single Crochet, Popcorn, Puff Stitch, Reverse Single Crochet, Scallop, Shell, Reverse Shell, Slanted Shell, Spider's Web, Star Stitch, Star Stitch Variation, V Stitch, Zigzag

FINISHED SIZE
36½ inches x 50½ inches

MATERIALS
❑ Worsted yarn:
    20 oz. off-white
    20 oz. lt. green
    20 oz. dk. green
❑ Tapestry needle
❑ G hook or size hook needed to obtain gauge for each Square

GAUGES
4 sc = 1 inch, 4 sc rows = 1 inch.
4 dc = 1 inch, 2 dc rows = 1 inch.
Each Square is 7 inches.

BASIC STITCHES
Ch, sl st, sc, hdc, dc, tr

NOTE
When **changing colors** *(see Stitch Guide on page 175),* drop unused color to wrong side of work; pick up again when needed. Do not fasten off unless otherwise stated.

INSTRUCTIONS
SQUARES
STAR STITCH DAISY
Special Stitches for this Square: *For* ***beginning star st (beg star st),*** *pull up a lp in second ch from hook, pull up a lp in next 3 chs or sts, yo, pull through all 5 lps on hook; for* ***eye, ch 1.***

For ***star st,*** *pull up a lp in last eye made, pull up a lp in same ch or st as last lp of previous star st, pull up a lp in each of next 2 chs or sts, yo, pull through all 5 lps on hook, for* ***eye, ch 1.***

Row 1: With dk. green, ch 27, **beg star st** *(see Special Stitches for this Square),* **star st** across, turn. *(12 eyes made)*

Row 2: Ch 1, 2 sc in each eye across, sc in last st, turn. *(25 sc)*

Row 3: Ch 2, beg star st, star st across, turn.

Rows 4–18: Repeat rows 2 and 3 alternately, ending with row 2. At end of last row, **do not turn.**

Rnd 19: With right side of Square facing you, working around outer edge, ch 1, evenly space 23 sc across each edge with 3 sc in each corner, join with sl st in first sc. Fasten off. *(Second sc of 3-sc group is corner st—4 corner sts, 25 sc on each side between corner sts; 104 sc total.)*

Rnd 20: Join off-white with sl st in any corner st, ch 3, (dc, ch 2, 2 dc) in same st as joining sl st, skip next st, (2 dc in next st, skip next st) across to next corner, *(2 dc, ch 2, 2 dc) in corner st, skip next st, (2 dc in next st, skip next st) across to next corner;

Classic Sampler

Continued from page 100

repeat from * around, join with sl st in top of ch-3. Fasten off. *(28 dc on each side between corner ch sps)*

FRONT POST STITCH

Row 1: With lt. green, ch 24, sc in second ch from hook, sc in next 2 chs, (tr in next ch, sc in next 3 chs) across, turn. *(23 sts made)*

Row 2: Ch 1, sc in each st across changing to dk. green in last st *(see Note),* turn.

Row 3: Ch 1, sc in first st, tr in next st, *sc in next st, **dc front post (fp,** *see Stitch Guide)* around next tr on row before last *(skip one st on last row behind each fp worked into previous row throughout);* sc in next st on last row, tr in next st; repeat from * 4 more times, sc in last st, turn.

Row 4: Ch 1, sc in each st across changing to lt. green in last st, turn.

Row 5: Ch 1, sc in first st, (fp around next tr on row before last, sc in next st on last row, tr in next st, sc in next st) 5 times, fp around next tr on row before last, sc in last st, turn.

Rows 6–22: Repeat rows 2–5 consecutively, ending with row 2. At end of last row, **do not turn or change to dk. green.**

Rnds 23–24: Repeat rnds 19 and 20 of Star Stitch Daisy Square.

STAR STITCH FILET

Special Stitches for this Square: *For **beginning star st variation (beg star st),** pull up a lp in first st, pull up a lp in next ch sp, pull up a lp in next st, yo, pull through all 4 lps on hook; for **eye, ch 1.***

*For **star st variation (star st),** pull up a lp in same st as last lp of previous star st, pull up a lp in next ch sp, pull up a lp in next st, yo, pull through all 4 lps on hook, ch 1.*

Row 1: With dk. green, ch 26, sc in second ch from hook, sc in each ch across, turn. *(25 sts made)*

Row 2: Ch 4 *(counts as first dc and ch-1 sp),* skip next st, dc in next st, (ch 1, skip next st, dc in next st) across, turn. *(13 dc, 12 ch sps)*

Row 3: Ch 2; **beg star st** *(see Special Stitches for this Square),* **star st** across, turn. *(12 eyes)*

Row 4: Ch 3 *(ch-1 of last eye made and ch-3 count as first dc and ch-1 sp),* skip last eye made, (dc in next eye, ch 1) 11 times, dc in top of ch-2, turn. *(13 dc, 12 ch sps)*

Rows 5–15: Repeat rows 3 and 4 alternately, ending with row 3. At end of last row, **do not turn.**

Rnds 16–17: Repeat rnds 19 and 20 of Star Stitch Daisy Square.

CONTRASTING SHELLS

Row 1: With dk. green, ch 26, (sc, 3 dc) in second ch from hook, *skip next 3 chs, (sc, 3 dc) in next ch; repeat from * 4 more times, skip next 3 chs, sc in last ch changing to lt. green *(see Note on page 100),* turn. *(3-dc groups form shells—6 shells, 7 sc made)*

Row 2: Ch 1, (sc, 3 dc) in first st, *skip next 3 dc, (sc, 3 dc) in next sc; repeat from * 4 more times, sc in last st changing to dk. green, turn.

Row 3: Ch 1, (sc, 3 dc) in first st, *skip next 3 dc, (sc, 3 dc) in next sc; repeat from * 4 more times, sc in last st changing to lt. green, turn.

Rows 4–15: Repeat rows 2 and 3 alternately.

Rnds 16–17: Repeat rnds 19 and 20 of Star Stitch Daisy Square on page 100.

PUFF STITCH

Special Stitch for this Square: *For **puff st,** yo, insert hook in next st, pull up ½-inch loop, (yo, insert hook in same st, pull up ½-inch loop) 2 times, yo, pull through all 7 lps on hook.*

Row 1: With dk. green, ch 26, sc in second ch from hook, sc in each ch across, turn. *(25 sts made)*

Row 2 and all even-numbered rows: Ch 1, sc in each st across, turn.

Row 3: Ch 1, sc in first 12 sts; **puff st** *(see Special Stitch for this Square),* sc in last 12 sts, turn.

Row 5: Ch 1, sc in first 10 sts, puff st, sc in next 3 sts, puff st, sc in last 10 sts, turn.

Row 7: Ch 1, sc in first 8 sts, puff st, sc in next 7 sts, puff st, sc in last 8 sts, turn.

Row 9: Ch 1, sc in first 6 sts, puff st, sc in next 11 sts, puff st, sc in last 6 sts, turn.

Row 11: Ch 1, sc in first 4 sts, puff st, (sc in next 7 sts, puff st) 2 times, sc in last 4 sts, turn.

Row 13: Ch 1, sc in first 2 sts, puff st, sc in next 7 sts, puff st, sc in next 3 sts, puff st, sc in next 7 sts, puff st, sc in last 2 sts, turn.

Row 15: Repeat row 11.

Row 17: Repeat row 9.

Row 19: Repeat row 7.

Row 21: Repeat row 5.

Row 23: Repeat row 3.

Row 24: Repeat row 2.

Rnds 25–26: Repeat rnds 19 and 20 of Star Stitch Daisy Square.

POPCORN MEDALLION

*Special Stitches for this Square: For **first popcorn (fpc),** ch 3, 3 dc in ring or ch-sp, drop lp from hook, insert hook through top ch of ch-3, return lp to hook and pull through.*

*For **dc popcorn (dcpc),** 4 dc in ring or ch-sp, drop lp from hook, insert hook through first dc of group, return lp to hook and pull through.*

*For **tr popcorn (trpc),** 4 tr in ch sp, drop lp from hook, insert hook through first tr of group, return lp to hook and pull through.*

Rnd 1: With lt. green, ch 4, sl st in first ch to form ring, **fpc** in ring *(see Special Stitches for this Square),* ch 3, (**dcpc** in ring —see Special Stitches for this Square, ch 3) 5 times, join with sl st in fpc. Fasten off. *(6 pc, 6 ch sps made)*

Rnd 2: Join dk. green with sl st in any ch sp, (fpc, ch 3, dcpc, ch 3) in same sp as sl st, (dcpc, ch 3, dcpc, ch 3) in each ch sp around, join. *(12 ch sps)*

Rnd 3: (Sl st, fpc, ch 3 at **corner,** dcpc, ch 3) in first ch sp, (dcpc in next ch sp, ch 3) 2 times, *(dcpc, ch 3 at **corner,** dcpc, ch 3) in next ch sp, (dcpc in next ch sp, ch 3) 2 times; repeat from * around, join. Fasten off. *(16)*

Rnd 4: Join lt. green with sl st in second ch sp past any corner ch sp, fpc, ch 4; **trpc** in next ch sp *(see Special Stitches for this Square),* ch 4, (trpc, ch 5 at **corner,** trpc, ch 4) in next ch sp, *trpc in next ch sp, ch 4, dcpc in next ch sp, ch 4, trpc in next ch sp, ch 4, (trpc, ch 5 at **corner,** trpc, ch 4) in next ch sp; repeat from * 2 more times, trpc in next ch sp, ch 4, join. *(20 pc, 20 ch sps)*

Rnd 5: (Sl st, ch 2, 3 hdc) in first ch sp, 5 hdc in next ch sp, *8 hdc in next corner ch sp, 5 hdc in next ch sp, (4 hdc in next ch sp) 2 times, 5 hdc in next ch sp; repeat from * 2 more times, 8 hdc in next corner ch sp, 5 hdc in next ch sp, 4 hdc in next ch sp, join with sl

st in top of ch-2. Fasten off. *(Fourth hdc of 8-hdc group is corner st—4 corner sts, 25 hdc on each side between corner sts; 104 hdc total.)*

Rnd 6: Repeat rnd 20 of Star Stitch Daisy Square.

GREEK CROSS

Rnd 1: With lt. green, ch 2, 8 sc in second ch from hook, join with sl st in first sc, turn. *(8 sc made)*

Rnd 2: (Ch 3, 2 dc) in first st, ch 2, 3 dc in next st, ch 1, (3 dc in next st, ch 2, 3 dc in next st, ch 1) around, join with sl st in top of ch-3. *(Ch-3 at beginning of row counts as first dc—24 dc, 8 ch sps.)*

Rnd 3: Sl st in next 2 sts, (sl st, ch 3, 2 dc, ch 3, 3 dc) in ch-2 sp, ch 1, 3 dc in next ch-1 sp, ch 1, *(3 dc, ch 3, 3 dc) in ch-2 sp, ch 1, 3 dc in next ch-1 sp, ch 1; repeat from * around, join. *(36 dc)*

Rnd 4: Sl st in next 2 sts, (sl st, ch 3, 2 dc, ch 3, 3 dc) in next ch-3 sp, ch 2, dc in next ch-1 sp, dc in next 3 dc, dc in next ch-1 sp, ch 2, *(3 dc, ch 3, 3 dc) in next ch-3 sp, ch 2, dc in next ch-1 sp, dc in next 3 dc, dc in next ch-1 sp, ch 2; repeat from * around, join. *(44)*

Rnds 5–6: Sl st in next 2 sts, (sl st, ch 3, 2 dc, ch 3, 3 dc) in next ch-3 sp, ch 2, dc in next ch sp, dc in each st across to next ch sp, dc in next ch sp, ch 2, *(3 dc, ch 3, 3 dc) in next ch-3 sp, ch 2, dc in next ch sp, dc in each st across to next ch sp, dc in next ch sp, ch 2; repeat from * around, join. *(52, 60)*

Rnd 7: Ch 1, sc in first 3 sts, *(5 sc in next ch sp at corner, sc in next 3 sts, 3 sc in next ch sp, sc in next 9 sts, 3 sc in next ch sp), sc in next 3 sts; repeat from * 2 more times; repeat between ( ), join with sl st in first sc. Fasten off. *(Third sc of 5-sc group is corner st—4 corner sts, 25 sc on each side between corner sts; 104 sc total.)*

Rnd 8: Repeat rnd 20 of Star Stitch Daisy Square.

LONG DC STRIPES

*Special Stitches for this Square: For **long dc (ldc),** working over ch-2 sp of last row, yo, insert hook in next skipped st on row before last, pull up long lp to same height as row being worked; complete as dc.*

Row 1: With dk. green, ch 26, dc in fourth ch from hook, dc in next ch, (ch 2, skip next 2 chs, dc in next 2 chs) 5 times, dc in last ch;

Classic Sampler

Continued from page 103

do not turn. Fasten off. *(3 chs at beginning of row count as first dc—14 dc, 5 ch-2 sps made.)*

Row 2: Join lt. green with sc in first st, ch 2, skip next 2 sts, ***ldc** *(see Special Stitch for this Square)* in each of next 2 skipped chs on row before last, ch 2, skip next 2 sts on last row; repeat from * across to last st, sc in last st; **do not turn.** Fasten off. *(2 sc, 10 dc, 6 ch-2 sps)*

Row 3: Join dk. green with sc in first st, ldc in next 2 skipped sts on row before last, (ch 2, skip next 2 sts on last row, ldc in next 2 skipped sts on row before last) 5 times, sc in last st on last row; **do not turn.** Fasten off. *(2 sc, 12 dc, 5 ch-2 sps)*

Row 4: Join lt. green with sc in first st, ch 2, skip next 2 sts, (ldc in each of next 2 skipped sts on row before last, ch 2, skip next 2 sts on last row) across to last st, sc in last st; **do not turn.** Fasten off. *(2 sc, 10 dc, 6 ch-2 sps)*

Rows 5–17: Repeat rows 3 and 4 alternately, ending with row 3.

Rnd 18: Join lt. green with sc in first st, 3 sc in same st as joining sc, sc in next 2 sts, (ldc in each of next 2 skipped sts on row before last, sc in next 2 sts on last row) across to last st, 3 sc in last st; continuing around outer edge, evenly space 23 sc in ends of rows across to row 1; working in starting ch on opposite side of row 1, 4 sc in first ch, sc in each ch across with 3 sc in last ch, evenly space 23 sc in ends of rows across to last row, join with sl st in first sc. Fasten off. *(Second sc of corner sc group is corner st—4 corner sts, 25 sc on each side between corner sts; 104 sc total.)*

Rnd 19: Repeat rnd 20 of Star Stitch Daisy Square on page 100.

SPIDER'S WEB

Row 1: With lt. green, ch 26, sc in second ch from hook, sc in each ch across, turn. *(25 sts made)*

Row 2: Ch 1, sc in first 3 sts, ch 4, skip next 3 sts, dc in next st, ch 4, skip next 3 sts, sc in next 5 sts, ch 4, skip next 3 sts, dc in next st, ch 4, skip next 3 sts, sc in last 3 sts, turn. *(11 sc, 2 dc, 4 ch sps)*

Row 3: Ch 3 *(counts as first dc)*, dc in next 2 sts, ch 3, sc in next ch sp, sc in next dc, sc in next ch sp, ch 3, skip next st, dc in next 3 sts, ch 3, sc in next ch sp, sc in next dc, sc in next ch sp, ch 3, dc in last 3 sts, turn. *(9 dc, 6 sc, 4 ch sps)*

Row 4: Ch 3, dc in next 2 sts, (ch 4, sc in next 3 sts, ch 4, dc in next 3 sts) 2 times, turn.

Row 5: Ch 1, sc in first 3 sts, ch 3, dc in third ch of next ch-5 sp, ch 3, skip next 3-sc group, sc in next ch sp, sc in next 3 sts, sc in next ch sp, ch 5, dc in third ch of next ch-5 sp, ch 3, sc in last 3 sts, turn.

Row 6: Ch 1, sc in each st across with 3 sc in each ch sp, turn. *(25 sc)*

Row 7: Ch 7 *(counts as first dc and ch-4 sp)*, skip next 3 sts, sc in next 5 sts, ch 4, skip next 3 sts, dc in next st, ch 4, skip next 3 sts, sc in next 5 sts, ch 4, skip next 3 sts, dc in next st, turn. *(10 sc, 3 dc, 4 ch sps)*

Row 8: Ch 1, sc in first st, sc in next ch sp, ch 3, skip next st, dc in next 3 sts, ch 3, skip next st, sc in next ch sp, sc in next st, sc in next ch sp, ch 3, skip next st, dc in next 3 sts, ch 3, skip next st, sc in next ch sp, skip next 4 chs of ch-7, sc in next ch, turn. *(6 dc, 7 sc, 4 ch sps)*

Row 9: Ch 1, sc in first 2 sts, ch 4, skip next ch sp, dc in next 3 sts, ch 4, skip next ch sp, sc in next 3 sts, ch 4, skip next ch sp, dc in next 3 sts, ch 4, skip next ch sp, sc in last 2 sts, turn.

Row 10: Ch 6, skip next st, sc in next ch sp, sc in next 3 sts, sc in next ch sp, ch 3, dc in center st of next 3-sc group, ch 3, skip next st, sc in next ch sp, sc in next 3 sts, sc in next ch sp, ch 3, dc in last st, turn.

Row 11: Ch 1, sc in each st across with 3 sc in each ch sp across to ch-6, 2 sc in ch-6 sp, sc in fourth ch of ch-6, turn.

Rows 12–16: Repeat rows 2–6. At end of last row, **do not turn.**

Rnds 17–18: Repeat rnds 19 and 20 of Star Stitch Daisy Square.

CROSSED X

Rnd 1: With lt. green, ch 5, sl st in first ch to form ring, ch 3, 2 dc in ring, (ch 2, 3 dc in ring) 3 times, ch 2, join with sl st in top of ch-3. *(Ch-3 at beginning of row counts as first dc—12 dc, 4 ch sps made.)*

Rnd 2: Ch 3, dc in next 2 sts changing to dk.

green in last st *(see Note on page 100; work over dropped color; **do not cut**),* *(2 dc, ch 2, 2 dc) in next ch sp changing to lt. green in last st, dc in next 3 sts changing to dk. green in last st; repeat from * 2 more times, (2 dc, ch 2, 2 dc) in last ch sp, join. *(28 dc)*

Rnd 3: Ch 3, dc in next 2 sts changing to lt. green in last st, *dc in next 2 sts changing to dk. green in last st, (2 dc, ch 2, 2 dc) in next ch sp changing to lt. green in last st, dc in next 2 sts changing to dk. green in last st, dc in next 3 sts changing to lt. green in last st; repeat from * 2 more times, dc in next 2 sts changing to dk. green in last st, (2 dc, ch 2, 2 dc) in next ch sp changing to lt. green in last st, dc in last 2 sts changing to dk. green in last st, join. *(44)*

Rnd 4: Ch 3, dc in next 4 sts changing to lt. green in last st, *dc in next 2 sts changing to dk. green in last st, (2 dc, ch 2, 2 dc) in next ch sp changing to lt. green in last st, dc in next 2 sts changing to dk. green in last st, dc in next 7 sts changing to lt. green in last st; repeat from * 2 more times, dc in next 2 sts changing to dk. green in last st, (2 dc, ch 2, 2 dc) in next ch sp changing to lt. green in last st, dc in next 2 sts changing to dk. green in last st, dc in last 2 sts, join. *(60)*

Rnd 5: Ch 3, dc in next 2 sts changing to lt. green in last st, *dc in next 6 sts changing to dk. green in last st, (2 dc, ch 2, 2 dc) in next ch sp changing to lt. green in last st, dc in next 6 sts changing to dk. green in last st, dc in next 3 sts changing to lt. green in last st; repeat from * 2 more times, dc in next 6 sts changing to dk. green in last st, (2 dc, ch 2, 2 dc) in next ch sp changing to lt. green in last st, dc in last 6 sts, join. *(76)*

Rnd 6: Ch 2, (hdc in each st across to last st before next ch sp, 2 hdc in next st, 5 hdc in next ch sp, 2 hdc in next st) 4 times, hdc in each st across, join with sl st in top of ch-2. Fasten off. *(Third hdc of 5-hdc group is corner st—4 corner sts, 25 hdc on each side between corner sts; 104 hdc total.)*

Rnd 7: Repeat rnd 20 of Star Stitch Daisy Square.

GRANNY SQUARE

Rnd 1: With dk. green, ch 4, sl st in first ch to form ring, ch 3 *(counts as first dc)*, 2 dc in ring, (ch 3, 3 dc in ring) 3 times, ch 1, join with hdc in top of first ch-3, **turn.** *(Ch-1 and hdc count as joining ch sp—12 dc, 4 ch sps made)*

Rnd 2: (Ch 3, 2 dc) in joining ch sp, *ch 1, (3 dc, ch 3 at corner, 3 dc) in next ch sp; repeat from * 2 more times, ch 1, 3 dc in joining ch sp, ch 1, join with hdc in first ch-3, **turn.** *(4 ch-1 sps, 4 corner ch sps)*

Rnd 3: (Ch 3, 2 dc) in joining ch sp, *ch 1, 3 dc in next ch-1 sp, ch 1, (3 dc, ch 3, 3 dc) in next corner ch sp; repeat from * 2 more times, ch 1, 3 dc in next ch-1 sp, ch 1, 3 dc in joining ch sp, ch 1, join with hdc in first ch-3, **turn.** *(8 ch-1 sps)*

Rnds 4–5: (Ch 3, 2 dc) in joining ch sp, ch 1, (3 dc in next ch-1 sp, ch 1) across to next corner ch sp, *(3 dc, ch 3, 3 dc) in corner ch sp, ch 1, (3 dc in next ch-1 sp, ch 1) across to next corner ch sp; repeat from * 2 more times, 3 dc in joining ch sp, ch 1, join with hdc in first ch-3, **turn.** *(12, 16 ch-1 sps)*

Rnd 6: Ch 1, 2 sc in joining ch sp, sc in each st and 2 sc in each ch-1 sp with 3 sc in each corner ch sp around to joining ch sp, sc in joining ch sp, join with sl st in first sc. Fasten off. *(Second sc of 3-sc group is corner st—4 corner sts, 25 sc on each side between corner sts; 104 sc total.)*

Rnd 7: Repeat rnd 20 of Star Stitch Daisy Square.

GRANNY'S STAR

Special Stitches for this Square: *For **beginning cluster (beg cluster)**, ch 2 (not worked into or counted as a st), (yo, insert hook in ring or ch sp, yo, pull lp through, yo, pull through 2 lps on hook) 2 times, yo, pull through all 3 lps on hook.*

*For **3-dc cluster (cluster)**, (yo, insert hook in ring or ch sp, yo, pull lp through, yo, pull through 2 lps on hook) 3 times, yo, pull through all 4 lps on hook.*

Motif A (make 2)
Rnd 1: With lt. green, ch 6, sl st in first ch to form ring, **beg cluster** in ring *(see Special Stitches for this Square)*, ch 3 at corner, **cluster** in ring *(see Special Stitches for this Square)*, (ch 2, cluster in ring, ch 3 at corner, cluster in ring) 3 times, ch 2, join with sl st in top of beg cluster. Fasten off. *(4 ch-2 sps, 4 ch-3 sps made)*

Rnd 2: Join dk. green with sl st in any ch-3 sp, (beg cluster, ch 5, cluster) in same sp as sl st, ch 3, cluster in next ch-2 sp, ch 3, *(cluster, ch 5 at corner, cluster) in next ch-3 sp, ch 3, cluster in next ch-2 sp, ch 3; repeat from * 2 more times, join. Fasten off.

Classic Sampler

Continued from page 105

Motif B

Rnd 1: Repeat rnd 1 of First Motif.

Rnd 2: With right side of all pieces facing you, join dk. green with sl st in any corner ch sp; *join Motifs as follows (see illustration):*
A: Beg cluster in same ch sp as sl st, ch 2, sc in any corner ch sp on one Motif A, ch 2, cluster in same ch sp on this Motif as beg cluster;
B: Ch 1, sc in next ch-2 sp on same Motif A, ch 1, cluster in next ch sp on this Motif;
C: Ch 1, sc in next ch-2 sp on same Motif A, ch 1, cluster in next corner ch sp on this Motif;
D: Ch 2, sc in next corner ch sp on same Motif A, sc in any corner ch sp on other Motif A, ch 2, cluster in same corner ch sp on this Motif;
E: Repeat steps B and C;
F: Ch 2, sc in next corner ch sp on same Motif A, ch 2, cluster in same corner ch sp on this Motif;
G: Ch 3, cluster in next ch-2 sp, ch 3, (cluster, ch 5, cluster) in next corner ch sp, ch 3, cluster in next ch-2 sp, ch 3, join. Fasten off.

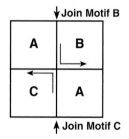

↓ **Join Motif B**

A	B
C	A

↑ **Join Motif C**

Motif C

Rnd 1: Repeat rnd 1 of Motif A.

Rnd 2: Working on other side edges of Motif A to form a square, repeat rnd 2 of Motif B *(see illustration on page 105).*

Rnd 3: For **border**, working around all edges of joined Motifs, join dk. green with sc in any corner ch sp, 6 sc in same ch sp, sc in each st and 2 sc in each ch-3 sp around with sc around side of each joining sc between Motifs and 7 sc in each corner ch sp, join with sl st in first sc. Fasten off. *(Fourth sc of 7-sc group is corner st—4 corner sts, 25 sc on each side between corner sts; 104 sc total.)*

Rnd 7: Repeat rnd 20 of Star Stitch Daisy Square.

ZIGZAG

Special Stitches for this Square: *For* **back zigzag st (bzs),** *skip next 3 sts, tr in next st; working behind tr just made, dc in first skipped st, dc in each of next 2 skipped sts.*

For **front zigzag st (fzs),** *skip next 3 sts, tr in next st; working in front of tr just made, dc in first skipped st, dc in each of next 2 skipped sts.*

Row 1: With dk. green, ch 23, sc in second ch from hook, sc in each ch across, turn. *(22 sc made)*

Row 2: Ch 3, **bzs** *(see Special Stitches for this Square)* across to last st, dc in last st, turn. *(2 dc, 5 bzs)*

Row 3: Ch 3, **fzs** *(see Special Stitches for this Square)* across to last st, dc in last st, turn. *(2 dc, 5 fzs)*

Rows 4–11: Repeat rows 2 and 3 alternately.

Rnds 12–13: Repeat rnds 19 and 20 of Star Stitch Daisy Square.

STRIPED PANELS

Panel (make 2 lt. green and 2 dk. green)
Ch 5, sl st in first ch to form ring, (ch 3, 5 dc in ring, ch 2, drop lp from hook, insert hook in top of last ch-3 made and through dropped lp, pull lp through to form ring) 9 times. Fasten off. *(9 shells made)*

Joining

Row 1: Working across long edge of one lt. green Panel, join dk. green with sc in first ring, (ch 3, sc in next ring on same Panel) 8 times, ch 3, (sc, ch 2, sc) in last ring; working across opposite long edge, of Panel, (ch 3, sc in next ring) 9 times; **do not turn.**

Row 2: Working across long edge of one dk. green Panel, ch 1, sc in first ring, ch 1, sc in next ch-3 sp on last Panel, ch 1, (sc in next ring on this Panel, ch 1, sc in next ch-3 sp on last Panel, ch 1) 8 times, (sc, ch 2, sc) in last ring; working across opposite long edge of second Panel, (ch 3, sc in next ring) 9 times; **do not turn.**

Row 3: Working across long edge of second lt. green Panel, repeat row 2.

Row 4: Working across long edge of second dk. green Panel, repeat row 2.

Rnds 5–6: Repeat rnds 19 and 20 of Star Stitch Daisy Square.

V STITCH

Special Stitches for this Square: *For* **V st,** *(dc, ch 1, dc) in ch indicated (on row 1 only), or in ch sp of next V st (on rows 2–12).*

Row 1: With dk. green, ch 28, **V st** in fifth ch from hook *(see Special Stitch for this Square),* (skip next 2 chs, V st in next ch) 7 times, skip next ch, dc in last ch, turn. *(3 chs at beginning of row count as first dc—8 V sts, 2 dc made)*

Rows 2–12: Ch 3 *(counts as first dc),* V st in each V st across with dc in last st, turn.

Rnds 13–14: Repeat rnds 19 and 20 of Star Stitch Daisy Square.

STAINED GLASS

Special Stitches for this Square: *For* **long sc (lsc),** *working over ch-2 sp of last row, insert hook in next skipped sc on row before last, pull up long lp to same height as row being worked; complete as sc.*

Rnd 1: With lt. green, ch 5, sl st in first ch to form ring, ch 3 *(counts at first dc),* 15 dc in ring, join with sl st in top of ch-3. Fasten off. *(16 dc made)*

Rnd 2: Join dk. green with sc in sp between any 2 dc, ch 2, skip next 2 dc, (sc in next sp between dc, ch 2, skip next 2 dc) around, join with sl st in first sc. Fasten off. *(8 sc, 8 ch-2 sps)*

Rnd 3: Join lt. green with sl st in any ch sp, (ch 3, dc, ch 1 at corner, 2 dc) in same sp as sl st; skipping each sc, 3 dc in next ch sp, *(2 dc, ch 1 at corner, 2 dc) in next ch sp, 3 dc in next ch sp; repeat from * around, join. Fasten off. *(28 dc, 4 corner ch sps)*

Rnd 4: Join dk. green with sc in any corner ch-1 sp, (ch 2 at corner, sc) in same sp as joining sc, ch 2; (skipping dc of last rnd, **lsc**—*see Special Stitch for this Square*—in next sc on rnd before last, ch 2) 2 times; *(sc, ch 2 at corner, sc) in next ch-1 sp on last rnd, ch 2, (lsc in next sc on rnd before last, ch 2) 2 times; repeat from * around, join. Fasten off. *(16 sc, 16 ch sps)*

Rnd 5: Join lt. green with sl st in any ch sp, (ch 3, dc, ch 1 at corner, 2 dc) in same sp as sl st; skipping each sc, 3 dc in each ch sp across to next corner ch sp, *(2 dc, ch 1, 2 dc) in corner ch sp, 3 dc in each ch sp across to next corner ch sp; repeat from * around, join. Fasten off. *(52 dc, 4 corner ch sps)*

Rnd 6: Join dk. green with sc in any corner ch-1 sp, (ch 2 at corner, sc) in same sp as joining sc, ch 2; (skipping dc of last rnd, lsc in next sc on rnd before last, ch 2) across to next corner ch sp; *(sc, ch 2 at corner, sc) in next ch-1 sp on last rnd, ch 2, (lsc in next sc on rnd before last, ch 2) across to next corner ch sp; repeat from * around, join. Fasten off. *(24 sc, 24 ch sps)*

Rnds 7–8: Repeat rnds 5 and 6. *(32 sc, 32 ch sps)*

Rnds 9–10: Repeat rnds 19 and 20 of Star Stitch Daisy Square.

COCKLE SHELLS

Row 1: With lt. green, ch 27, sc in second ch from hook, sc in next ch, (ch 2, skip next 2 chs, sc in next 2 chs) across, turn. *(14 sc, 6 ch sps made)*

Row 2: Ch 3 *(counts as first dc),* 4 dc in each ch-2 sp across, dc in last st, turn. *(26 dc)*

Row 3: Ch 1, sc in first 2 sts, (ch 2, skip next 2 sts, sc in next 2 sts) across, turn. *(14 sc, 6 ch sps)*

Rows 4–15: Repeat rows 2 and 3 alternately.

Rnds 16–17: Repeat rnds 19 and 20 of Star Stitch Daisy Square.

PINWHEEL

Row 1: With lt. green, ch 26, sc in second ch from hook, sc in each ch across, turn. *(25 sc made)*

Rows 2–4: Ch 1, sc in each st across, turn.

Rows 5–19: Changing colors according to corresponding row of Pinwheel Graph *(see*

Pinwheel Graph

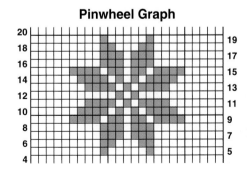

Pinwheel Key
☐ **Lt. Green Sc**
▓ **Dk. Green Sc**

Classic Sampler

Continued from page 107

Note on page 100) and working over dropped color as you go, ch 1, sc in each st across, turn. At end of last row, fasten off dk. green.

Rows 20–23: With lt. green, ch 1, sc in each st across, turn.

Rnds 24–25: Repeat rnds 19 and 20 of Star Stitch Daisy Square.

BASKETWEAVE

Row 1: With lt. green, ch 28, dc in fourth ch from hook, dc in each ch across, turn. *(26 dc made)*

Row 2: Ch 3 *(counts as first dc),* ***dc back post (fp,** see Stitch Guide on page 175)* around next 2 sts, **dc front post (bp)** around next 2 sts; repeat from * across to last st, dc in last st, turn.

Row 3: Ch 2, (bp around next 2 sts, fp around next 2 sts) across to last st, dc in last st, turn.

Rows 4–14: Repeat rows 2 and 3 alternately, ending with row 2. At end of last row, **do not turn.**

Rnds 15–16: Repeat rnds 19 and 20 of Star Stitch Daisy Square.

STARBURST

Special Stitches for this Square: *For* **reverse shell (r-shell),** *(yo, pull up a lp in next st, yo, pull through 2 lps on hook) 8 times, yo, pull through all 9 lps on hook; for* **eye,** *ch 1.*

For **half reversed shell (half r-shell),** *(yo, pull up a lp in next st, yo, pull through 2 lps on hook) 4 times, yo, pull through all 5 lps on hook; for* **eye,** *ch 1.*

Row 1: With lt. green, ch 23, sc in second ch from hook, (skip next 2 chs, 7 dc in next ch, skip next 2 chs, sc in next ch) 3 times, skip next 2 chs, 4 dc in last ch, turn. Fasten off. *(29 sts made)*

Row 2: Working this row in **back lps** *(see Stitch Guide),* join dk. green with sc in first st, ***ch 2, r-shell** (see Special Stitches for this Square),* ch 2, sc in same st as last st of r-shell; repeat from * 2 more times, ch 2, **half r-shell** *(see Special Stitches for this Square),* turn.

Row 3: Working in **both lps,** ch 2, 3 dc in first st; skipping each ch-2, sc in next sc, (7 dc in eye of next r-shell, sc in next sc) 3 times, turn. Fasten off. *(29 sts made)*

Row 4: Working in **back lps,** join lt. green with sl st in first st, ch 2, half r-shell, ch 2, sc in same st as last st of r-shell, (ch 2, r-shell, ch 2, sc in same st as last st of r-shell) 3 times, turn.

Row 5: Working in **both lps,** ch 1, sc in first st; skipping each ch-2, (7 dc in eye of next r-shell, sc in next sc) 3 times, half r-shell, turn. Fasten off.

Rows 6–12: Repeat rows 2–5 consecutively, ending with row 4. At end of last row, **do not turn.**

Rnds 13–14: Repeat rnds 19 and 20 of Star Stitch Daisy Square.

GRANNY'S FILET

Rnd 1: With dk. green, ch 5, sl st in first ch to form ring, ch 4 *(counts at first dc and ch-1 sp),* (2 dc in ring, ch 1) 7 times, dc in ring, join with sl st in third ch of ch-4. *(16 dc, 8 ch sps made)*

Rnd 2: (Sl st, ch 1, sc) in first ch sp, ch 2, skip next 2 dc, (sc in next ch sp, ch 2, skip next 2 dc) around, join with sl st in first sc. *(8 sc, 8 ch-2 sps)*

Rnd 3: (Sl st, ch 4, 2 dc, ch 1) in first corner ch sp; skipping each sc, (3 dc, ch 1) in next ch sp, *(2 dc, ch 1, 2 dc, ch 1) in next corner ch sp, (3 dc, ch 1) in next ch sp; repeat from * around, dc in first ch sp, join with sl st in third ch of ch-4. *(12 ch sps)*

Rnd 4: (Sl st, ch 1, sc) in first ch sp at corner, *[ch 2; skipping each dc, (sc in next ch-1 sp, ch 2) across to next corner ch sp], (sc, ch 3, sc) in corner ch sp; repeat from * 2 more times; repeat between [ ], sc in first ch sp, ch 1, join with hdc in first sc. *(Ch 1 and hdc form joining ch sp—12 ch-2 sps, 4 corner ch sps.)*

Rnd 5: (Ch 5, 2 dc, ch 1) in joining ch sp; skipping each sc, (3 dc in next ch-1 sp, ch 1) across to next corner, *(2 dc, ch 2, 2 dc, ch 1) in next corner ch sp, (3 dc in next ch sp, ch 1) across to next corner; repeat from * around, dc in joining ch sp, join with sl st in third ch of ch-5. *(16 ch-1 sps, 4 corner ch sps)*

Rnd 6: Repeat rnd 4. *(20 ch-2 sps, 4 corner ch sps)*

Rnd 7: (Ch 5, 2 dc, ch 1) in joining ch sp; skipping each sc, 2 dc in next ch sp, ch 1, (3 dc in next ch-1 sp, ch 1) 3 times, 2 dc in next ch sp, ch 1, *(2 dc, ch 2, 2 dc, ch 1) in next corner ch sp, 2 dc in next ch sp, ch 1, (3 dc in next ch-1 sp, ch 1) 3 times, 2 dc in next ch sp, ch 1; repeat from * around, dc in joining ch sp, join with sl st in third ch of ch-5. *(24 ch-1 sps, 4 corner ch sps)*

Rnds 8–9: Repeat rnds 19 and 20 of Star Stitch Daisy Square on page 100.

REVERSE SHELL

Special Stitches for this Square: *For* ***reverse shell (r-shell),*** *(yo, pull up a lp in next st, yo, pull through 2 lps on hook) 4 times, yo, pull through all 5 lps on hook.*

For ***shell,*** *4 dc in next st.*

Row 1: With dk. green, ch 26, sc in second ch from hook, sc in each ch across changing to lt. green in last st *(see Note on page 100),* turn. *(25 sts made)*

Row 2: With lt. green, ch 2, skip next st, **shell** *(see Special Stitches for this Square),* (skip next 3 sts, shell) 5 times, skip next st, dc in last st, turn. *(2 dc, 6 shells)*

Row 3: Ch 4 *(counts as first dc and ch-1 sp),* **r-shell** *(see Special Stitches for this Square),* (ch 3, r-shell) 5 times, ch 1, dc in last st changing to dk. green, turn.

Row 4: With dk. green, ch 1, sc in first st, sc in next ch sp, sc in next st, (3 sc in next ch sp, sc in next st) 5 times, sc in next ch sp, sc in last st, turn. *(25 sts)*

Row 5: Ch 1, sc in each st across changing to lt. green in last st, turn.

Rows 6–16: Repeat rows 2–5 consecutively, ending with row 4.

Rnds 17–18: Repeat rnds 19 and 20 of Star Stitch Daisy Square.

CATTY CORNER

Row 1: With dk. green, ch 13, sc in second ch from hook, sc in each ch across, turn. *(12 sc made)*

Rows 2–12: Ch 1, sc in each st across, turn.

Rnd 13: Working around outer edge, ch 1, 3 sc in first st, sc in next 10 sts, 3 sc in next st; working in ends of rows, evenly space 10 sc across to next corner; working in starting ch on opposite side of row 1, 3 sc in first ch, sc in next 10 chs, 3 sc in next ch; working in

ends of rows, evenly space 10 sc across to next corner, join with sl st in first sc. *(52)*

Rnd 14: (Sl st, ch 1, sc) in next st, *[skip next st, hdc in next st, dc in next st, ch 3, sc in next st, hdc in next st, 2 dc in next st, ch 2 *(this will now be corner ch sp),* 2 dc in next st, hdc in next st, sc in next st, ch 3, dc in next st, hdc in next st, skip next st], sc in next st; repeat from * 2 more times; repeat between [ ], join. *(52 sts, 8 ch-3 sps, 4 ch-2 sps)*

Rnd 15: Ch 1, sc in first 3 sts, *[sc in next ch-3 sp, ch 3, skip next st, sc in next st, hdc in next st, dc in next st, (dc, ch 2 at corner, dc) in next ch-2 sp, dc in next st, hdc in next st, sc in next st, ch 3, skip next st, sc in next ch-3 sp], sc in next 5 sts; repeat from * 2 more times; repeat between [ ], sc in last 2 sts, join. *(60 sts, 4 corner ch-sps)*

Rnd 16: Ch 1, sc in first 4 sts, *[sc in next ch-3 sp, ch 3, skip next st, sc in next st, hdc in next st, dc in next st, (dc, ch 2 at corner, dc) in next ch-2 sp, dc in next st, hdc in next st, sc in next st, ch 3, skip next st, sc in next ch-3 sp], sc in next 7 sts; repeat from * 2 more times; repeat between [ ], sc in last 3 sts, join. *(68 sts, 4 corner ch-sps)*

Rnd 17: Working around outer edge, ch 1, sc in each st around with 3 sc in each ch sp, join. Fasten off. *(Second sc of 3-sc group at corner is corner st—4 corner sts, 25 sc on each side between corner sts; 104 sc total.)*

Rnd 18: Repeat rnd 20 of Star Stitch Daisy Square.

FLOWER

Special Stitches for this Square: *For* ***shell,*** *(3 dc, ch 2, 3 dc) in ch sp.*

For ***scallop,*** *9 dc in ch sp of next shell.*

Rnd 1: With lt. green, ch 6, sl st in first ch to form ring, ch 3 *(counts at first dc),* 23 dc in ring, join with sl st in top of ch-3. Fasten off. *(24 dc made)*

Rnd 2: (Ch 5, dc) in first st, skip next 2 sts, *(dc, ch 2, dc) in next st, skip next 2 sts; repeat from * around, join with sl st in third ch of ch-5. *(8 ch-2 sps)*

Rnd 3: (Sl st, ch 3, 2 dc, ch 2, 3 dc) in first ch sp, **shell** *(see Special Stitches for this Square)* in each ch sp around, join with sl st in top of ch-3.

Rnd 4: Ch 1, sc back into sp between first and last dc of rnd 3, **scallop** *(see Special*

Classic Sampler

Continued from page 109

Stitches for this Square) in next shell, (sc in next sp between shells, scallop in next shell) around, join with sl st in first sc. Fasten off. *(8 sc, 8 scallops)*

Rnd 5: Join dk. green with sl st in any sc, (ch 5, dc) in same sc as sl st, *[ch 3, skip next 4 dc on next scallop, sc in any upper strand at back of next dc, ch 3, skip next 4 dc, sc in next sc, ch 3, skip next 4 dc on next scallop, sc in any upper strand at back of next dc, ch 3, skip next 4 dc], (dc, ch 2, dc) in next sc; repeat from * 2 more times; repeat between [ ], join with sl st in third ch of ch-5. *(Ch-2 sps are at corners—4 ch-2 sps, 16 ch-3 sps.)*

Rnd 6: (Sl st, ch 3, dc, ch 2, 2 dc) in first ch-2 sp, *ch 2, (sc in next ch sp, ch 2) 4 times, (2 dc, ch 2, 2 dc) in next corner ch sp; repeat from * 2 more times, ch 2, (sc in next ch sp, ch 2) 4 times, join with sl st in top of ch-3. *(24 ch sps)*

Rnd 7: Sl st in next st, (sl st, ch 3, dc, ch 3, 2 dc) in next ch-2 sp, *ch 2, (sc in next ch sp, ch 2) 5 times, (2 dc, ch 3, 2 dc) in next corner ch sp; repeat from * 2 more times, ch 2, (sc in next ch sp, ch 2) 5 times, join. *(28 ch sps.)*

Rnd 8: Ch 1, sc in each st and 2 sc in each ch-2 sp around with 5 sc in each corner ch-3 sp, join with sl st in first sc. Fasten off. *(Third sc of 5-sc group is corner st—4 corner sts, 25 sc on each side between corner sts; 104 sc total.)*

Rnd 9: Repeat rnd 20 of Star Stitch Daisy Square.

GRANNY'S POPCORN

Special Stitches for this Square: For popcorn (pc), 4 dc in next st, drop lp from hook, insert hook through first dc of group, return lp to hook and pull through, ch 1 (do not work into or count ch-1 of pc).

Rnd 1: With dk. green, ch 6, sl st in first ch to form ring, ch 5, (3 dc in ring, ch 2) 3 times, 2 dc in ring, join with sl st in third ch of ch-5. *(12 dc, 4 ch sps made)*

NOTE: *All rnds are worked in* **back lps** *(see Stitch Guide).*

Rnd 2: Working in **back lps** *(see Note),* (sl st, ch 5, 2 dc) in first ch sp, dc in next 3 sts, *(2 dc, ch 2, 2 dc) in next ch sp, dc in next 3 sts; repeat from * around, dc in first ch sp, join in third ch of ch-5. *(28 dc, 4 ch sps)*

Rnd 3: (Sl st, ch 5, 2 dc) in first ch sp, dc in next 3 sts, **pc** *(see Special Stitch for this Square),* dc in next 3 sts, *(2 dc, ch 2, 2 dc) in next ch sp, dc in next 3 sts, pc, dc in next 3 sts; repeat from * around, dc in first ch sp, join in third ch of ch-5. *(44 sts)*

Rnd 4: (Sl st, ch 5, 2 dc) in first ch sp, dc in next 3 sts, (pc, dc in next 3 sts) 2 times, *(2 dc, ch 2, 2 dc) in next ch sp, dc in next 3 sts, (pc, dc in next 3 sts) 2 times; repeat from * around, dc in first ch sp, join in third ch of ch-5. *(60)*

Rnd 5: (Sl st, ch 5, 2 dc) in first ch sp, dc in next 3 sts, (pc, dc in next 3 sts) 3 times, *(2 dc, ch 2, 2 dc) in next ch sp, dc in next 3 sts, (pc, dc in next 3 sts) 3 times; repeat from * around, dc in first ch sp, join in third ch of ch-5. *(76)*

Rnds 6–7: Repeat rnds 19 and 20 of Star Stitch Daisy Square on page 100.

FAN SHELLS

Special Stitches for this Square: For **shell,** *5 dc in same ch or ch sp*

Row 1: With lt. green, ch 28, 2 dc in fourth ch from hook (skip next 2 chs, sc in next ch, skip next 2 chs, **shell**—*see Special Stitch for this Square*—in next ch) 3 times, skip next 2 chs, sc in next ch, skip next 2 chs, 3 dc in last ch, turn. *(3 chs at beginning of row count as first dc—6 dc, 4 sc, 3 shells made.)*

Row 2: Ch 1, sc in first dc, shell in next sc, (sc in center dc of next shell, shell in next sc) 3 times, sc last dc, turn. Fasten off. *(4 shells, 5 sc)*

Row 3: Working this row in **back lps** *(see Stitch Guide),* join dk. green with sl st in first st, (ch 3, 2 dc) in same st as sl st, sc in third dc of next shell, (shell in next sc, sc in third dc of next shell) 3 times, 3 dc in last sc, turn. *(6 dc, 4 sc, 3 shells)*

Row 4: Ch 1, sc in first st, shell in next sc, (sc in third dc of next shell, shell in next sc) 3 times, sc last st, turn. Fasten off.

Row 5: Working this row in **back lps,** join lt. green with sl st in first st, (ch 3, 2 dc) in same st as sl st, sc in third dc of next shell, (shell in next sc, sc in third dc of next shell) 3 times, 3 dc in last sc, turn. *(29 sts made)*

Rows 6–14: Repeat rows 2–5 consecutively, ending with row 2.

Rnds 15–16: Repeat rnds 19 and 20 of Star Stitch Daisy Square.

DOUBLE DIAMOND

Special Stitches for this Square: For **berry st (berry),** tr in next st (berry sts are worked in sc rows on wrong side of work and pushed to right side of work).

Row 1: With lt. green, ch 24, sc in second ch from hook, sc in each ch across, turn. *(23 sc made)*

Rows 2–3: Ch 1, sc in each st across, turn.

Row 4: Ch 1, sc in first 6 sts, dc in next st, sc in next 9 sts, dc in next st, sc in last 6 sts, turn.

Row 5: Ch 1, sc in each st across, turn.

NOTE: For **dc front post (fp),** see Stitch Guide.

Row 6: Ch 1, sc in first 5 sts, (fp—see Note—around next dc on row before last, skip next st on last row, sc in next st, fp around same dc on row before last, skip next st on last row), sc in next 7 sts; repeat between ( ), sc in last 5 sts, turn.

Front of row 6 is right side of work.

Row 7: Ch 1, sc in each st across, turn.

Row 8: Ch 1, sc in first 4 sts, (fp around next fp on row before last, skip next st on last row, sc in next 3 sts, fp around next fp on row before last, skip next st on last row), sc in next 5 sts; repeat between ( ), sc in last 4 sts, turn.

Row 9: Ch 1, sc in first 6 sts, **berry** (see Special Stitch for this Square), sc in next 9 sts, berry, sc in last 6 sts, turn.

Row 10: Ch 1, sc in first 3 sts, (fp around next fp on row before last, skip next st on last row, sc in next 5 sts, fp around next fp on row before last, skip next st on last row, sc in next 3 sts) 2 times, turn.

Row 11: Ch 1, sc in first 5 sts, berry, sc in next st, berry, sc in next 7 sts, berry, sc in next st, berry, sc in last 5 sts, turn.

Row 12: Ch 1, sc in first 2 sts, (fp around next fp on row before last, skip next st on last row, sc in next 7 sts, fp around next fp on row before last, skip next st on last row), sc in next st; repeat between ( ), sc in last 2 sts, turn.

Row 13: Ch 1, sc in first 4 sts, berry, (sc in next st, berry) 2 times, sc in next 5 sts, berry, (sc in next st, berry) 2 times, sc in last 4 sts, turn.

Rows 14–19: Working in reverse order, repeat rows 12–7.

Row 20: Ch 1, sc in first 5 sts, (fp around next fp on row before last, skip next st on last row, sc in next st, fp around next fp on row before last, skip next st on last row), sc in next 7 sts; repeat between ( ), sc in last 5 sts, turn.

Row 21: Ch 1, sc in each st across, turn.

Row 22: Ch 1, sc in first 6 sts; to **fp next 2 fp tog,** fp around next fp on row before last leaving last 2 lps on hook, fp around next fp on row before last leaving last 3 lps on hook, yo, pull through all 3 lps on hook, skip next st on last row *(fp next 2 fp tog made),* sc in next 9 sts, fp next 2 fp tog, skip next st on last row, sc in last 6 sts, turn.

Rows 23–25: Ch 1, sc in each st across, turn.

Rnds 26–27: Repeat rnds 19 and 20 of Star Stitch Daisy Square.

LATTICE

Rnd 1: With dk. green, ch 4, sl st in first ch to form ring, ch 3 *(counts as first dc),* 2 dc in ring, (ch 3, 3 dc in ring) 3 times, ch 1, join with hdc in top of first ch-3. *(Ch-1 and hdc count as joining ch sp—12 dc, 4 ch sps made.)*

Rnd 2: (Ch 3, 2 dc) in joining ch sp, *ch 2, (3 dc, ch 3 for corner, 3 dc) in next ch sp; repeat from * 2 more times, ch 2, 3 dc in joining ch sp, ch 1, join with hdc in first ch-3. *(4 ch-2 sps, 4 corner ch sps)*

Rnd 3: (Ch 3, 2 dc) in joining ch sp, ch 2, 3 dc in next ch-1 sp, ch 2, *(3 dc, ch 3, 3 dc) in next corner ch sp, ch 2, 3 dc in next ch sp, ch 2; repeat from * 2 more times, 3 dc in joining ch sp, ch 1, join with hdc in first ch-3. *(8 ch-2 sps, 4 corner ch sps)*

Rnds 4–6: (Ch 3, 2 dc) in joining ch sp, ch 2, (3 dc in next ch-2 sp, ch 2) across to next corner ch sp, *(3 dc, ch 3, 3 dc) in corner ch sp, ch 2, (3 dc in next ch-2 sp, ch 2) across to next corner ch sp; repeat from * 2 more times, 3 dc in joining ch sp, ch 1, join with hdc in first ch-3. At end of last rnd, fasten off. *(12, 16, 20 ch-2 sps, 4 corner ch sps)*

Lattice Chains

With wrong side of work facing you, join lt. green with sl st in first ch-2 sp past any

Classic Sampler

Continued from page 111

corner on rnd 5 *(see "Begin here" arrow on Lattice Illustration);* working diagonally across Square in ch-2 sps at base of 3-dc groups, *work as follows:*

1: Following red dots and arrows on Illustration, *(ch 2, sc) in ch-2 sp on rnd 4, then on rnds 3, 2, 1, 1, 2, 3, 4 and 5; continue across three ch-2 sps at corner of rnd 5; turn piece around and repeat from *;

2: Ch 2, sl st in first sc of step 1 *(first red dot);* following teal dots and arrows on Illustration, ch 2, sc in next ch-2 sp on rnd 5 before 3-dc group; complete in same manner as step 1;

3: Ch 2, sl st in first sc of step 2 *(first teal dot);* following peach dots and arrows on Illustration, ch 2, sc in next ch-2 sp on rnd 5 before 3-dc group; complete in same manner as previous steps;

4: Ch 2, sl st in first sc of step 3 *(first peach dot);* following purple dots and arrows on Illustration, ch 2, sc in next ch-2 sp on rnd 5 before 3-dc group; complete in same manner as previous steps;

5: Ch 2, sl st in first sc of step 3 *(first purple dot);* following green dots and arrows on Illustration, ch 2, sc in next ch-2 sp on rnd 5 before 3-dc group; complete in same manner as previous steps. Fasten off *(see "End here" arrow).*

Lattice Illustration

End here. Begin here.

Rnd 7: Join lt. green with sc in any ch-2 sp on rnd 6, 3 sc in same ch sp as joining sc, work 4 sc in each ch-2 sp and 6 sc in each corner ch-3 sp around, join with sl st in first

sc. Fasten off. *(Third sc of 6-sc group is corner st—4 corner sts, 25 sc on each side between corner sts; 104 sc total.)*

Rnd 8: Repeat rnd 20 of Star Stitch Daisy Square on page 100.

FILET

Row 1: With lt. green, ch 24, sc in second ch from hook, sc in each ch across, turn. *(23 sc made)*

Row 2: Ch 3 *(counts as first dc),* dc in next 4 sts, (ch 1, skip next st, dc in next 5 sts) across, turn. *(23 sts and chs)*

Row 3: Ch 1, sc in each st and in each ch across, turn.

Row 4: Ch 3, dc in next st, (ch 1, skip next st, dc in next 2 sts) across, turn.

Row 5: Ch 1, sc in each st and in each ch across, turn.

Rows 6–17: Repeat rows 2–5 consecutively. At end of last row, **do not turn.**

Rnds 18–19: Repeat rnds 19 and 20 of Star Stitch Daisy Square.

MEDALLION

Special Stitches for this Square: *For* **beginning cluster (beg cl),** *(ch 2, dc) in ring or ch sp.*

For **cluster,** *(yo, pull up lp in ring or ch sp, yo, pull through 2 lps on hook) 2 times, yo, pull through all 3 lps on hook.*

Rnd 1: With lt. green, ch 5, sl st in first ch to form ring, **beg cl** *(see Special Stitches for this Square),* ch 2, **(cluster,** ch 2) 7 times, join with sl st in top of beg cl. Fasten off. *(8 ch sps made)*

Rnd 2: Join dk. green with sl st in any ch sp, (beg cl, ch 2, cluster, ch 1) in same ch sp as sl st, (cluster, ch 2, cluster, ch 1) in each ch sp around, join. Fasten off. *(16 ch sps)*

Rnd 3: Join lt. green with sl st in any ch-2 sp, (beg cl, ch 2, cluster) in same ch sp as sl st, (cluster, ch 2, cluster) in each ch sp around, join. Fasten off.

Rnd 4: Join dk. green with sl st in any ch sp, beg cl in same ch sp, (ch 2, cluster) 3 times in same ch sp as sl st *(corner made),* (cluster, ch 2, cluster) in each of next 3 ch sps, *cluster in next ch sp, (ch 2, cluster) 3 times in same ch sp as last cluster *(corner made),* (cluster, ch 2, cluster) in each of next 3 ch sps; repeat from * around, join. Fasten off. *(24 ch sps)*

Rnd 5: Join lt. green with sl st in any center corner ch sp, (beg cl, ch 2, cluster) in same ch sp as sl st, (cluster, ch 2, hdc) in next ch sp, (hdc, ch 2, hdc) in each of next 3 ch sps, (hdc, ch 2, cluster) in next ch sp, *(cluster, ch 2, cluster) in next ch sp, (cluster, ch 2, hdc) in next ch sp, (hdc, ch 2, hdc) in each of next 3 ch sps, (hdc, ch 2, cluster) in next ch sp; repeat from * around, join.

Rnd 6: (Sl st, ch 2, 3 dc, hdc) in first ch sp, hdc in next sp between clusters, (3 sc in next ch sp, hdc in next sp between hdc) 4 times, 3 sc in next ch sp, hdc in next sp between clusters, *(hdc, 3 dc, hdc) in next ch sp, hdc in next sp between clusters, (3 sc in next ch sp, hdc in next sp between hdc) 4 times, 3 sc in next ch sp, hdc in next sp between clusters; repeat from * around, join with sl st in top of ch-2. Fasten off. *(Second dc of 3-dc group is corner st—4 corner sts, 25 sts on each side between corner sts; 104 sts total.)*

Rnd 7: Repeat rnd 20 of Star Stitch Daisy Square.

KNOBBY STITCH

Row 1: With dk. green, ch 24, sc in second ch from hook, (skip next ch, 3 sc in next ch) 10 times, skip next ch, sc in last ch, turn. *(32 sc made)*

Rows 2–26: Ch 1, sc in first st, (skip next 2 sts, 3 sc in next st) 10 times, sc in last st, turn. At end of row 26, **do not turn.**

Rnds 27–28: Repeat rnds 19 and 20 of Star Stitch Daisy Square.

LONG STITCH

Special Stitches for this Square: For long sc (lsc), pull up lp in designated st on previous row, pull up to height of row being worked, complete as sc.

Row 1: With dk. green, ch 23, sc in second ch from hook, sc in each ch across, turn. *(22 sc made)*

Rows 2–3: Ch 1, sc in each st across, turn. At end of last row, fasten off.

Row 4: Join lt. green with sc in first st, ***lsc** (see Special Stitch for this Square) in next st on second row below, lsc in next st on third row below, lsc in each of next 2 sts on fourth row below, lsc in next st on third row below, lsc in next st on second row below, sc in next st on last row; repeat from * 2 more times, turn.

Rows 5–7: Ch 1, sc in each st across, turn. At end of last row, fasten off.

Row 8: Join dk. green with sc in first st,*lsc in next st on second row below, lsc in next st on third row below, lsc in each of next 2 sts on fourth row below, lsc in next st on third row below, lsc in next st on second row below, sc in next st on last row; repeat from *2 more times, turn.

Rows 9–11: Ch 1, sc in each st across, turn. At end of last row, fasten off.

Rows 12–32: Repeat rows 4–11 consecutively, ending with row 8. At end of last row, **do not turn.**

Rnds 33–34: Repeat rnds 19 and 20 of Star Stitch Daisy Square.

LACY SHELL

*Special Stitches for this Square: For **V st,** (dc, ch 2, dc) in ch or ch-sp.*

*For **shell,** (2 dc, ch 1, 2 dc) in ch or ch-sp.*

Row 1: With dk. green, ch 27, **V st** *(see Special Stitch for this Square)* in fifth ch from hook, skip next 3 chs, **shell** *(see Special Stitch for this Square)* in next ch, (skip next 3 chs, V st in next ch, skip next 3 chs, shell in next ch) 2 times, skip next ch, dc in last ch, turn. *(3 V sts, 3 shells, 2 dc made)*

Rows 2–11: Ch 3, (V st in next shell, shell in next V st) across with dc in last st, turn.

Rnds 12–13: Repeat rnds 19 and 20 of Star Stitch Daisy square.

CHECKERBOARD

*NOTE: When **changing colors** (see Stitch Guide), drop unused color to wrong side of work; pick up again when needed. Use separate ball of yarn for each section of color. Always change to next color in last st made.*

Row 1: With lt. green, ch 26, hdc in third ch from hook, hdc in next 3 chs changing to dk. green *(see Note)* in last st, hdc in next 5 chs changing to lt. green, hdc in next 5 chs changing to dk. green, hdc in next 5 chs changing to lt. green, hdc in last 5 chs, turn. *(2 chs at beginning of row counts as first hdc—25 hdc made.)*

Rows 2–3: Ch 2; changing colors to match last row, hdc in each st across, turn. At end of last row, fasten off both colors.

Row 4: Join dk. green with sl st in first st, ch 2, hdc in next 4 sts changing to lt. green, hdc in

Classic Sampler

Continued from page 113

next 5 sts changing to dk. green, hdc in next 5 sts changing to lt. green, hdc in next 5 sts changing to dk. green, hdc in last 5 sts, turn.

Rows 5–7: Ch 2; changing colors to match last row, hdc in each st across, turn. At end of last row, fasten off both colors.

Row 8: Join lt. green with sl st in first st, ch 2, hdc in next 4 sts changing to dk. green, hdc in next 5 sts changing to lt. green, hdc in next 5 sts changing to dk. green, hdc in next 5 sts changing to lt. green, hdc in last 5 sts, turn.

Rows 9–11: Ch 2; changing colors to match last row, hdc in each st across, turn. At end of last row, fasten off both colors.

Rnds 12–16: Repeat rows 4–8.

Rows 17–18: Ch 2; changing colors to match last row, hdc in each st across, turn. At end of last row, fasten off dk. green only.

Rnds 19–20: Repeat rnds 19 and 20 of Star Stitch Daisy Square.

SLANTED SHELL

Special Stitches for this Square: For **slanted shell (shell),** *(2 dc, ch 2, sc) in ch or ch-sp.*

For **beginning slanted shell (beg shell),** *(ch 2, dc, ch 2, sc) in ch-sp.*

Row 1: With dk. green, ch 25, (dc, ch 2, sc) in fourth ch from hook *(counts as first shell)*, (skip next 2 chs, **shell**—*see Special Stitches for this Square*—in next ch) across, turn. *(8 shells made)*

Rows 2–13: Beg shell *(see Special Stitches for this Square)* in first ch-2 sp, (shell in ch sp of next shell) across, turn.

Rnd 14: Ch 1, 2 sc in first ch-2 sp, (hdc in next sc, 2 sc in next ch sp) across *(23 sts made)*; working in ends of rows, 3 sc in first row, evenly space 23 sc across each of remaining 3 edges with 3 sc in each corner, join with sl st in first sc. Fasten off. *(Second sc of 3-sc group is corner st—4 corner sts, 25 sc on each side between corner sts; 104 sts total.)*

Rnd 15: Repeat rnd 20 of Star Stitch Daisy Square on page 160.

FINISHING

ASSEMBLY

Place Squares five wide and seven long in desired arrangement.

Using tapestry needle and off-white yarn, matching sts, sew squares together through **back lps.**

BORDER

Rnd 1: Working around outer edge of assembled Squares, join off-white with sl st in any corner ch sp, (ch 3, dc, ch 2, 2 dc) in same ch sp as joining sl st; counting each seam as a 2-dc group, 2 dc in each sp between 2-dc groups and in each ch sp at corner of square around with (2 dc, ch 2, 2 dc) in each corner ch sp, join with sl st in top of ch-3.

Rnd 2: Ch 1; working from left to right, **reverse sc** *(see Stitch guide on page 175)* in each st and in each ch around, join with sl st in first reverse sc. Fasten off.

Keep Me in Stitches

Continued from page 99

next 3 dc, dc in next vertical bar on second row below, pull up a lp in next 6 vertical bars) 4 times, pull up a lp in last 2 vertical bars; work lps off hook.

Row 12: Skip first vertical bar, pull up a lp in next 4 vertical bars, (dcfp around each of next 3 dc, dc in next vertical bar on second row below, pull up a lp in next 6 vertical bars) 4 times, pull up a lp in last vertical bar; work lps off hook.

Row 13: Skip first vertical bar, pull up a lp in next 5 vertical bars, (dcfp around each of next 3 dc, dc in next vertical bar on second row below, pull up a lp in next 6 vertical bars) 4 times; work lps off hook.

Row 14: Skip first vertical bar, (pull up a lp in next 6 vertical bars, dcfp around each of next 3 dc, dc in next vertical bar on second row below) 4 times, pull up a lp in next 5 vertical bars; work lps off hook.

Row 15: Skip first vertical bar, pull up a lp in next 5 vertical bars, (dcfp around each of next 4 dc, pull up a lp in next 6 vertical bars) 4 times; work lps off hook.

Row 16: Skip first vertical bar, pull up a lp in next 5 vertical bars, dc in next vertical bar on second row below, dcfp around each of next 3 dc, (pull up a lp in next 6 vertical bars, dc in next vertical bar on second row below, dcfp around each of next 3 dc) 3 times, pull up a lp in last 6 vertical bars; work lps off hook.

Rows 17–199: Repeat rows 5–16 consecutively, ending with row 7.

Rows 200–202: Work in afghan st. At end of last row, fasten off.

Row 203: With right side of work facing you, working in ends of rows on left edge of Panel, using crochet hook, join ivory with sc in row 202, sc in next 6 rows, **half-shell cluster** *(see Special Stitches for this Panel),* sc in next 7 rows, half-shell cluster, (sc in next 6 rows, half-shell cluster, sc in next 7 rows, half-shell cluster) 12 times, sc in last 6 rows. Fasten off.

SIDE PANELS ASSEMBLY

NOTE: When joining Panels, have row 1 of all Panels at same end of work.

1: For **first seam,** with wrong sides together, hold Chain Links Panel behind Rickrack Panel; matching sc sts on row 203 of Rickrack Panel to ends of rows on Chain Links Panel.

2: Using crochet hook and working through both layers as one, join ivory with sc in first st/row at corner, sc across long edge to next corner. Fasten off.

3: For **second seam,** with wrong sides together, holding Rickrack Panel behind right edge of assembled Center Panel and working behind Border into ends of rows on Center Section, repeat step 2.

4: For **third seam,** with wrong sides together, holding Dragonflies Panel behind left edge of assembled Center Panel and working behind Border into ends of rows on Center Section, repeat step 2.

5: For **fourth seam,** with wrong sides together, holding Zigzag Panel behind Dragonflies Panel, repeat step 2.

6: Taking care that stitches don't show, sew edge of Center Border to Panels.

BORDER

Row 1: Working in starting chs across row-1 edge of assembled Panels, using crochet hook, join ivory with sc in first ch, sc in each ch and in end of each seam across all Panels. Fasten off.

Row 2: Working across row 202 edge of assembled Panels, join ivory with sc in first st, sc in each st and in end of each seam across all Panels. Fasten off.

Rnd 3: Working around outer edge in sts and in ends of rows, join burgundy with sc in any corner st, sc in same st as joining sc, sc in each st and in end of each row around with 3 sc in each corner st, sc in same st as joining sc, join with sl st in first sc, **turn.**

Rnd 4: Ch 1, 3 sc in first st, sc in each st around with 3 sc in each center corner st, join, **turn.** Fasten off.

Rnd 5: Join gray with sc in any center corner st, sc in same st as joining sc, sc in each st around with 3 sc in each center corner st, sc in same st as joining sc, join with sl st in first sc, **turn.**

Rnd 6: Repeat rnd 4.

Rnd 7: With blue, repeat rnd 5.

Rnd 8: Repeat rnd 4.

TASSEL (make 24)

For each **Tassel,** wrap ivory yarn 24 times around 7-inch cardboard; tightly tie a separate 14-inch double strand ivory through center of all wraps and remove cardboard. Using double-strand ends, tie to Border at stitch designated below, run ends back through loops to hide. Run separate 12-inch strand ivory through stitch on Border one inch below first knot, tightly wrap around all Tassel loops and tie securely. Cut loops, trim ends even.

On each end of Panels, working on row 1 of Border, tie top of one Tassel at end of each seam and one at center of each 46-stitch side Panel; at each side edge of Border, tie one Tassel to rnd 6, about 1¼ inches from corner, so it is even with other Tassels *(see photo).*❦

Just Geese by Diane Poellot

TECHNIQUE
Color Change

FINISHED SIZE
35 inches x 58 inches

MATERIALS
❑ Red Heart Super Saver Art. E300 and Art.
E301 by Coats & Clark or worsted yarn:
19 oz. Black #312
42 oz. of desired geese
colors —shown are:
Frosty Green #661,
Amethyst #356,
Cherry Red #319,
Pale Green #363,
Lavender #358,
Pumpkin #254,
Emerald #676,
Light Coral #246,
Royal Blue #385,
Blue #886,
Petal Pink 3#73,
Lilac #571,
Bright Yellow #324,
Orange #245,
Light Plum #531,
Delft Blue #885,
Lt. Raspberry #774,
Gold #321,
Cornmeal #220,
Burgundy #376,
Paddy Green #368,
Light Blue #381
❑ Tapestry needle
❑ G hook or size hook needed to
obtain gauge

GAUGE
7 sc = 2 inches; 7 sc rows = 2 inches.

BASIC STITCHES
Ch, sl st, sc

NOTE
For **color change** (see Stitch Guide on page
175), drop last color; pick up again when
needed. **Do not work over dropped color**
unless otherwise stated; use separate strand
for each section of color. Always change to
next color in last st made.

INSTRUCTIONS

STRIP (make 11)
Row 1: With first goose color, ch 12, sc in
second ch from hook, sc in each ch across
changing to black (see Note), turn. (11
sc made)

Row 2: Ch 1, sc in first st changing to goose
color, sc in next 9 sts changing to separate
strand black, sc in last st, turn.

Row 3: Ch 1, sc in first 2 sts changing to
same goose color in last st, sc in next 7 sts
changing to black, sc in last 2 sts, turn.

Row 4: Ch 1, sc in first 3 sts changing to
same goose color in last st, sc in next 5 sts
changing to black, sc in last 3 sts, turn.

Row 5: Ch 1, sc in first 4 sts changing to
same goose color in last st, sc in next 3 sts
changing to black, sc in last 4 sts, turn.

Row 6: Ch 1, sc in first 5 sts changing to
same goose color in last st, sc in next st
changing to black, sc in last 5 sts, turn.
Fasten off goose color.

Row 7: Working over dropped black on each
side, join next goose color with sc in first st,
sc in each st across, turn.

Next rows: Using each of the separate
goose colors before repeating any colors,
repeat rows 2–7 consecutively until you have
34 geese in Strip, ending with row 6. At end
of last row, fasten off black.

ASSEMBLY
Arrange Strips matching first row on one Strip
to last row on next Strip so color pattern is
inverted on alternate Strips.

Using tapestry needle and black, sew ends
of rows together, pulling end stitches flush
and snug without forming a ridge.

EDGING
Working around entire outer edge of
assembled Strips, join black with sc in any
st, sc in each st or ch and in end of each row
around with 3 sc in each corner, join with sl st
in first sc. Fasten off. ❧

Fairy Fluff by Nancy Nehring

TECHNIQUES
Hairpin Lace, Mile-A-Minute

SPECIAL STITCH
Back Loops

FINISHED SIZE
44 inches x 46 inches

MATERIALS
❑ Red Heart Yarns by Coats & Clark or baby yarn:
TLC Baby Art. E511:
5 oz. Powder Pink #5737
5 oz. Powder Blue #5881
5 oz. Naptime #5964 *(variegated)*
4 oz. Powder Yellow #5322
Baby Teri Art. E716:
6 oz. Pink #9137
6 oz. Blue #9181
6 oz. Yellow #9121
❑ Bobby pins for markers
❑ H hook
❑ Hairpin lace frame set at 2 inches wide

GAUGE
4-loop bundle and ch-2 = 1 inch; 4 dc = 1 inch; Panel = 4 inches across.

BASIC STITCHES
Ch, sl st, sc, dc

NOTE
Refer to Hairpin Lace Basic Technique on page 45 for additional information.

INSTRUCTIONS

PANEL
(make 4 blue, 4 pink, 3 yellow)
Row 1: For **first bundle,** with designated color Baby Teri yarn, wrap around one prong of hairpin frame and tie at center, wrap around other prong ending at back, wrap 7 more times around both prongs and end at back *(8 loops on each prong);* insert crochet hook under all wraps, yo, pull to front; working loosely, (yo above wraps, insert hook under wraps, yo, pull to front) 3 times, yo, pull through all loops on hook, ch 2;

For **next bundle** *(make 42),* wrap yarn 4 times around both prongs and end at back *(4 loops on each prong);* working loosely, (yo above wraps, insert hook in second ch of ch-2 and under wraps, yo, pull through ch to front) 3 times, yo, pull through all loops on hook, ch 2;

For **last bundle,** wrap yarn 8 times around both prongs and end at back *(8 loops on each prong);* working loosely, (yo above wraps, insert hook in second ch of ch-2 and under wraps, yo, pull through ch to front) 3 times, yo, pull through all loops on hook, ch 1. Fasten off.

Rnd 2: Now working in rnds, with same color TLC yarn, removing loops from prong as you go, join with sc in first loop, sc in each loop across one prong of hairpin lace frame, then across other prong, forming a long oval, join with sl st in first sc. *(368 sc made)*

Rnd 3: Working this rnd in **back lps** *(see Stitch Guide on page 175),* ch 3, dc next st, 2 dc in next st, dc in next 2 sts, 2 dc in next st, dc in next 171 sts, (2 dc in next st, dc in next 2 sts) 5 times, dc in next 169 sts, (2 dc in next st, dc in next 2 sts) 2 times, 2 dc in last st, join with sl st in top of ch-3. Fasten off. *(378 dc)*

ASSEMBLY
1: On each Panel, mark center 18 dc at each end leaving 171 dc along each straight edge.

2: Lay Panels right side up in the following order: blue, pink, yellow, pink, blue, yellow, blue, pink, yellow, pink and blue.

3: For each **seam,** matching long straight edges, hold two Panels with wrong sides together; working in **back lps** of both layers as one, join variegated TLC yarn with sc in next st past marked st, sc in next 169 sts. Fasten off.

4: Working around outer edge, join variegated with sc in any st; skipping each seam, sc in each st around entire assembled Afghan, join with sl st in first sc. Fasten off. ❧

Star Stitch Scrap by Susie Maxfield and Linda McGinn

TECHNIQUE
Weaving Assembly

SPECIAL STITCHES
Back Loops, Star Stitch

FINISHED SIZE
45 inches x 54 inches

MATERIALS
❑ Red Heart Super Saver Art. E300 by Coats & Clark or worsted yarn:
   16 oz. Black #312
   8 oz. Soft White #316
   8 oz. Light Sage #631
   8 oz. Paddy Green #368
   8 oz. Warm Brown #336 *(light brown)*
   8 oz. Brown #328 *(dark brown)*
   8 oz. Country Rose #374
   8 oz. Burgundy #376
   8 oz. Vibrant Orange #534
❑ 12 large safety pins
❑ G hook or size hook needed to obtain gauge

GAUGE
4 sc = 1 inch. Strip = 1½ inches x 7¾ inches. Block is 8¾ inches square.

BASIC STITCHES
Ch, sl st, sc, hdc, dc

INSTRUCTIONS

BLOCK (make 30)

Strip (make 8—one each white, green, dark brown, light brown, sage, rose, burgundy and orange)
Row 1: Ch 32, hdc in third ch from hook, hdc in each ch across, turn. *(2 chs at beginning of row count as first st—31 hdc made.)*

Row 2: For **star st** row, ch 3, insert hook in second ch from hook, yo, pull through, insert hook in next ch, yo, pull through, (insert hook in next st on row 1, yo, pull through) 2 times, yo, pull through all 5 lps on hook, ch 1 for **eye** *(first star st made);* *insert hook in eye of last star st, yo, pull through, insert hook in last worked st on row 1, yo, pull through, (insert hook in next st, yo, pull through) 2 times, yo, pull through all 5 lps on hook, ch 1 for **eye** *(next star st made);* repeat from * across to last st, hdc in top of ch-2, turn. *(15 star sts, one hdc)*

Front of row 2 is right side of work.

Row 3: Ch 1, 2 hdc in each eye across, hdc in top of ch-3, turn. *(31 hdc)*

Row 4: Ch 2, hdc in each st across. Fasten off.

With right side of all Strips facing you, weave Strips together according to Block Weaving illustration; pin in place with safety pins.

Block Weaving

Edging
Rnd 1: Matching sts and ends of rows and working through both lengthwise and crosswise layers as one, join black with sc in first st past any corner, working in each st of Strip *(lengthwise)* and evenly spacing 7 sts in ends of rows on each Strip *(crosswise)*, *sc across to corner, 3 sc in corner; repeat from * around, join with sl st in first sc, **do not** turn. *(29 sc across each side; 3 sts in each corner—128 sts total)*

Rnd 2: Ch 1, sc in each st around with (hdc, dc, hdc) in each center corner st, join. Fasten off.

ASSEMBLY
Arrange Blocks five wide and six long with each color in same position on each Block.

Using yarn needle and black, sew together through **back lps** *(see Stitch Guide on page 175)* of sts on last rnd.

BORDER
Rnd 1: With right side of assembled Blocks facing you, working around outer edge, join black with sc in any st, sc in each st around with (sc 2 corner dc tog) at each seam and with 3 sc in each center corner st, join with sl st in first sc.

Rnd 2: Ch 2, hdc in each st around with (hdc, dc, hdc) in each center corner st, join with sl st in top of ch-2. Fasten off. ❦

All Your Wishes by Rosalie DeVries

SPECIAL STITCH
Popcorn Variation

FINISHED SIZE
48 inches x 60 inches

MATERIALS
❑ Red Heart Super Saver Art. E300 by Coats
   & Clark or worsted yarn:
   11 oz. Claret #378
   8 oz. Lt. Raspberry #774
   8 oz. Raspberry #375
❑ 28 oz. Jet Stream #0598 *(variegated)*
   Natura Delux Art. 1982-O by Caron or
   worsted yarn
❑ G hook or size hook needed to
   obtain gauge

GAUGE
In pattern: 5 dc, pc, 5 dc and tr = 2 inches;
6 rows = 7 inches.

BASIC STITCHES
Ch, sl st, sc, hdc, dc, tr

SPECIAL STITCH
For **popcorn variation (pc),** 2 dc in fourth
ch from hook, remove loop from hook, insert
hook in last ch made and pull loop through,
ch 3, sl st in same ch as dc sts.

INSTRUCTIONS
Row 1: With variegated, ch 8, **pc** *(see
Special Stitch),* (ch 9, pc) 23 times, ch 4.
Fasten off. *(24 pc, 25 ch sps made)*

NOTE: Do not turn *at ends of rows.*

Row 2: Skip first ch on row 1, join claret
with sl st in second ch, (5 dc in ch-3 sp at
side of next pc, ch 4, pc, 5 dc in ch-3 sp
on other side of same pc, sl st in third ch of
next ch sp) across, leaving last ch on row 1
unworked. Fasten off.

Row 3: Join variegated with sl st in skipped
first ch on row 1, ch 4 *(counts as first tr),* *sl
st in fourth dc of next 5-dc group, 5 dc in
ch-3 sp at side of next pc, ch 4, pc, 5 dc
in ch-3 sp on other side of same pc, sl st in
second dc of next 5-dc group, tr in next sl st
between 5-dc groups; repeat from * across
with last tr in unworked ch at end of row 1.
Fasten off.

Row 4: Join lt. raspberry with sl st in top of
ch-4 on last row, ch 4, *sl st in fourth dc of
next 5-dc group, 5 dc in ch-3 sp at side of
next pc, ch 4, pc, 5 dc in ch-3 sp on other
side of same pc, sl st in second dc of next
5-dc group, tr in next tr; repeat from * across.
Fasten off.

Rows 5–49: Working in color sequence as
follows, repeat row 4:
   One row variegated
   One row lt. raspberry
   One row variegated
   One row claret
   One row variegated
   One row lt. raspberry

Row 50: Join claret with sl st in top of ch-4 on
last row, ch 4, *sl st in fourth dc of next 5-dc
group, (4 dc, ch 3, sl st) in ch-3 sp at side
of next pc, ch 1, (sl st, ch 3, 4 dc) in ch-3 sp
on other side of same pc, sl st in second dc
of next 5-dc group, tr in next tr; repeat from *
across. Fasten off.

Row 51: Join variegated with sl st in first tr,
ch 4, *skip 4 dc, sc in first ch of next ch-3,
sc in same ch-3 sp, sc in next ch-1 sp, sc in
next ch-3 sp, sc in third ch of same ch-3, tr
in next tr; repeat from * across. **Do not** fasten
off. *(145 sts)*

BORDER
Rnd 1: Working in ends of rows and spacing
sts evenly, ch 1, 3 sc across tr at end of row
51, work 4 sc across tr at end of each row
across to row 1 with 3 sc across tr at end of
row 1; working in starting ch on opposite side
of row 1, 5 sc in first ch, (2 sc in each ch-2
sp with sc at base of each pc and at base
of each tr) across to last ch at corner, 5 sc in
last ch; working in ends of rows, work 3 sc
across tr at end of row 1, work 4 sc across tr
at end of each row across to row 51 with 3 sc
across tr at end of row 51, 5 sc in first tr on
row 51, sc in each st across with 5 sc in last
st, join with sl st in first sc.

Rnd 2: Ch 2 *(counts as first hdc),* hdc in
each st around with 5 hdc in center st of
5-sc group at each corner, join with sl st in
top of ch-2.

Continued on page 126

Crib Coverlet by Julene Watson

TECHNIQUE
Fringe Embellishment

SPECIAL STITCHES
Bobble, Bouclé Loop, Chain Loop, Front Post, Post Stitch Cluster, Rib Stitch

FINISHED SIZE
36 inches square, not including fringe

MATERIALS
❑ Bouclé sport yarn:
   18 oz. white
   18 oz. yellow
   18 oz. pink
   18 oz. blue
❑ ¼-inch dowel or pencil *(unsharpened)*
❑ 5-inch square cardboard
❑ Tapestry needle
❑ G hook or size hook needed to obtain gauge

GAUGE
9 sc = 2 inches. Each color section = 2 inches x 9 inches.

BASIC STITCHES
Ch, sl st, sc, dc

SPECIAL STITCHES
For **bobble,** (yo, insert hook in st, yo, pull lp through, yo, pull through 2 lps) 5 times all in same st, yo, pull through all 6 lps on hook. Bobble is worked on a wrong-side row; push bobble to back of work.

For **bouclé loop,** holding pencil behind work and using pencil to keep loops consistent size, (insert hook in next sc, wrap yarn around pencil, yo, pull lp through, yo, pull through 2 lps) across, sliding loops along pencil and off other end as new sts are formed.

For **rib st,** (yo, insert hook around **front post**—*see Stitch Guide on page 175*—of next st, yo, pull lp through) 2 times all in same st, yo, pull through all 5 lps on hook.

For **chain loop,** ch 5, sc around **front post** of next sc.

INSTRUCTIONS

SQUARE (make 16)
Row 1: With pink, ch 41, sc in second ch from hook, sc in each ch across, turn. *(40 sc made)*

Row 2: Ch 1, **bobble** *(see Special Stitches)* in first st, (sc in next 2 sts, bobble in next st) across, turn. *(14 bobbles, 26 sc)*

Back of row 2 is right side of work.

Row 3: Ch 1, sc in each st across, turn.

Row 4: Ch 1, sc in first 2 sts, (bobble in next st, sc in next 2 sts) across to last 2 sts, bobble in next st, sc in last st, turn. *(13 bobbles, 27 sc)*

Row 5: Ch 1, sc in each st across, turn.

Row 6: Ch 1, sc in first st, (bobble in next st, sc in next 2 sts) across, turn. *(13 bobbles, 27 sc)*

Row 7: Ch 1, sc in each st across, turn.

Row 8: Repeat row 2.

Row 9: Ch 1, sc in each st across, turn.

Row 10: Repeat row 4.

Row 11: Ch 1, sc in each st across, turn. Fasten off.

Row 12: Join white with sl st in first sc, ch 1, **bouclé loop** *(see Special Stitches)* across to last st, sc in last st, turn. *(39 bouclé loops, 1 sc)*

Back of row 12 is right side of work.

Row 13: Ch 1, sc in each st across, turn.

Row 14: Ch 1, bouclé loop across to last st, sc in last st, turn

Rows 15–23: Repeat rows 12 and 13 alternately, ending with row 12. At end of last row, fasten off.

Row 24: Join yellow with sc in first st, sc in each st across, turn.

Row 25: Ch 1, sc in first st, **(rib st** —*see Special Stitches,* sc in next 2 sts) across, turn. *(13 rib sts, 27 sc)*

Row 26: Ch 1, sc in each st across, turn.

Rows 27–37: Repeat rows 25 and 26 alternately, ending with row 25. At end of last row, fasten off.

Row 38: Join blue with sc in first st, sc in each st across, turn. *(40 sc)*

Rows 39–48: Ch 1, sc in each st across, turn. At end of last row, rotate piece so row 48 is next to you and row 1 is away from you.

Crib Coverlet

Continued from page 124

Row 49: With right side of work facing you and holding yarn on right side of work, work loops on front surface of blue section as follows:
A: Ch 1, skip row 48, sc fp around first st on row 47, **chain loop** *(see Special Stitches)* in each st across to last st, sc in last st;
B: Rotate piece so row 1 is next to you and last chain loop row is away from you; ch 1, skip next row, sc front post around first st of row 45, chain loop in each st across to last st, sc in last st;
C: Rotate piece so last chain loop row is next to you and row 1 is away from you; ch 1, skip next row, sc front post around first st of row 43, chain loop in each st across to last st, sc in last st;
D: Working in row 41, repeat step B.
E: Working in row 39, repeat step C. Fasten off.

Fold here.

FINISHING

1: With right sides facing you, sew squares together edge-to-edge according to Assembly illustration.

2: For each **fringe,** wrap white yarn three times around 5-inch cardboard; remove from cardboard *(do not cut);* holding all loops together as one, fold at center opposite ends *(see illustration).* Insert hook from back to front through first st or row at edge of Afghan, pull fold through Afghan, pull loops and ends through fold, pull snug.

3: Fringe ½ inch apart across each edge of Afghan.❧

Assembly

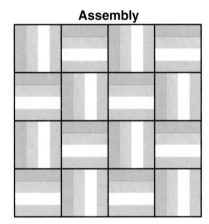

All Your Wishes

Continued from page 122

Rnd 3: Ch 1, sc in each st around with 5 sc in center st of 5-hdc group at each corner, join with sl st in first sc. Fasten off.

Rnd 4: Join claret with sl st in any st, insert hook from **back to front** through next st, complete as sl st, (insert hook from **front to back** through next st, complete as sl st, insert hook from **back to front** through next st, complete as sl st) around, join with sl st in first sl st. Fasten off.

Rnd 5: With back of rnds 1–4 facing you and yarn behind work, join claret with sl st in any hdc of rnd 2, sl st in each st around, join with sl st in first sl st. Fasten off.

Rnd 6: Working in sc of rnd 1, repeat rnd 5.❧

Floral Cables by Diane Poellot

TECHNIQUE
Surface Chains

SPECIAL STITCHES
Back Loops, Cable Stitch, Star Stitch

FINISHED SIZE
45 inches x 61 inches

MATERIALS
❏ Worsted yarn:
  42 oz. tan
  15 oz. variegated
❏ I hook or size hook needed to obtain gauge

GAUGE
3 sc = 1 inch; 3 sc rows = 1 inch. 3 star sts = 2 inches; 3 star st rows and 3 sc rows = 3 inches.

BASIC STITCHES
Ch, sl st, sc, dc, tr

SPECIAL STITCHES
To **attach ch lp,** insert hook in next sc and in **back bar** *(see illustration)* of fifth ch in designated ch-9 lp, yo, pull through ch and sc, yo, pull through 2 lps on hook.

Back Bar of Ch

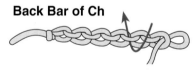

For **star stitch,** pulling all lps up to height of first st, pull up a lp in 2 threads at top of last st made, pull up a lp in 2 threads at center of same st; working in last row, pull up a lp in sc on last row at base of last st made, pull up a lp in next 2 sc, yo, pull through all 6 lps on hook, ch 1.

For **half-flower,** (sc, ch 9, sc, ch 9, sc, ch 9, sc) all in next ch.

INSTRUCTIONS

CENTER PANEL
Row 1: With variegated, ch 182, sc in second ch from hook, sc in next 4 chs; work **half-flower**—see Special Stitches—in next ch, (sc in next 9 chs, half-flower in next ch) across to last 5 chs, sc in next 4 chs, (sc, ch 1, sl st) in last ch; **do not turn,** rotate piece so starting ch is at top. *(235 sc, 54 ch-9 lps made)*

Row 2: Continuing on opposite side of starting ch on row 1, ch 1, sc in first 5 chs, half-flower in next ch *(this is same ch as half-flower of row 1),* (sc in next 9 chs, half-flower in next ch) across to last 5 chs, sc in last 5 chs, turn. Fasten off.

Front of rows 1–2 is right side of work.

Row 3: With wrong side of work facing you, join tan with sc in first st on row 2, sc in next 4 sts; *[holding ch-9 lps out of way at back, skip first sc of half-flower, sc next 2 sc tog, skip last sc of half-flower], sc in next 9 sts; repeat from * 16 more times; repeat between [ ], sc in last 5 sts, turn. *(181 sc)*

Row 4: Ch 1, sc in each st across, turn.

Row 5: Ch 1, sc in first 2 sts; **attach ch lp** *(see Special Stitches)* in first ch-9 of first half-flower, sc in next 5 sts on last row, skip second ch-9 of half-flower, attach ch lp in next ch-9, (sc in next 3 sc on last row, attach ch lp in first ch-9 of next half-flower, sc in next 5 sts on last row, skip second ch-9 of half-flower, attach ch lp in next ch-9) across to last 2 sts, sc in last 2 sts, turn.

Row 6: Ch 1, sc in each st across, turn.

Row 7: Ch 1, sc in first 5 sts, attach ch lp in skipped ch-9 of first half-flower, (sc in next 9 sc on last row, attach ch lp in skipped ch-9 of next half-flower) across to last 5 sts, sc in last 5 sts, turn.

Row 8: Ch 1, sc in each st across, turn. Pull up long loop and remove hook; **do not** fasten off.

Row 9: With wrong side of work facing you, working this row in **back lps** *(see Stitch Guide on page 175),* join variegated with sc in first st, sc in each st across, **do not** turn. Fasten off.

Row 10: Return dropped tan loop to hook; working this row in remaining **front lps** of row 8, ch 1, sc in each st across, turn.

Row 11: Ch 3; pulling all lps up to height of ch-3, pull up a lp in second ch from hook; working in last row, pull up a lp in sc on last row at base of ch-3, pull up a lp in next 2 sc, yo, pull through all 5 lps on hook, ch 1 *(first star st made),* **star st** *(see Special Stitches)* across, turn. *(90 star sts)*

Floral Cables

Continued from page 127

Row 12: Ch 1, sc in each st across, turn. *(181 sc)*

Rows 13–33: Repeat rows 11 and 12 alternately, ending with row 11. At end of last row, fasten off.

CABLE PANEL

Row 1: Working on row 1 of Center Panel, repeat row 3 of Center Panel.

Rows 2–6: Repeat rows 4–8 of Center Panel. At end of last row, **do not turn.**

Row 7: With right side of work facing you, join variegated with sc in first st; (for **cable,** ch 3, skip next 2 sts, sc in next st, **turn,** work 5 sc in ch-3 sp just made—*cable made,* **turn,** sc in each of 2 skipped sc on last row) across, turn. Fasten off. *(181 sc, 60 cables)*

Row 8: With wrong side of work facing you, return dropped tan loop to hook; skipping sts worked into ch-3 sp, ch 1, sc in first st, (skip next st, 2 sc in next st, sc in next st) across, turn. *(181 sc)*

Row 9: Ch 3, dc in next st, (skip next 3 sts, tr in next st; working behind tr just made, dc in each of 3 skipped sts) across to last 3 sts, dc in last 3 sts, turn.

Row 10: Ch 3, dc in next 2 sts, (skip next 3 sts, tr in next st; working in front of tr just made, dc in each of 3 skipped sts) across to last 2 sts, dc in last 2 sts, turn.

Row 11: Ch 1, sc in each st across. Fasten off.

Row 12: With right side of work facing you, join variegated with sc in first st; (for **cable,** ch 3, skip next 2 sts, sc in next st, **turn,** work 5 sc in ch-3 sp just made *(cable made),* **turn,** sc in each of 2 skipped sc on last row) across, turn. Fasten off.

RIGHT SIDE PANEL

Rows 1–10: Repeat rows 1–10 of Center Panel.

Rows 11–19: Repeat rows 11 and 12 of Center Panel alternately, ending with row 11. At end of last row, fasten off.

Row 20: Working on row 1 of Right Side Panel, repeat row 3 of Center Panel.

Rows 21–25: Repeat rows 4–8 of Center Panel. At end of last row, fasten off leaving long strand for sewing.

Matching stitches, sew last row of Right Side Panel and row 12 of Cable Panel together.

LEFT SIDE PANEL

First Section

Rows 1–10: Repeat rows 1–10 of Center Panel. At end of last row, fasten off leaving long strand for sewing.

Matching stitches, sew last row to row 33 of Center Panel.

Rows 11–16: Working on row 1 of Left Side Panel First Section, repeat rows 3–8 of Center Panel. At end of last row, fasten off.

Second Section

Rows 1–10: Repeat rows 1–10 of Center Panel.

Rows 11–19: Repeat rows 11 and 12 of Center Panel alternately, ending with row 11. At end of last row, fasten off.

Row 20: Working on row 1 of Left Side Panel Second Section, repeat row 3 of Center Panel.

Rows 21–25: Repeat rows 4–8 of Center Panel.

Rows 26–31: Repeat rows 7–12 of Cable Panel. At end of last row, fasten off leaving long strand for sewing.

Matching stitches, sew last rows of Left Side Panel First and Second Sections together.

BORDER

With right side of assembled Panels facing you, working around outer edge, join tan with sc in any st, sc in each st and in each ch around with 4 sc evenly spaced across ends of every 2 rows and with 3 sc in each corner, join with sl st in first sc. Fasten off. ❦

Baby Blocks by Jessica Gardner

TECHNIQUES
Color Change, Crochet On the Double

SPECIAL STITCH
Puff Stitch

FINISHED SIZE
About 30 inches x 33 inches, not including Ruffle

MATERIALS
❑ Worsted yarn:
  16 oz. white
  8 oz. pink
  8 oz. yellow
  8 oz. turquoise
❑ Yarn needle
❑ H crochet hook
❑ H double-ended crochet hook or size needed to obtain gauge

GAUGE
8 sts = 2 inches. Each Motif is 10 inches wide x 11 inches long.

BASIC STITCHES
Ch, sl st, sc, dc

NOTES
See General Instructions in Crochet On the Double Basic Technique on page 33.

Always skip first vertical bar of row unless otherwise stated.

When picking up a lp in horizontal bar, insert hook under **top strand** only *(see illustration)*.

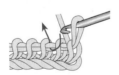

INSTRUCTIONS

WAVES MOTIF (make 4)
Row 1: With double-ended hook and pink, ch 38 loosely; pull up a lp in second ch from hook *(see Notes above),* pull up a lp in each ch across, turn. *(38 lps on hook)* Cut yarn. *Slide lps to opposite end of hook.*

Row 2: With yellow, to **work lps off hook,** working from left to right, yo, pull through first lp on hook, (yo, pull through 2 lps on hook) across, **do not turn.** *(One lp on hook)*

Row 3: With yellow, working from right to left, ch 1, pull up a lp in each of first 2 horizontal bars *(see Notes),* skip next vertical bar, pull up a lp in each of next 2 vertical bars, *pull up a lp in each of next 2 horizontal bars, skip next vertical bar, (yo, insert hook in next vertical bar, yo, pull through 2 lps on hook) 4 times, pull up a lp in each of next 2 horizontal bars, skip next vertical bar, pull up a lp in each of next 2 vertical bars; repeat from * 2 more times, pull up a lp in last 3 horizontal bars, turn. *(38 lps on hook) Slide lps to opposite end of hook.*

Row 4: With turquoise, work lps off hook, **do not turn.** *(One lp on hook)*

Row 5: With turquoise, working from right to left, ch 1, pull up a lp in first horizontal bar, skip next vertical bar, (yo, insert hook in next vertical bar, yo, pull through 2 lps on hook) 4 times, pull up a lp in next 2 horizontal bars, *skip next vertical bar, pull up a lp in each of next 2 vertical bars, pull up a lp in each of next 2 horizontal bars, skip next vertical bar, (yo, insert hook in next vertical bar, yo, pull through 2 lps on hook) 4 times, pull up a lp in each of next 2 horizontal bars; repeat from * 2 more times, turn. *(38 lps on hook)* Cut yarn. *Slide lps to opposite end of hook.*

Rows 6–7: With pink, repeat rows 2 and 3.

Rows 8–9: With yellow, repeat rows 4 and 5.

Rows 10–11: With turquoise, repeat rows 2 and 3.

Rows 12–13: With pink, repeat rows 4 and 5.

Rows 14–60: Working color sequence as established in rows 2–13, repeat rows 2–5 consecutively, ending with row 4.

Row 61: Continuing in color sequence as established, ch 1, sl st in each horizontal bar across. Fasten off.

WHITE MOTIF (make 2)
Rows 1–61: Using two skeins white yarn and carrying dropped yarn along ends of rows without cutting, repeat rows 1–61 of Waves Motif.

Baby Blocks

Continued from page 132

A-1 MOTIF

Row 1: With double-ended hook and pink, ch 39 loosely; pull up a lp in second ch from hook, pull up a lp in each ch across, turn. *(39 lps on hook)* Drop yarn; **do not cut.**

Row 2: With white, work lps off hook, **do not turn.** *(One lp on hook)*

Row 3: With white, working from right to left, ch 1, pull up a lp in each horizontal bar across, turn. Drop yarn. *Slide lps to opposite end of hook.*

Row 4: With pink, work lps off hook, **do not turn.** *(One lp on hook)*

Row 5: With pink, working from right to left, ch 1, pull up a lp in each horizontal bar across, turn. Drop yarn. *Slide lps to opposite end of hook.*

Rows 6–12: Repeat rows 2–5 consecutively, ending with row 4.

NOTES: *For **puff st**, yo, pull up a lp in corresponding opposite-color vertical bar 4 rows below, (yo, pull up a lp in same bar 4 rows below) 2 times, yo, pull through 7 lps on hook, ch 1 to close; skip one lp on last row behind puff st.*

*When working puff st into **previous puff st**, insert hook under vertical bar formed by ch-1 at top of puff st.*

Row 13: To position beginning of letter **"A,"** with pink, working from right to left on white side of work, ch 1, pull up a lp in first 6 horizontal bars *(7 lps on hook),* *work **puff st** (see Notes above), pull up a lp in next horizontal bar on last row, work puff st**, pull up a lp in next 21 horizontal bars; repeat from * to **, pull up a lp in last 6 horizontal bars, turn. *(39*

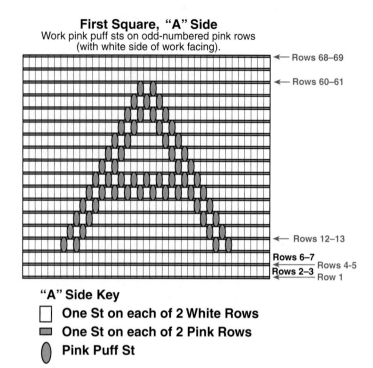

First Square, "A" Side
Work pink puff sts on odd-numbered pink rows
(with white side of work facing).

← Rows 68–69
← Rows 60–61
← Rows 12–13
Rows 6–7
Rows 2–3
Rows 4–5
Row 1

"A" Side Key
☐ One St on each of 2 White Rows
▨ One St on each of 2 Pink Rows
⬭ Pink Puff St

First Square, "1" Side
Work white puff sts on odd-numbered white rows
(with pink side of work facing).

← Rows 68–69
← Rows 62–63
← Rows 14–15
Rows 8–9
Rows 4–5 — Rows 2–3
Row 1

"1" Side Key
▨ One St on each of 2 Pink Rows
☐ One St on each of 2 White Rows
() White Puff St

lps on hook) Cut yarn. *Slide lps to opposite end of hook.*

Row 14: With pink, work lps off hook.

Row 15: To position beginning of number **"1",** with white, working from right to left on pink side of work, ch 1, pull up a lp in first 18 horizontal bars *(19 lps on hook),* work puff st, pull up a lp in next horizontal bar, work puff st, pull up a lp in last 18 horizontal bars, turn. *(39 lps on hook)* Cut yarn. *Slide lps to opposite end of hook.*

Rows 16–63: Repeat rows 2–5 consecutively as follows:
Work **pink puff sts** over rows 16–61 according to Letter A graph.
Work **white puff sts** over rows 16–63 according to Number "1" graph.

Rows 64–68: Repeat rows 2–5 consecutively, ending with row 2.

Row 69: With pink, ch 1, sl st in each horizontal bar across. Fasten off.

B-2 MOTIF
Rows 1–10: Using yellow instead of pink, repeat rows 1–10 of A-1 Motif.

Row 11: To position beginning of number **"2,"** with white, working from right to left on yellow side of work, ch 1, skip first horizontal bar, pull up a lp in next 7 horizontal bars *(8 lps on hook),* work puff st, (pull up a lp in next horizontal bar, work puff st) 11 times, pull up a lp in last 8 horizontal bars, turn. *(39 lps on hook)* Cut yarn. *Slide lps to opposite end of hook.*

Row 12: With yellow, work lps off hook, **do not turn.** *(One lp on hook)*

Row 13: To position beginning of letter **"B,"** with yellow, working from right to left on white side of work, ch 1, skip first horizontal bar, pull up a lp in next 9 horizontal bars *(10 lps on hook),* work

Second Square,"B" Side
Work yellow puff sts on odd-numbered yellow rows
(with white side of work facing).

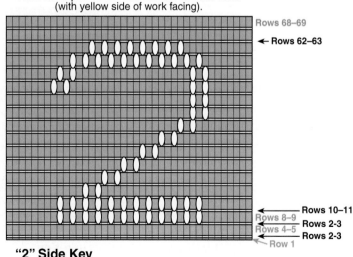

← Rows 68–69
← Rows 60–61
← Rows 12–13
Rows 6–7
Rows 4-5
Rows 2–3
Row 1

"B" Side Key
☐ **One St on each of 2 White Rows**
▣ **One St on each of 2 Yellow Rows**
⬭ **Yellow Puff St**

Second Square, "2" Side
Work white puff sts on odd-numbered white rows
(with yellow side of work facing).

Rows 68–69
← Rows 62–63
Rows 8–9
Rows 4–5
Row 1
Rows 10–11
Rows 2–3
Rows 2–3

"2" Side Key
▣ **One St on each of 2 Yellow Rows**
☐ **One St on each of 2 White Rows**
⬭ **White Puff St**

Baby Blocks

Continued from page 133

puff st, (pull up a lp in next horizontal bar, work puff st) 11 times, pull up a lp in last 6 horizontal bars, turn. *(39 lps on hook)* Cut yarn. *Slide lps to opposite end of hook.*

Row 14: With white, work lps off hook, **do not turn.** *(One lp on hook)*

Row 15: Work according to row 15 of Letter "B" graph, ch 1, pull up a lp in each horizontal bar across, turn. Drop yarn. *Slide lps to opposite end of hook.*

Rows 16–63: Repeat rows 2–5 consecutively as follows: Work **yellow puff sts** over rows 16–61 according to Letter "B" graph. Work **white puff sts** over rows 16–63 according to Number "2" graph.

Rows 64–68: Repeat rows 2–5 consecutively, ending with row 2.

Row 69: With yellow, ch 1, sl st in each horizontal bar across. Fasten off.

C-3 MOTIF

Rows 1–10: Using turquoise instead of pink, repeat rows 1–10 of A-1 Motif.

Row 11: To position beginning of number **"3,"** with turquoise side facing you, using white, working from right to left, ch 1, skip first horizontal bar, pull up a lp in next 15 horizontal bars *(16 lps on hook),* work puff st, (pull up a lp in next horizontal bar, work puff st) 4 times, pull up a lp in last 14 horizontal bars, turn. *(39 lps on hook)* Cut yarn. *Slide lps to opposite end of hook.*

Row 12: With turquoise, work lps off hook, **do not turn.** *(One lp on hook)*

Third Square, "C" Side
Work turquoise puff sts on odd-numbered turquoise rows
(with white side of work facing).

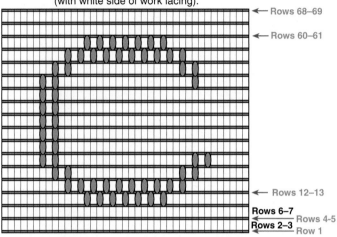

← Rows 68–69
← Rows 60–61

← Rows 12–13
Rows 6–7
← Rows 4-5
Rows 2–3
Row 1

"B" Side Key

☐ **One St on each of 2 White Rows**

▬ **One St on each of 2 Turquoise Rows**

⬤ **Turquoise Puff St**

Third Square, "3" Side
Work white puff sts on odd-numbered white rows
(with turquoise side of work facing).

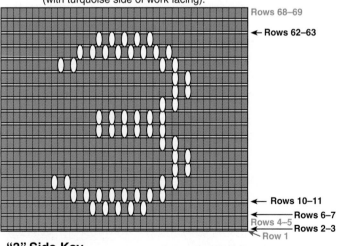

Rows 68–69
← Rows 62–63

← Rows 10–11
← Rows 6–7
Rows 4–5
Rows 2–3
← Row 1

"3" Side Key

■ **One St on each of 2 Turquoise Rows**

☐ **One St on each of 2 White Rows**

◗ **White Puff St**

Row 13: To position beginning of letter **"C,"** with white side facing you, using turquoise, working from right to left, ch 1, skip first horizontal bar, pull up a lp in next 12 horizontal bars *(13 lps on hook)*, work puff st, (pull up a lp in next horizontal bar, work puff st) 6 times, pull up a lp in last 13 horizontal bars, turn. *(39 lps on hook)* Cut yarn. *Slide lps to opposite end of hook.*

Rows 14–63: Repeat rows 2–5 consecutively as follows:
Work **turquoise puff sts** over rows 14–61 according to Letter "C" graph.
Work **white puff sts** over rows 14–63 according to Number "3" graph.

Rows 64–68: Repeat rows 2–5 consecutively, ending with row 2.

Row 69: With turquoise, ch 1, sl st in each horizontal bar across. Fasten off.

ASSEMBLY

1: Lay Motifs flat as shown in Assembly Diagram.

2: For first **vertical seam,** using crochet hook, join white with sc at corner of one Motif *(see red X on Assembly Diagram),* sc edges of two Motifs together across all three pairs of Motifs. Fasten off at red dot on Diagram. Repeat for second vertical seam.

3: For **horizontal seams,** turn Motifs to side and repeat step 2.

Assembly Diagram

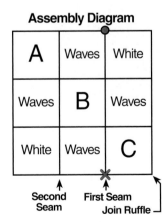

Second Seam   First Seam   Join Ruffle

RUFFLE

Rnd 1: Join white with sl st in corner of assembled Afghan *(see black arrow on Assembly Diagram),* ch 3 *(counts as first dc),* dc in same corner, evenly space 41 dc in ends of rows across each Motif on long edges *(total of 123 dc in ends of rows across long edge)* and dc in each st or ch across each short edge *(total of 115 dc in sts across short edge)* with (2 dc, ch 2, 2 dc) in each corner, ending with 2 dc in same corner as joining, ch 2, join with sl st in top of ch-3, **turn.** Fasten off. *(127 dc on each long edge, 119 dc on each short edge, 4 ch sps made)*

Rnd 2: With wrong side of last rnd facing, join pink with (sl st, ch 5, dc) in any corner ch sp, dc in next dc, (2 dc in next dc, dc in next dc) across to next corner ch sp, *(dc, ch 2, dc) in ch sp, dc in next dc, (2 dc in next dc, dc in next dc) across to next corner ch sp; repeat from * 2 more times, join with sl st in third ch of ch-5, **turn.** Fasten off. *(192 dc on each long edge, 180 dc on each short edge, 4 corner ch sps)*

Rnd 3: With wrong side of last rnd facing, join yellow with (sl st, ch 5, dc) in any corner ch sp, (2 dc in next dc, dc in next dc) across to next corner ch sp, *(dc, ch 2, dc) in ch sp, (dc in next dc, 2 dc in next dc) across to next corner ch sp; repeat from * 2 more times, join with sl st in third ch of ch-5, **turn.** Fasten off. *(290 dc on each long edge, 272 dc on each short edge, 4 corner ch sps)*

Rnd 4: With wrong side of last rnd facing, join turquoise with (sl st, ch 5, dc) in any corner ch sp, 2 dc in next dc, dc in each dc across to one dc before next corner ch sp, 2 dc in next dc, *(dc, ch 2, dc) in ch sp, 2 dc in next dc, dc in each dc across to one dc before next corner ch sp, 2 dc in next dc; repeat from * 2 more times, join with sl st in third ch of ch-5, **turn.** Fasten off.

Rnd 5: With wrong side of last rnd facing, join white with sc in any corner ch sp, (ch 2, sc, ch 2) in same ch sp, (sc, ch 2) in each st around with (sc, ch 2, sc, ch 2) in each corner ch sp, join with sl st in first sc. Fasten off. ❦

FINISHING-TOUCH
EMBELLISHMENTS

Want to take a table from drab to dramatic? Add a small bouquet. Want to dress up a package? Add a little bow. As simple as it sounds, adding one small "extra" can transform any basic project into a stunning heirloom. The next time you want something that's a little more than ordinary, try these easy additions for a truly personal touch.

Raindrops on the Pond by Marilyn Mezer

TECHNIQUES
Color Change, Ripple, Tunisian, Beads, Buttons, Embroidery and Tassels Embellishments

SPECIAL STITCHES
Afghan Stitch, Back Loops/Front Loops, Reverse Single Crochet

FINISHED SIZE
51 inches x 55 inches, not including Tassels

MATERIALS
❑ Worsted yarn:
  28 oz. med. aqua
  21 oz. white/aqua fleck *(white fleck)*
  18 oz. dk. aqua
  Small amounts each lt. orange, dk. orange, black, lt. pink, dk. pink, burgundy, lt. green, dk. green, brown, gold, white, lt. gray, blue-gray, lt. yellow, med. yellow, dk. yellow, lt. blue and med. blue *(for embroidery)*
❑ About 100 crystal iridescent pony beads
❑ Novelty buttons:
  8 yellow ½-inch dragonflies
  8 green ¾-inch dragonflies
  8 green ¾-inch frogs
❑ 6-inch square of cardboard
❑ Sewing thread to match buttons
❑ Sewing needle *(for buttons)*
❑ Tapestry needle (for embroidery)
❑ G crochet hook or size hook needed to obtain gauge
❑ Size J afghan hook or size hook needed to obtain gauge

GAUGE
J hook; 8 afghan sts = 2 inches; 7 rows = 2 inches.

G hook; 22 sts in ripple pattern = 4½ inches; 7 rows = 2 inches.

BASIC STITCHES
Ch, sl st, sc

INSTRUCTIONS

WIDE PANEL (make 3)
NOTES: *Refer to Basic Tunisian Crochet Technique on page 49 to work afghan st.*

*When **changing colors in afghan st,** work off all lps across to last 2 lps on hook; with next color, pull through last 2 lps on hook. Cut off last color and secure end.*

Row 1: With J afghan hook and white fleck, ch 50 loosely; pull up a lp in second ch from hook, pull up a lp in each ch across *(50 lps on hook);* **work lps off hook** *(see Note—one lp remains on hook).*

Row 2: To **work in afghan st,** skip first vertical bar, pull up a lp in each vertical bar across *(50 lps on hook);* work lps off hook *(one lp on hook).*

Rows 3–29: Work in afghan st. At end of last row, change to med. aqua *(see Notes).*

Rows 30–54: With med. aqua, work in afghan st. At end of last row, change to dk. aqua.

Rows 55–79: With dk. aqua, work in afghan st. At end of last row, change to med. aqua.

Rows 80–106: With med. aqua, work in afghan st. At end of last row, change to dk. aqua.

Rows 107–131: With dk. aqua, work in afghan st. At end of last row, change to med. aqua.

Rows 132–156: With med. aqua, work in afghan st. At end of last row, change to white fleck.

Rows 157–185: With white fleck, work in afghan st. At end of last row, **do not fasten off.**

NOTE: *Fasten off each color when no longer needed.*

Rnd 186: With G hook, working around entire Panel, **changing colors** to match rows *(see Stitch Guide on page 175),* ch 1, sc in each st across, ch 1, sc in end of each row across to row 1; working in starting ch on opposite side of row 1, ch 1, sc in each ch across, ch 1, sc in end of each row across to row 185, ch 1, join with sl st in first sc. Fasten off.

Panel Embroidery
1: Hold one Wide Panel so row 1 is next to you. Using **cross stitch** *(see illustration),* stitching through beads as indicated, embroider according to Left Panel Bottom Section

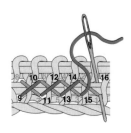

Left Panel Bottom Section

Raindrops on the Pond

Continued from page 137

graph and Top Section graph on page 140; sew buttons in place.

2: In same manner, embroider next Wide Panel according to Center Panel Bottom Section graph on page 143 and Top Section graph on page 147; sew buttons in place.

Key
Afghan Stitches
- Dk. Aqua
- Med. Aqua
- White Fleck

Cross Stitches
- Lt. Orange
- Dk. Orange
- Black
- Lt. Pink
- Dk. Pink
- Burgundy
- Lt. Green
- Dk. green
- Brown
- Gold
- White
- Lt. Gray
- Blue-Gray
- Lt. Yellow
- Med. Yellow
- Dk. Yellow
- Lt. Blue
- Med. Blue

Backstitches
- Lt. Pink
- Lt. Blue

Placements
- ✖ Large Dragonfly
- ✖ Small Dragonfly
- ✖ Frog
- ○ Bead

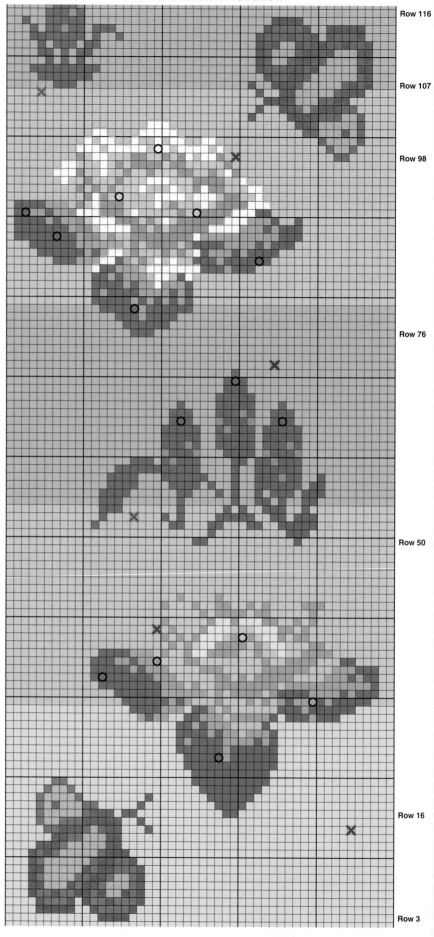

Row 116
Row 107
Row 98
Row 76
Row 50
Row 16
Row 3

Raindrops on the Pond

Continued from page 138

3: In same manner, embroider last Wide Panel according to Right Panel Bottom Section graph on page 141 and Top Section graph on page 142; sew buttons in place.

RIPPLE PANEL (make 2)

Row 1: With G crochet hook and white fleck, ch 23, sc in second ch from hook, sc in next ch, skip next ch, sc in next 3 chs, 3 sc in next ch, sc in next 3 chs, skip next 2 chs, sc in next 3 chs, 3 sc in next ch, sc in next 3 chs, skip next ch, sc in last 2 chs, turn. *(22 sc made)*

Row 2: Working in **back lps** *(see Stitch Guide on page 175),* ch 1, sc in each st across, turn.

Row 3: Working in **back lps,** ch 1, sc in first 2 sts, skip next st, sc in next 3 sts, 3 sc in next st, sc in next 3 sts, skip next 2 sts, sc in next 3 sts, 3 sc in next st, sc in next 3 sts, skip next st, sc in last 2 sts, turn.

Rows 4–29: Repeat rows 2 and 3 alternately. At end of last row, fasten off.

Left Panel Top Section

Key
Afghan Stitches
- Dk. Aqua
- Med. Aqua
- White Fleck

Cross Stitches
- Lt. Orange
- Dk. Orange
- Black
- Lt. Pink
- Dk. Pink
- Burgundy
- Lt. Green
- Dk. green
- Brown
- Gold
- White
- Lt. Gray
- Blue-Gray
- Lt. Yellow
- Med. Yellow
- Dk. Yellow
- Lt. Blue
- Med. Blue

Backstitches
- Lt. Pink
- Lt. Blue

Placements
- ✕ Large Dragonfly
- ✕ Small Dragonfly
- ✕ Frog
- O Bead

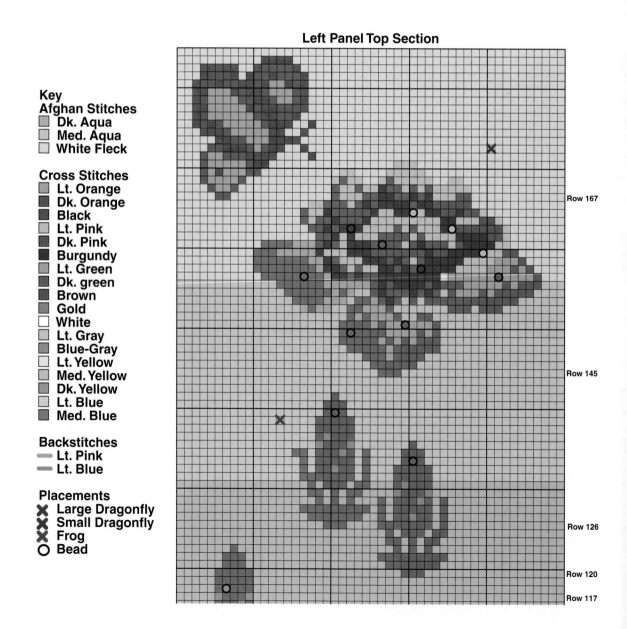

Row 167

Row 145

Row 126

Row 120

Row 117

Row 30: Join med. aqua with sc in first st, sc in each st across, turn.

Rows 31–54: Repeat rows 3 and 2 alternately, ending with row 2. At end of last row, fasten off.

Row 55: Working in **back lps,** join dk. aqua with sc in first st, sc in next st, skip next st, sc in next 3 sts, 3 sc in next st, sc in next 3 sts, skip next 2 sts, sc in next 3 sts, 3 sc in next st, sc in next 3 sts, skip next st, sc in last 2 sts, turn.

Rows 56–79: Repeat rows 2 and 3 alternately. At end of last row, fasten off.

Row 80: Join med. aqua with sc in first st, sc in each st across, turn.

Rows 81–106: Repeat rows 3 and 2 alternately. At end of last row, fasten off.

Row 107: Repeat row 55.

Rows 108–131: Repeat rows 2 and 3 alternately. At end of last row, fasten off.

Row 132: Join med. aqua with sc in first st, sc in each st across, turn.

Rows 133–156: Repeat rows 3 and 2 alternately, ending with row 2. At end of last row, fasten off.

Row 157: With white fleck, repeat row 55.

Rows 158–185: Repeat rows 2 and 3 alternately. At end of last row, **do not fasten off.**

Rnd 186: With G hook, working around entire Panel, changing colors to match rows, sc in end of each row across to row 1, ch 1 at corner; working in starting ch on opposite side of row 1, sc in each ch across, ch 1 at corner, sc in end of each row across to row 185, ch 1 at corner, sc in each st across, ch 1 at corner, join with sl st in first sc. Fasten off.

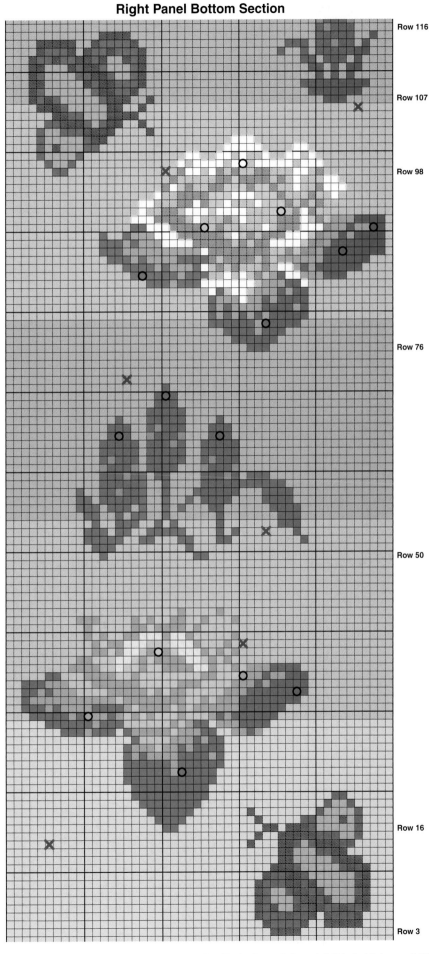

Row 116

Row 107

Row 98

Row 76

Row 50

Row 16

Row 3

Raindrops on the Pond

Continued from page 141

ASSEMBLY

1: Assemble Panels from right to left in this order: Right Wide, Ripple, Center Wide, Ripple, Left Wide.

2: For first **seam,** with wrong sides together, matching sts at ends of rows and working through both layers as one in **back lps** of front Panel and **front lps** of back Panel, join white with sc in first st past ch-1 at corner; changing colors to match, sc in each st across to ch-1 at next corner. Fasten off.

3: Repeat step 2 until all Panels are joined.

BORDER

Rnd 1: With G hook, join dk. aqua with sc in any unworked corner ch sp of assembled Panels, 2 sc in same ch sp as joining sc; working in **back lps,** sc in each st around all Panels with 3 sc in each corner ch sp, join with sl st in first sc.

Rnds 2–3: Ch 1; working in **back lps,** sc in each st around with 3 sc in each center corner st, join.

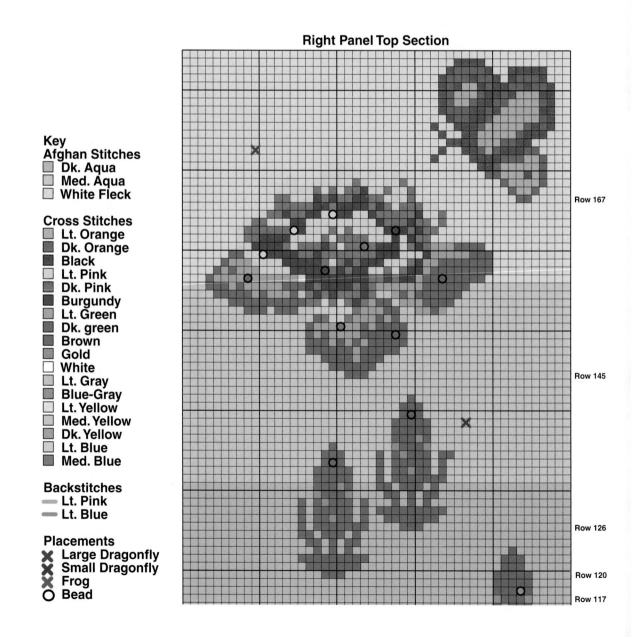

Right Panel Top Section

Key

Afghan Stitches
- Dk. Aqua
- Med. Aqua
- White Fleck

Cross Stitches
- Lt. Orange
- Dk. Orange
- Black
- Lt. Pink
- Dk. Pink
- Burgundy
- Lt. Green
- Dk. green
- Brown
- Gold
- White
- Lt. Gray
- Blue-Gray
- Lt. Yellow
- Med. Yellow
- Dk. Yellow
- Lt. Blue
- Med. Blue

Backstitches
- Lt. Pink
- Lt. Blue

Placements
- X Large Dragonfly
- X Small Dragonfly
- X Frog
- O Bead

Row 167

Row 145

Row 126

Row 120

Row 117

Center Panel Bottom Section

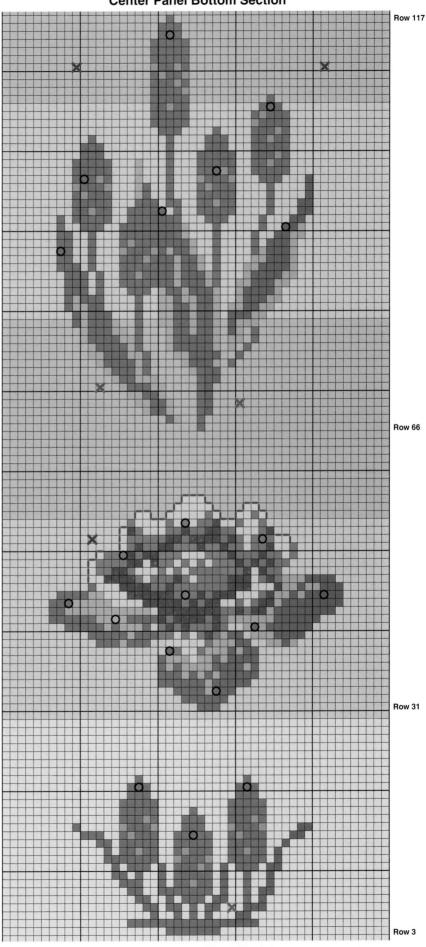

Row 117

Row 66

Row 31

Row 3

Rnd 4: Ch 1, **reverse sc** *(see Stitch Guide on page 175)* in first st, ch 1, skip next st, (reverse sc, ch 1, skip next st) around with 3 reverse sc in each center corner st instead of one, join with sl st in first reverse sc. Fasten off.

TASSEL
(make 12 white, make 70 dk. aqua)

For **each Tassel,** wrap yarn 20 times around 6-inch square of cardboard. Run a separate 14-inch strand of same-color yarn under all wraps at one edge of cardboard; remove wraps from cardboard and tie 14-inch strand very tightly around loops. Holding 14-inch strand apart, fold loops at knot and tightly tie separate 10-inch strand of same-color yarn around all loops one inch below first knot; run ends inside loops to hide. Cut loops; trim even.

Using ends of 14-inch strands, tie tassels evenly spaced across each short edge of Afghan in this order:
One white, 10 dk. aqua
One white, three dk. aqua
One white, nine dk. aqua
One white, three dk. aqua
One white, 10 dk. aqua
One white

Run ends of 14-inch strands back through Tassels to hide.❦

Graphs continued on page 147

Spring Violets by Darla Sims

TECHNIQUE
Ribbon Embroidery Embellishment

SPECIAL STITCH
Front Post

FINISHED SIZE
39 inches x 53 inches including Border

MATERIALS
❑ 40 oz. Pastel Green #156 Pound of Love Art. 550 by Lion Brand Yarn or worsted yarn
❑ Satin Ribbon:
  15 yds. of ⅝-inch purple
  7 yds. of ¼-inch sheer teal
  4 yds. of ⅛-inch pale yellow
❑ Sewing thread to match each ribbon
❑ Sewing needle
❑ Size 20 chenille needle
❑ I and J hooks or size hook needed to obtain gauge

GAUGE
J hook; 7 sc = 2 inches; 9 sc rows = 2 inches.

BASIC STITCHES
Ch, sl st, sc, dc, tr

INSTRUCTIONS
Row 1: With J hook and yarn, ch 117, sc in second ch from hook, sc in each ch across, turn. *(116 sc made)*

Row 2 and all even-numbered rows: Ch 1, sc in each st across, turn.

NOTES: *All sc sts are worked into last row.*

After row 3, work all fp sts around fp st on row before last, pull up to height of row being worked.

Skip one st on last row behind each fp.

Row 3: Ch 1, sc in first 9 sts, **dc front post (fp**—*see Stitch Guide on page 175)* around each of 2 sts on row before last directly below next 2 sts, skip next 2 sts on last row *(see Notes),* (sc in next 14 sts, fp around each of 2 sts on row before last directly below next 2 sts) across to last 9 sts, sc in last 9 sts, turn.

Front of row 3 is right side of work.

Row 5: Ch 1, sc in first 8 sts, fp around first

fp, sc in next 2 sts, fp around next fp, (sc in next 12 sts, fp around next fp, sc in next 2 sts, fp around next fp) across to last 8 sts, sc in last 8 sts, turn.

Row 7: Ch 1, sc in first 7 sts, fp around first fp, sc in next 4 sts, fp around next fp, (sc in next 10 sts, fp around next fp, sc in next 4 sts, fp around next fp) across to last 7 sts, sc in last 7 sts, turn.

Row 9: Ch 1, sc in first 6 sts, fp around first fp, sc in next 6 sts, fp around next fp, (sc in next 8 sts, fp around next fp, sc in next 6 sts, fp around next fp) across to last 6 sts, sc in last 6 sts, turn.

Row 11: Ch 1, sc in first 5 sts, fp around first fp, sc in next 8 sts, fp around next fp, (sc in next 6 sts, fp around next fp, sc in next 8 sts, fp around next fp) across to last 5 sts, sc in last 5 sts, turn.

Row 13: Ch 1, sc in first 4 sts, fp around first fp, sc in next 10 sts, fp around next fp, (sc in next 4 sts, fp around next fp, sc in next 10 sts, fp around next fp) across to last 4 sts, sc in last 4 sts, turn.

Row 15: Ch 1, sc in first 3 sts, fp around first fp, sc in next 12 sts, fp around next fp, (sc in next 2 sts, fp around next fp, sc in next 12 sts, fp around next fp) across to last 3 sts, sc in last 3 sts, turn.

Row 16: Ch 1, sc in each st across, turn.

Row 17: Ch 1, sc in first 2 sts, fp around next fp, sc in next 14 sts, (fp around each of next 2 fp, sc in next 14 sts) across to last 3 sts, fp around next fp, sc in last 2 sts, turn.

Row 19: Ch 1, sc in first 3 sts, fp around first fp, sc in next 12 sts; (skip next fp, fp around next fp, sc in next 2 sts; working in front of last fp, fp around skipped fp, sc in next 12 sts) across to last 4 sts, fp around next fp, sc in last 3 sts, turn.

Row 21: Ch 1, sc in first 4 sts, fp around first fp, sc in next 10 sts, fp around next fp, (sc in next 4 sts, fp around next fp, sc in next 10 sts, fp around next fp) across to last 4 sts, sc in last 4 sts, turn.

Row 23: Ch 1, sc in first 5 sts, fp around first fp, sc in next 8 sts, fp around next fp, (sc in

Spring Violets

Continued from page 144

next 6 sts, fp around next fp, sc in next 8 sts, fp around next fp) across to last 5 sts, sc in last 5 sts, turn.

Row 25: Ch 1, sc in first 6 sts, fp around first fp, sc in next 6 sts, fp around next fp, (sc in next 8 sts, fp around next fp, sc in next 6 sts, fp around next fp) across to last 6 sts, sc in last 6 sts, turn.

Row 27: Ch 1, sc in first 7 sts, fp around first fp, sc in next 4 sts, fp around next fp, (sc in next 10 sts, fp around next fp, sc in next 4 sts, fp around next fp) across to last 7 sts, sc in last 7 sts, turn.

Row 29: Ch 1, sc in first 8 sts, fp around first fp, sc in next 2 sts, fp around next fp, (sc in next 12 sts, fp around next fp, sc in next 2 sts, fp around next fp) across to last 8 sts, sc in last 8 sts, turn.

Row 31: Ch 1, sc in first 9 sts, fp around

each of next 2 fp, (sc in next 14 sts, fp around each of next 2 fp) across to last 9 sts, sc in last 9 sts, turn.

Row 33: Ch 1, sc in first 8 sts, skip next fp, fp around next fp, sc in next 2 sts; working in front of last fp, fp around skipped fp, (sc in next 12 sts, skip next fp, fp around next fp, sc in next 2 sts; working in front of last fp, fp around skipped fp) across to last 8 sts, sc in last 8 sts, turn.

Rows 34–199: Repeat rows 6–33 consecutively, ending with row 31. At end of last row, **do not turn or fasten off.**

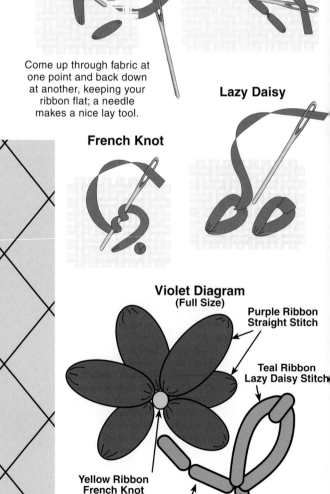

Straight Stitch

Backstitch

Come up through fabric at one point and back down at another, keeping your ribbon flat; a needle makes a nice lay tool.

Lazy Daisy

French Knot

Violet Diagram
(Full Size)

Purple Ribbon
Straight Stitch

Teal Ribbon
Lazy Daisy Stitch

Yellow Ribbon
French Knot

Teal Ribbon
Backstitch

Center Violet Placement

BORDER

Rnd 1: With right side of work facing you, using I hook, sc in end of each row and in each st around with 3 sc in each corner st, join with sl st in first sc. *(638 sts made)*

Rnd 2: Ch 4 *(counts as first dc and ch 1)*, skip next st, (dc in next st, ch 1, skip next st) around with (dc, ch 1, dc, ch 1, dc) in each center corner st, join with sl st in third ch of ch-4. *(319 ch-1 sps)*

Rnd 3: Ch 1, sc in first ch sp, ch 1; skipping each dc, (2 dc, ch 3, 2 dc) in next ch sp, *sc in next ch sp, ch 1, (2 dc, ch 3, 2 dc) in next ch sp; repeat from * around, join with sl st in first sc.

Rnd 4: Ch 1, sc in first sc, *ch 3, skip next 2 dc, (tr, ch 5, tr) in next ch sp, ch 3, skip next

2 dc**, sc in next sc; repeat from * around ending last repeat at **, join.

Rnd 5: Ch 1, work 3 sc in each ch-3 sp and (3 sc, ch 3, sl st in third ch from hook, 3 sc) in each ch-5 sp around, join. Fasten off.

FINISHING

With chenille needle, using Straight Stitch, French Knot, Lazy Daisy Stitch and Backstitch *(see illustrations)*, embroider nine violets *(see Violet Diagram)* in diamonds at center of Afghan according to Center Violet Placement. To secure, use sewing needle and matching thread to stitch ribbon ends in place on wrong side

In same manner, embroider a violet in each full diamond around outer edge of Afghan *(see photo).*

Raindrops on the Pond

Continued from page 143

Key
Afghan Stitches
- Dk. Aqua
- Med. Aqua
- White Fleck

Cross Stitches
- Lt. Orange
- Dk. Orange
- Black
- Lt. Pink
- Dk. Pink
- Burgundy
- Lt. Green
- Dk. green
- Brown
- Gold
- White
- Lt. Gray
- Blue-Gray
- Lt. Yellow
- Med. Yellow
- Dk. Yellow
- Lt. Blue
- Med. Blue

Backstitches
- — Lt. Pink
- — Lt. Blue

Placements
- ✖ Large Dragonfly
- ✖ Small Dragonfly
- ✖ Frog
- ○ Bead

Center Panel Top Section

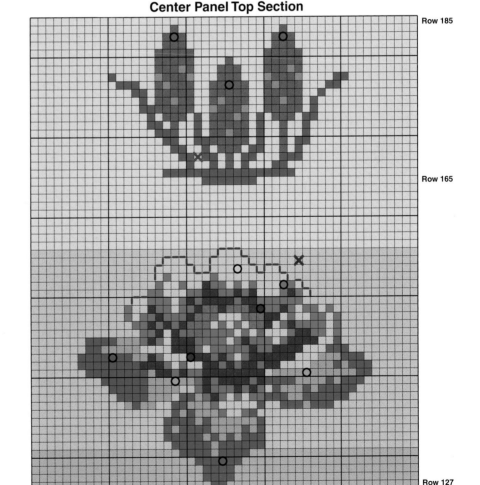

Row 185

Row 165

Row 127

No embroidery on rows 118 –126

Experimenting with Embellishments

by Donna Jones and Jennifer McClain

There are any number of ways to spruce up an otherwise plain or drab piece of crochet. Appliqués, buttons, bows, beads, charms and embroidery can all be added to the fabric to lend interesting dimension and a personal touch. There are several examples in this book, but don't be afraid to try your own design adaptation.

The "Kitty on Fence Motif" motif pattern on page 150 is a good example of using **embroidery** to add detail and emphasis to plain single crochet stitches. The facial features and the leg and tail detail on the body are all done with embroidery, along with shading in the clouds. While in the same pattern, crocheted sunflowers are appliquéd in place, adding depth and feeling to the overall piece. While these appliqués were crocheted, purchased appliqués also could have been used, either alone or in conjunction with the crocheted ones.

When using **appliqués** to enhance a crochet project, sewing is the best method for securing them. Especially on designs for young children, appliqués should be sewn carefully, but even on items for adults or decoration, don't be tempted to use fabric glue as it will not hold up over time.

For those of you who enjoy **cross-stitch** as well as crochet, "Raindrops on the Pond" on page 135 is a great example of how well these two techniques can blend and complement each other. And, as a further use of embellishments, clear pony beads and novelty buttons add life and movement to the cross-stitched design. Cross-stitch can easily be embroidered from a standard chart onto any plain single crochet or afghan stitch background.

Any embroidery can be used to liven up crochet, including **ribbon embroidery** as illustrated in "Spring Violets" on page 144. Here, a very plain single crochet base is transformed into a beautiful decorative accessory through the addition of embroidery embellishment.

Another way to embellish your crochet is to utilize things you already have on hand like the beads from old necklaces, bracelet charms, buttons or appliqués, which have been clipped off an item you were ready to throw away, and other adornments you may have stored in your craft box. With a little imagination and forethought, you can add stunning embellishments that will truly make a crochet piece stand out from the others.

When working embroidery or cross-stitch on crochet, always use a blunt-tipped tapestry needle to prevent splitting the yarn and never use a hoop. It is also very important to choose yarns, threads or ribbons with the same fiber content as the crocheted piece, so cleaning or laundering the piece will not cause the embroidery to shrink or stretch and distort the stitching. If you use ribbon, it is best to dry-clean the project either professionally or using the at-home dryer method. Consult each yarn wrapper of both the fabric yarn and the embroidery materials for blocking and laundering instructions.

When transferring a design for embroidery to your crocheted piece, use a contrasting color thread to baste an outline of the area to be embroidered. When stitching, work between the crochet stitches whenever possible for the best results. However, if you are working small embroidery stitches, you may wish to trace the design onto a piece of waste canvas, then baste the canvas in place on the crocheted piece. As you embroider each stitch, run the needle all the way through both the waste canvas and the crocheted fabric. When finished embroidering the design, remove the waste canvas as directed.

Always avoid pulling embroidery stitches too tight, as this will cause the crochet to pucker and the embroidery stitches to shrink into the fabric and become less visible. When finishing your embroidery design, weave in all yarn ends rather than tie them (Be sure to leave long ends at the beginning and end of the work to weave in on the back side.), as knots on the back side will eventually come apart.

When you have completed the embroidery, steam block the embroidery design lightly using a steam iron or garment steamer, allowing the steam to penetrate the fibers. Pat the stitches lightly into shape while being careful not to touch the yarn with the iron. After blocking, allow the crochet piece to dry thoroughly before moving it.

With a little planning and forethought, embroidery and other added embellishments can add a lovely finishing touch to your crochet for a one-of-a-kind creation. 🐾

Afghan
Index

Craft a tiny piece of your heart into everything you crochet when you personalize with embellishments.

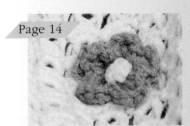

Page 14

Page 42

Page 137

Page 144

Page 158

Kitty on Fence Motif by Carol Mittal

TECHNIQUES
Appliqué and Embroidery Embellishments, Color change

SPECIAL STITCHES
Back Posts/Front Posts, Long Single Crochet

FINISHED SIZE
12 inches x 12½ inches

MATERIALS FOR ONE MOTIF
❑ Worsted yarn:
   2 oz. lt. blue
   2 oz. black
   Small amount each white, lt. gray, lt. green, dk. green, yellow, rust and dk. brown
❑ Black and gold rayon embroidery floss
❑ Med. pink, dk. pink and beige cotton embroidery floss
❑ 2 spools each dk. blue and lt. green sewing thread
❑ Tear-away embroidery stabilizer
❑ Sewing and tapestry needles
❑ G and H hooks or size hook needed to obtain gauge

GAUGE
H hook, 7 sc = 2 inches; 8 rows = 2 inches.

BASIC STITCHES
Ch, sl st, sc, hdc, dc

SPECIAL STITCH
For **long sc,** inserting hook around **front post** (see Stitch Guide on page 175) on right-side rows or around **back post** on wrong-side rows so sts fall on right side of work, insert hook around corresponding sc on third row below, yo, pull through and pull up to height of row being worked, yo, pull through 2 lps on hook; skip st on last row behind long sc.

NOTE
When **changing colors** (see Stitch Guide on page 175), drop last color to wrong side of work. Pick up again when needed. Do not work over dropped color; use separate strand for each section of color. Fasten off each color when no longer needed.

INSTRUCTIONS
MOTIF
Row 1: Using H hook, with dk. green yarn and two strands lt. green sewing thread held together as one, ch 43, sc in second ch from hook, sc in each ch across, turn. *(42 sc made)*

***Front** of row 1 is right side of work.*

Rows 2–4: Ch 1, sc in each st across, turn. At end of last row, fasten off.

Row 5: Join rust with sc in first st, sc in each st across, turn.

Row 6: Ch 1, sc in each st across, turn. Fasten off.

Row 7: Join lt. gray with sc in first st, sc in next 5 sts, **long sc** (see Special Stitch), (sc in next 5 sts, long sc) across to last 6 sts, sc in last 6 sts, turn. Fasten off.

Row 8: Join rust with sc in first st, sc in each st across, turn.

Row 9: Ch 1, sc in each st across, turn. Fasten off.

Row 10: Join lt. gray with sc in first st, sc in next st, long sc, (sc in next 5 sts, long sc) across to last 3 sts, sc in last 3 sts, turn. Fasten off.

Row 11: Join rust with sc in first st, sc in each st across, turn.

Row 12: Ch 1, sc in each st across, turn. Fasten off.

Row 13: Join lt. gray with sc in first st, sc in next 4 sts, (long sc, sc in next 5 sts) across to last st, sc in last st, turn.

Row 14: Ch 1, sc in each st across, turn.

Rows 15–16: Changing colors *(see Note)* according to corresponding row of Kitty On Fence graph on page 152, ch 1, sc in each st across, turn. At end of last row, fasten off lt. gray.

Row 17: With lt. blue yarn and two strands dk. blue sewing thread held together as one, join with sc in first st; changing colors according to row 17 of graph, sc in each st across, turn.

Rows 18–48: Changing colors according to corresponding row of graph, ch 1, sc in each st across, turn.

Rows 49–50: With lt. blue yarn and two strands dk. blue sewing thread only, ch 1, sc in each st across, turn. At end of last row, fasten off.

APPLIQUÉS

Flower (make 3)

Rnd 1: With G hook and dk. brown yarn, ch 3, sl st in first ch to form ring, ch 1, 3 sc in each ch around, join with sl st in first sc. Fasten off. *(9 sc made)*

Rnd 2: Join yellow with sl st in any st, (ch 5, sl st in second ch from hook, sc in next ch, hdc in next ch, sc in next ch, sl st in next sc on rnd 1) 9 times, ending with last sl st in joining sl st. Fasten off.

Double Stem

With G hook and lt. green yarn, ch 18, sl st in second ch from hook, sl st in next 6 chs, ch 7, sl st in second ch from hook, sl st in next 5 chs, sl st in each remaining ch of ch-18. Fasten off.

Stem With Leaf

With G hook and lt. green yarn, ch 15, sl st in second ch from hook, sl st in next 4 chs, ch 7, sl st in second ch from hook, sc in next ch, hdc in next ch, dc in next ch, hdc in next ch, sc in next ch, sl st in each remaining ch of ch-15. Fasten off.

FINISHING

1: Using yarn needle with two strands black yarn, work backstitch *(see illustration)* for chin line as shown on Kitty On Fence graph.

2: Using one strand white yarn for legs and tail and one strand lt. gray yarn for cloud, work backstitches as shown on graph.

3: Trace facial features on piece of tear-away stabilizer fabric; pin or baste stabilizer in place on right side of Motif.

Kitty on Fence Motif

Continued from page 151

4: Using sewing needle and 6-strand rayon or cotton floss with satin stitch *(see illustration)*, embroider face through stabilizer and crochet piece as follows:

Backstitch

Satin Stitch

Eyes—gold rayon floss

Pupils—black rayon floss

Nose—med. pink cotton floss

5: Using 6-strand cotton floss for backstitch, embroider mouth with dk. pink and whiskers with beige.

6: Remove stabilizer fabric.

7: Pin flowers and stems to lower corners *(see photo);* sew in place with tapestry needle and matching yarn.

NOTE: There are several ways to use the Kitty on Fence Motif to make an afghan.

For a square lapghan or child's afghan, make one Motif as shown; then add a simple single crochet edge around it, working three stitches in each corner. Working out from this motif as the center, add the border of your choice until the afghan is as large as you like.

For a quilt-style afghan, stitch 12 of the Kitty Motifs. Add a single crochet edging around each and sew them together three wide and four long. A simple tailored edging would complete your afghan. If you do not wish to embroider that many motifs, stitch six Kitty motifs as shown and six more with just the fence (bottom) portion only. This will make the fence appear to go all the way across the afghan. Alternate motifs when sewing them together, then add an edging.❧

Full Size Facial Features

Worsted Yarn Key

☐ **Lt. Blue with Dk. Blue Thread Sc**

■ **Black Sc**

☐ **White Sc**

☐ **Lt. gray Sc**

■ **Rust Sc**

Surface Stitches (work last)

●━● **2-Strand Black Yarn Backstitch**

●━● **White Yarn Backstitch**

●━● **Lt. Gray Yarn Backstitch**

Kitty On Fence

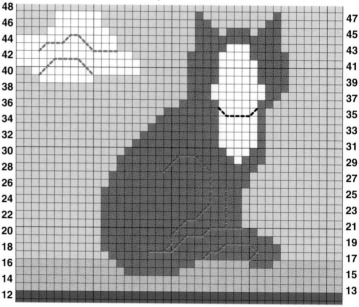

Diagonal Chains by Rena Stevens

TECHNIQUES
Fringe Embellishment, Surface Slip Stitch

SPECIAL STITCH
Shell

FINISHED SIZE
53 inches x 69 inches, without Fringe

MATERIALS
❑ Worsted yarn:
  45 oz. med. teal
  10½ oz. dk. teal
  10½ oz. navy
  10½ oz. burgundy
  10½ oz. purple
❑ Tapestry needle
❑ Size Q or S crochet hook or any oversize hook
❑ H hook or size hook needed to obtain gauge

GAUGE
3 shells and 3 sc = 4 inches; 4 rows in pattern = 2 inches.

BASIC STITCHES
Ch, sl st, sc, dc

SPECIAL STITCH
For **shell,** (dc, ch 1, dc, ch 1, dc) in st or ch.

INSTRUCTIONS
Row 1: With H hook and med. teal, ch 224, sc in second ch from hook, *(skip next 2 chs, **shell**—see Special Stitch—in next ch, skip next 2 chs, sc in next ch) 4 times, (ch 5, skip next 4 chs, sc in next ch) 2 times, (skip next 2 chs, shell in next ch, skip next 2 chs, sc in next ch) 2 times, (ch 5, skip next 4 chs, sc in next ch) 4 times; repeat from * 2 more times, (skip next 2 chs, shell in next ch, skip next 2 chs, sc in next ch) 4 times, turn. *(41 sc, 22 shells, 18 ch-5 sps made)*

NOTE: *Work sc in center dc of shell unless otherwise stated.*

Row 2: (Ch 3—*counts as first dc,* dc) in first sc, sc in next shell *(see Note),* (shell in next sc, sc in next shell*)* 3 times, *(ch 5, sc in next ch sp) 4 times, (shell in next sc, sc in next shell) 2 times, (ch 5, sc in next ch sp) 2 times, (shell in next sc, sc in next shell) 4 times; repeat from * 2 more times, 2 dc in last sc, turn.

Row 3: Ch 1, sc in first dc, ch 5, sc in next shell, *(shell in next sc, sc in next shell or ch sp*)* 4 times, (ch 5, sc in next ch sp or shell) 2 times, (shell in next sc, sc in next shell or ch sp) 2 times, (ch 5, sc in next ch sp or shell) 4 times; repeat from * 2 more times, (shell in next sc, sc in next shell) 2 times, shell in next sc, skip next dc, sc in last dc, turn.

Row 4: (Ch 3, dc) in first sc, sc in next shell*,* (shell in next sc, sc in next shell*)* 2 times, *(ch 5, sc in next ch sp) 4 times, (shell in next sc, sc in next shell) 2 times, (ch 5, sc in next ch sp) 2 times, (shell in next sc, sc in next shell) 4 times; repeat from * 2 more times, ch 5, sc in next ch sp, ch 2, dc in last sc, turn.

Row 5: Ch 1, sc in first dc, ch 5, skip next ch-2 sp, sc in next ch-5 sp, ch 5, sc in next shell, *(shell in next sc, sc in next shell or ch sp*)* 4 times, (ch 5, sc in next ch sp or shell) 2 times, (shell in next sc, sc in next shell or ch sp) 2 times, (ch 5, sc in next ch sp or shell) 4 times; repeat from * 2 more times, shell in next sc, sc in next shell, shell in next sc, skip next dc, sc in last dc, turn.

Row 6: (Ch 3, dc) in first sc, sc in next shell, shell in next sc, sc in next shell, *(ch 5, sc in next ch sp) 4 times, (shell in next sc, sc in next shell) 2 times, (ch 5, sc in next ch sp) 2 times, (shell in next sc, sc in next shell) 4 times; repeat from * 2 more times, (ch 5, sc in next ch sp) 2 times, ch 2, dc in last sc, turn.

Row 7: Ch 1, sc in first dc, skip next ch-2 sp, (ch 5, sc in next ch sp or shell) 3 times, *(shell in next sc, sc in next shell or ch sp*)* 4 times, (ch 5, sc in next ch sp or shell) 2 times, (shell in next sc, sc in next shell or ch sp) 2 times, (ch 5, sc in next ch sp or shell) 4 times; repeat from * 2 more times, shell in next sc, skip next dc, sc in last dc, turn.

Row 8: (Ch 3, dc) in first sc, sc in next shell*,* *(ch 5, sc in next ch sp) 4 times, (shell in next sc, sc in next shell) 2 times, (ch 5, sc in next ch sp) 2 times, (shell in next sc, sc in next shell) 4 times; repeat from * 2 more times, (ch 5, sc in next ch sp) 3 times, ch 2, dc in last sc, turn.

Diagonal Chains

Continued from page 153

Row 9: Ch 1, sc in first dc, skip next ch-2 sp, *(ch 5, sc in next ch sp or shell) 4 times, (shell in next sc, sc in next shell or ch sp) 4 times, (ch 5, sc in next ch sp or shell) 2 times, (shell in next sc, sc in next shell or ch sp) 2 times; repeat from * 2 more times, (ch 5, sc in next ch sp) 3 times, ch 5, skip next dc, sc in last dc, turn.

Row 10: (Ch 3, dc) in first sc, sc in next ch sp, (ch 5, sc in next ch sp) 3 times, *(shell in next sc, sc in next shell) 2 times, (ch 5, sc in next ch sp) 2 times, (shell in next sc, sc in next shell) 4 times, (ch 5, sc in next ch sp) 4 times; repeat from * 2 more times, 2 dc in last sc, turn.

Row 11: Ch 1, sc in first dc, skip next dc, shell in next sc, sc in next ch sp, *(ch 5, sc in next ch sp or shell) 4 times, (shell in next sc, sc in next shell or ch sp) 4 times, (ch 5, sc in next ch sp or shell) 2 times, (shell in next sc, sc in next shell or ch sp) 2 times; repeat from * 2 more times, (ch 5, sc in next ch sp) 2 times, ch 5, skip next dc, sc in last dc, turn.

Row 12: (Ch 3, dc) in first sc, sc in next ch sp, (ch 5, sc in next ch sp) 2 times, *(shell in next sc, sc in next shell) 2 times, (ch 5, sc in next ch sp) 2 times, (shell in next sc, sc in next shell) 4 times, (ch 5, sc in next ch sp) 4 times; repeat from * 2 more times, shell in next sc, sc in next shell, 2 dc in last sc, turn.

Row 13: Ch 1, sc in first dc, skip next dc, (shell in next sc, sc in next shell or ch sp) 2 times, *(ch 5, sc in next ch sp or shell) 4 times, (shell in next sc, sc in next shell or ch sp) 4 times, (ch 5, sc in next ch sp or shell) 2 times, (shell in next sc, sc in next shell or ch sp) 2 times; repeat from * 2 more times, ch 5, sc in next ch sp, ch 5, skip next dc, sc in last dc, turn.

Row 14: (Ch 3, dc) in first sc, sc in next ch sp, ch 5, sc in next ch sp, *(shell in next sc, sc in next shell) 2 times, (ch 5, sc in next ch sp) 2 times, (shell in next sc, sc in next shell) 4 times, (ch 5, sc in next ch sp) 4 times; repeat from * 2 more times, (shell in next sc, sc in next shell) 2 times, ch 2, dc in last sc, turn.

Row 15: Ch 1, sc in first dc, ch 5, sc in next shell, (shell in next sc, sc in next shell or ch sp) 2 times, *(ch 5, sc in next ch sp or shell)

4 times, (shell in next sc, sc in next shell or ch sp) 4 times, (ch 5, sc in next ch sp or shell) 2 times, (shell in next sc, sc in next shell or ch sp) 2 times; repeat from * 2 more times, ch 5, skip next dc, sc in last dc, turn.

Row 16: (Ch 3, dc) in first sc, sc in next ch sp, *(shell in next sc, sc in next shell) 2 times, (ch 5, sc in next ch sp) 2 times, (shell in next sc, sc in next shell) 4 times, (ch 5, sc in next ch sp) 4 times; repeat from * 2 more times, (shell in next sc, sc in next shell) 2 times, ch 5, sc in next ch sp, ch 2, dc in last sc, turn.

Row 17: Ch 1, sc in first dc, skip next ch-2 sp, *(ch 5, sc in next ch sp or shell) 2 times, (shell in next sc, sc in next shell or ch sp) 2 times, (ch 5, sc in next ch sp or shell) 4 times, (shell in next sc, sc in next shell or ch sp) 4 times; repeat from * 2 more times, (ch 5, sc in next ch sp or shell) 2 times, shell in next sc, sc in next shell, shell in next sc, skip next dc, sc in last dc, turn.

Row 18: (Ch 3, dc) in first sc, sc in next shell, shell in next sc, sc in next shell, *(ch 5, sc in next ch sp) 2 times, (shell in next sc, sc in next shell) 4 times, (ch 5, sc in next ch sp) 4 times, (shell in next sc, sc in next shell) 2 times; repeat from * 2 more times, (ch 5, sc in next ch sp) 2 times, 2 dc in last sc, turn.

Row 19: Ch 1, sc in first dc, skip next dc, shell in next sc, sc in next ch sp, *(ch 5, sc in next ch sp or shell) 2 times, (shell in next sc, sc in next shell or ch sp) 2 times, (ch 5, sc in next ch sp or shell) 4 times, (shell in next sc, sc in next shell or ch sp) 4 times; repeat from * 2 more times, (ch 5, sc in next ch sp or shell) 2 times, shell in next sc, skip next dc, sc in last dc, turn.

Row 20: (Ch 3, dc) in first sc, sc in next shell, *(ch 5, sc in next ch sp) 2 times, (shell in next sc, sc in next shell) 4 times, (ch 5, sc in next ch sp) 4 times, (shell in next sc, sc in next shell) 2 times; repeat from * 2 more times, (ch 5, sc in next ch sp) 2 times, shell in next sc, sc in next shell, 2 dc in last sc, turn.

Row 21: Ch 1, sc in first dc, skip next dc, (shell in next sc, sc in next shell or ch sp) 2 times, *(ch 5, sc in next ch sp or shell) 2 times, (shell in next sc, sc in next shell or ch sp) 2 times, (ch 5, sc in next ch sp or shell) 4 times, (shell in next sc, sc in next shell or ch sp) 4 times; repeat from * 2 more times, ch 5, sc in next ch sp, ch 2, skip next dc, sc in last dc, turn.

Diagonal Chains

Continued from page 154

Row 22: (Ch 3, dc) in first sc, sc in next ch sp, ch 5, sc in next ch sp, *(shell in next sc, sc in next shell) 4 times, (ch 5, sc in next ch sp) 4 times, (shell in next sc, sc in next shell) 2 times, (ch 5, sc in next ch sp) 2 times; repeat from * 2 more times, (shell in next sc, sc in next shell) 2 times, 2 dc in last sc, turn.

Row 23: Ch 1, sc in first dc, skip next dc, (shell in next sc, sc in next shell or ch sp) 3 times, *(ch 5, sc in next ch sp or shell) 2 times, (shell in next sc, sc in next shell or ch sp) 2 times, (ch 5, sc in next ch sp or shell) 4 times, (shell in next sc, sc in next shell or ch sp) 4 times; repeat from * 2 more times, shell in next sc, skip next dc, sc in last dc, turn.

Row 24: (Ch 3, dc) in first sc, sc in next shell, *(shell in next sc, sc in next shell) 4 times, (ch 5, sc in next ch sp) 4 times, (shell in next sc, sc in next shell) 2 times, (ch 5, sc in next ch sp) 2 times; repeat from * 2 more times, (shell in next sc, sc in next shell) 3 times, 2 dc in last sc, turn.

Row 25: Ch 1, sc in first dc, skip next dc, *(shell in next sc, sc in next shell or ch sp) 4 times, (ch 5, sc in next ch sp or shell) 2 times, (shell in next sc, sc in next shell or ch sp) 2 times, (ch 5, sc in next ch sp or shell) 4 times; repeat from * 2 more times, (shell in next sc, sc in next shell or ch sp) 3 times, shell in next sc, sc in last dc, turn.

Row 26: (Ch 3, dc) in first sc, sc in next shell, (shell in next sc, sc in next shell) 3 times, *(ch 5, sc in next shell) 4 times, (shell in next sc, sc in next shell) 2 times, (ch 5, sc in next shell) 2 times, (shell in next sc, sc in next shell) 4 times; repeat from * 2 more times, 2 dc in last sc, turn.

Rows 27–139: Repeat rows 3–26 consecutively, ending with row 19. At end of last row, fasten off.

STRIPES

For **each Diagonal Stripe,** using oversize hook and three strands of stripe-color yarn held together as one, join with sl st in edge of Afghan at beginning of Stripe *(see Diagonal Stripes illustration)*; working diagonally toward the upper left in same row of openings, (sl st in corresponding ch-5 sp on next row) across, ending with last sl st at edge of Afghan. Fasten off. Hide ends.

In same manner, using color sequence shown in Diagonal Stripes illustration, make Stripes in each diagonal row of openings over entire Afghan *(Stripes go from lower right to upper left, beginning in row 1 and in ends of rows along long right edge).*

FRINGE

For each **Fringe,** cut eight strands yarn each 16 inches long. Holding all strands together as one, fold in half, insert hook from back to front through edge of Afghan, pull fold through, pull ends through fold, pull snug.

On both short edges, using same color as Diagonal Stripe, make Fringe at end of each Stripe. Using med. teal, make Fringe evenly spaced across remaining med. teal shell-pattern sections *(see Diagonal Stripes illustration).*

Trim Fringe ends even. ❧

Diagonal Stripes

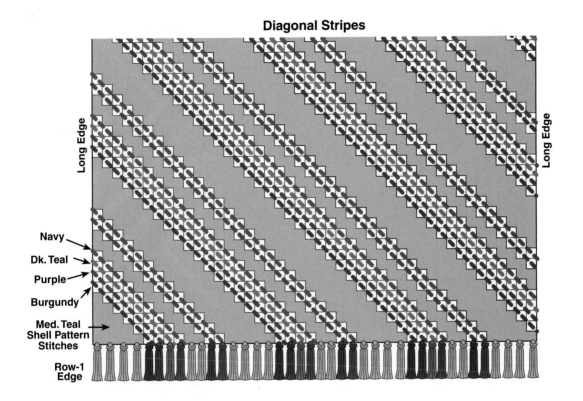

Long Edge

Long Edge

Navy

Dk. Teal

Purple

Burgundy

Med. Teal
Shell Pattern
Stitches

Row-1
Edge

Faux Ripple by Norma Gale

TECHNIQUE
Surface Slip Stitch

FINISHED SIZE
49½ inches x 64½ inches, before adding "ripple" design

MATERIALS
❑ Worsted yarn:
  16 oz. black
  48 oz. of assorted colors—each row requires about 11½ yds.
❑ H hook or size hook needed to obtain gauge

GAUGE
7 sts and chs = 2 inches;
7 sc rows = 2 inches.

BASIC STITCHES
Ch, sl st, sc

READ BEFORE STARTING
All rows are worked with right side facing. Fasten off at end of each row; **do not turn.**

Work over yarn ends as you go.

Make random stripes of 1 to 4 rows of color in no particular order as desired.

INSTRUCTIONS
Row 1: With first color, ch 200, sc in second ch from hook, (sc in next 2 chs, ch 1, skip next ch) 2 times, sc in next 5 chs, ch 1, skip next ch, *(sc in next 2 chs, ch 1, skip next ch) 4 times, sc in next 5 chs, ch 1, skip next ch; repeat from * across to last 6 chs, sc in next 2 chs, ch 1, skip next ch, sc in last 3 chs. Fasten off; **do not turn** (see Read Before Starting). (199 sc and ch-1 sps made)

NOTE: Both sc and ch-1 sps of previous row are referred to as **sts**.

Row 2: Join desired color with sc in first st, *(ch 1, skip next st, sc in next 2 sts—**see Note**) 2 times, ch 1, skip next st, sc in next 3 sts, (ch 1, skip next st, sc in next 2 sts) 2 times, ch 1, skip next st, sc in next st; repeat from * across. Fasten off.

Row 3: Join desired color with sc in first st, sc in next st; *complete the row as follows:
A: (Ch 1, skip next st, sc in next 2 sts) 2 times, ch 1, skip next st, sc in next st, (ch 1,

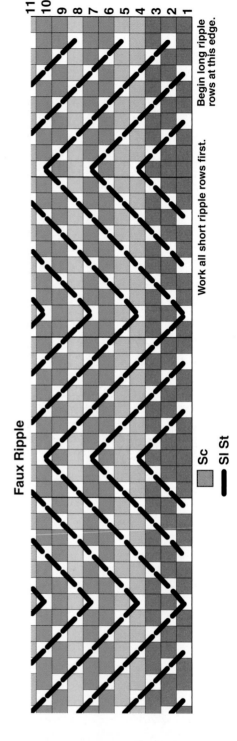

Faux Ripple

Begin long ripple rows at this edge.

Work all short ripple rows first.

☐ Sc
━ Sl St

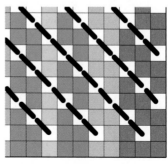

End long ripple rows at this edge.

Faux Ripple
Continued from page 158

skip next st, sc in next 2 sts) 2 times, ch 1, skip next st, sc in next 3 sts;

B: Repeat step A to last 17 sts;

C: (Ch 1, skip next st, sc in next 2 sts) 2 times, ch 1, skip next st, sc in next st, (ch 1, skip next st, sc in next 2 sts) 3 times. Fasten off.

Row 4: Join desired color with sc in first st, sc in next 2 sts, (ch 1, skip next st, sc in next 2 sts) across to last st, sc in last st. Fasten off.

Row 5: Join desired color with sc in first st, *(ch 1, skip next st, sc in next 2 sts) 2 times, ch 1, skip next st, sc in next 3 sts, (ch 1, skip next st, sc in next 2 sts) 2 times, ch 1, skip next st, sc in next st; repeat from * across. Fasten off.

Rows 6–237: Repeat rows 3–5 consecutively, ending with row 3.

Row 238: Join desired color with sc in first st, sc in next 2 sts, *(ch 1, skip next st, sc in next 2 sts) 4 times, ch 1, skip next st, sc in next 5 sts; repeat from * across to last 16 sts, (ch 1, skip next st, sc in next 2 sts) 4 times, ch 1, skip next st, sc in last 3 sts. Fasten off.

TOP STITCH "RIPPLE" DESIGN

For **each row of "ripples",** holding black yarn at back of work and working on front, join with sl st in first skipped ch of sl st "ripple" row *(see graph on page 158),* working according to graph in ch-1 sps of Afghan and keeping sts loose, (sl st in each ch-1 sp up to point, sl st in each ch-1 sp down to base of V) across. At end, remove hook from last loop, insert hook from back through last ch-1 sp, return loop to hook and pull to back of work. Fasten off.

BORDER

Rnd 1: Join black with sc in first st on last row of Afghan; working around all edges and spacing sts so edge lies flat, sc in sts, in ends of rows and in chs on opposite side of row 1 around with 3 sc in each corner, join with sl st in first sc. **Do not fasten off.**

Rnd 2: Ch 1, sc in each st around with 3 sc in each center corner st, join, **turn.**

Rnd 3: Sl st in each st around, join with sl st in first sl st. Fasten off. 🐞

Joining Techniques

By Jennifer McClain

Crochet designers know that proper joining techniques are an asset to any design and often incorporate different methods into a project to enhance its overall appeal. Regardless of the type of joining they choose, they all know that well-made seams, whether sewn or crocheted, are what keep an afghan looking lovely for years to come.

The two most common joining techniques are **sewn seams** and **crocheted seams**. Sewing squares or strips together as shown in "Classic Sampler" on page 100

and "Butterfly Quilt" on page 164 is relatively easy, but not necessarily quick, and care must be taken to keep the seams from showing.

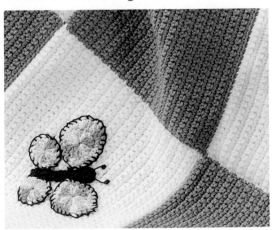

If your seams are to be "invisible," you should always use a blunt-tipped tapestry needle and the same color and/or texture of yarn to match the edges of the strips or motifs. If sewing a dark-colored strip or square to a light-colored one, the light color yarn should be used for the seams. Always leave a long length of yarn at the beginning and end of the seams to allow enough to secure it properly. Do not tie the ends in knots. This will leave a bump and the knots will eventually come loose, causing the seam to come apart.

As you begin the seam, secure the strand by running the needle back and forth through the back side of a few stitches. Be careful not to make the stitches too tight, and always make stitches in the same direction. Once the seam is complete, secure the end as you did at the beginning, then hide the long "tails" by weaving back and forth through the back of the stitches for several inches. Pull the end slightly and clip close to the afghan. This will let the end retract back into the stitches and if done correctly, the end will not show or pop out later.

For those who find sewing too tedious and time-consuming, crocheting the edges together is a much quicker method. "Keep Me in Stitches" on page 94,

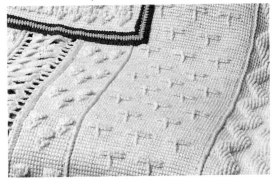

Joining Techniques

Continued from page 162

"Fairy Fluff" on page 118, and "Baby Blocks" on page 130 show the seam created when two pieces are joined using a single crochet stitch. Variations of this method are worked using a taller stitch such as half-double or double-crochet stitches. If taller stitches are used, a wide seam will be formed. Crocheted seams are often worked on the right side of the work so a ridge will separate the pieces, but this method can also be worked from the wrong side of the piece to produce a more "invisible" seam, similar to a sewn seam.

As with sewn seams, be sure to secure your ends well and work the stitches with a good, even tension using the same gauge as the afghan. If the stitches are too tight or too loose, the seam will appear sloppy and the pieces will pucker or separate unevenly.

Crocheted seams can also be worked as part of the design by using chain loops or another combination of stitches. In "Ripple Hairpin Lace" on page 46 and

"Golden Pineapples" on page 61, two strips are held right sides together and are joined by a series of single crochet stitches and chains worked in a pattern. This method creates a "seam" that appears as part of the finished design.

An alternate method of attaching motifs or strips is the **join-as-you-go** technique. This is definitely the preferred technique of some crocheters who do not like to hide the seemingly "hundreds" of ends you can have on an afghan that is sewn together. By working the pieces together as the afghan is made, it saves time and there are fewer ends since the joining yarn is usually just a continuation of the motif or strip. "Granny's Flower Garden" on page 84 is a classic example of a join-as-you-go design. As each tiny motif is stitched, it is joined to the ones next to it. In "Autumn Fields" on page 18 and

"Pretty Baby Pastels" on page 82, the joinings are incorporated as part of the crochet technique and the end result appears to be a one-piece afghan, even though it is comprised of multiple pieces.

Since designers love to be inventive, other joinings are also used, such as the **weaving** method in "Star Stitch Scrap" on page 120. In this afghan, strips are

crocheted, then woven together and attached at the outer edges with an edging. In "Gold & Jewels" on page 28, an embroidery-type stitch is used to "weave" the edges of two panels together and form a beautiful raised design.

As you can see from these examples, joining seams don't have to be dull and boring. They can add a whole new dimension to your afghan and can beautifully enhance the overall design. With patience and practice, you can learn to use the joining techniques shown here to create your own unique variations by combining methods or using different colors or fibers to add personality and visual appeal to your handcrafted afghans. ❧

Afghan
Index

Lend lasting beauty and function to any crocheted project by taking extra care with seams and joinings.

Page 124

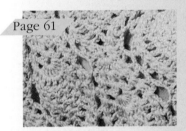

Page 61

Page 118

Page 55

Page 84

Butterfly Quilt by Susie Spier Maxfield

TECHNIQUES
Appliqué and Embroidery Embellishments

FINISHED SIZE
45 inches x 46 inches

MATERIALS
❑ Worsted yarn:
   17½ oz. light purple
   17½ oz. off-white
❑ Cotton sport yarn:
   2 oz. black
   2 oz. variegated
❑ Tapestry needle
❑ H hook or size hook needed to
   obtain gauge

GAUGE
7 sc = 2 inches; 8 sc rows = 2 inches. Each Block is 9 inches x 9¼ inches.

BASIC STITCHES
Ch, sl st, sc, hdc, dc

INSTRUCTIONS

BLOCK (make 13 light purple, 12 off-white)
Row 1: Ch 33, sc in second ch from hook, sc in each ch across, turn. *(32 sc made)*

Rows 2–36: Ch 1, sc in each st across, turn. At end of last row, fasten off.

Alternating colors, matching stitches and rows, sew Blocks together in five rows of five Blocks each *(see photo).*

Blanket Stitch

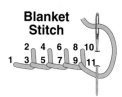

French Knot

Border
Rnd 1: Join off-white with sc in any corner, 2 sc in same corner; working around outer edge, sc in each st and in end of each row around with 3 sc in each corner, join with sl st in first sc. Fasten off.

Rnd 2: Join light purple with sl st in any st, ch 1; working from left to right, reverse sc *(see Stitch Guide on page 175)* in each st around with 2 reverse sc in each center corner st, join. Fasten off.

BUTTERFLY (make 12)
Body
Starting at **head,** with black, ch 2, 6 sc in second ch from hook; for **body,** ch 12, sc in second ch from hook, sc in each ch across, join with sl st in first sc. Fasten off.

Large Wing (make 2)
Rnd 1: With variegated, ch 4, dc 14 times in fourth ch from hook, join with sl st in top of ch-3. *(15 dc made)*

Rnd 2: Ch 1, 2 sc in each of first 2 sts, sc in next 3 sts, 2 sc in next st, 2 hdc in next st, 2 dc in each of next 4 sts, 2 hdc in next st, 2 sc in next st, sc in next st, 2 sc in next st, join with sl st in first sc. Fasten off.

Small Wing (make 2)
With variegated, ch 4, dc 13 times in fourth ch from hook, join with sl st in top of ch-3. Fasten off. *(14 dc)*

With black, using blanket stitch *(see illustration)*, sew Butterfly Body and Wings across each off-white Block facing in same direction *(see photo).*

With black, using straight stitches and French knots *(see illustrations)*, sew two antennae above head on each Block *(see photo).*☙

Straight Stitch

Berry Purple by Diane Simpson

SPECIAL STITCH
Berry Stitch

FINISHED SIZE
48½ inches x 63½ inches

MATERIALS
❑ 56 oz. Purple #27 Canadiana by Patons or worsted yarn
❑ Tapestry needle
❑ I hook or size hook needed to obtain gauge

GAUGE
3 sc = 1 inch; 7 rows = 2 inches.

BASIC STITCHES
Ch, sl st, sc

SPECIAL STITCH
For **berry st (b-st),** insert hook in next st, yo, pull lp through, (yo, pull through one lp on hook) 3 times, yo, pull through 2 lps on hook; push to right side of work.

INSTRUCTIONS

SQUARE (make 12)

Row 1: Ch 45, sc in second ch from hook, sc in each ch across, turn. *(44 sc made)*

Front of row 1 is right side of work.

Rows 2–5: Ch 1, sc in each st across, turn.

Rows 6–10: Ch 1, sc in first 5 sts, **b-st** *(see Special Stitch),* (sc in next st, b-st) across to last 4 sts, sc in last 4 sts, turn. *(18 b-sts, 26 sc)*

Rows 11–16: Ch 1, sc in first 5 sts, b-st, sc in next st, b-st, sc in next 27 sts, (b-st, sc in next st) 2 times, b-st, sc in last 4 sts, turn. *(5 b-sts, 39 sc)*

Rows 17–32: Ch 1, sc in first 5 sts, b-st, sc in next st, b-st, sc in next 6 sts, b-st, (sc in next st, b-st) 7 times, sc in next 6 sts, (b-st, sc in next st) 2 times, b-st, sc in last 4 sts, turn. *(13 b-sts, 31 sc)*

Rows 33–38: Repeat row 11.

Rows 39–43: Repeat row 6.

Rows 44–49: Ch 1, sc in each st across, turn.

Rnd 50: Working around outer edge, ch 1, sc in each st or ch and in end of each row around with ch 2 at each corner, join with sl st in first sc. Fasten off.

ASSEMBLY

1: To join first two rows of Squares, matching sts, hold two Squares with wrong sides together; working through both layers as one, join with *sc in first sc past corner ch sp, (b-st, sc in next st) across to next corner ch sp**, b-st in corner ch sp; pick up next two Squares and repeat from *; continue in this manner until four pairs of Squares are joined, ending last repeat at **. Fasten off.

2: To join third row of Squares, in same manner, join remaining four Squares to one side of assembled Squares forming an afghan three Squares wide and four Squares long.

3: Turn assembled Squares to side and join adjacent loose edges in same manner.

BORDER

Rnd 1: Working around entire outer edge, join with sc in first sc past any corner ch sp, sc in each st around with (sc, ch 2, sc) in each corner ch sp, join with sl st in first sc. *(End with an even number of sts between corner ch sps on each edge.)*

Rnds 2–4: Ch 1, sc in first st, (b-st, sc in next st) around with (sc, ch 2, sc) in each corner ch sp, join, **turn.** At end of last rnd, fasten off.❧

Endless Edgings

by Jennifer McClain

Just as the sewn edges of a garment give it a finished appearance, an edging on an afghan does the same. Whether you choose a simple single crochet edging or something much more elaborate, adding that last little bit to your afghan will be well worth the effort.

Edgings come in all shapes and sizes and, in most cases, you may change the pattern to suit your taste with little difficulty. A **simple single crochet** edging as is used in "Just Geese" on page 116 finishes the edges of the afghan without detracting from the design. For just a tad more impact, use a **reverse single crochet** edging instead *(see "Butterfly Quilt" on page 164)*. These super easy edging treatments work great on almost any design.

To take the plain single crochet edging just a step farther, a **tailored edging** keeps the look simple, yet adds lots of visual appeal. The most common tailored edging is made using several rounds of single crochet as shown in "Checks & Chains" on page 8. The last round can be plain, or use either reverse single or a picot.

Tailored edgings can also be crocheted from taller stitches such as in "Checks & Chains" on page 8, or from pattern stitches *(see "Berry Purple" on page 166 and "Flower Broomstick" on page 14)*. If you use tall stitches, some compensation may need to be made at the corners by adding extra stitches to assure that they lay flat. For **pattern stitches**, you will need to figure the amount of stitches needed for the "repeat," then adjust as needed by skipping a stitch here or there,

or adding an extra at a corner to keep the pattern going correctly. Adjustments to the stitch count can usually be made in the first round of the edging where an extra stitch or two can be added, but you can also make adjustments in the first pattern round by skipping more or less stitches when needed.

For a tailored edging with a touch of femininity, add increases to the second round of the edging and create a **ruffle**. In "Baby Blocks" on page 130, easy double crochet stitches are used to make a gently flowing ruffle around the edge without a lot of work. Just be careful not to add too many increases, or your ruffle will look out of proportion.

Shells are another way to keep the border simple yet more appealing than just a plain flat edging. A single row of shells or scallops as shown in "Spring Fling" on page 34 or "Ripple Hairpin Lace" on page 46 are a sleek addition to an already striking design. Several rounds of shells worked onto each other as illustrated in "Flower Broomstick" on page 14 also make a neat, clean edging but still dress up the design. Be sure to check the number of stitches you will need to keep your pattern repeats even, and adjust accordingly before working the bulk of the edging.

When your afghan just seems to cry out for something really special, a stunning **lace** edging is just the thing you need to add striking beauty. From simply elegant like "Tweed Stripes" on page 50 to the more elaborate style of "Fair Isle" on page 90, lace borders bring a flair unmatched by a plain edging.

For those who like to personalize their projects, beads, ribbon and specialty yarns can be incorporated into an edging for a unique twist. **Specialty yarns** like mohair, boucle or lamé can be used as accents in borders to add texture and color but should be used sparingly so as not to overpower the body of the design. You may add a specialty yarn either by using it for a single row or round, or by holding it together with the regular yarn used for the pattern.

To add **beads,** string the number of beads you will need onto the yarn before you begin stitching and push them back along the yarn until needed. When needed, pull up a bead and complete the stitch or chain around the bead to secure it. Proper placement of the beads is crucial, so be sure to plan ahead. Larger pony or wooden beads work best with yarn, but if a smaller bead is desired, simply string them onto a smaller yarn or thread and hold this together with the regular yarn and work as one.

Ribbon is an easy addition to any border and is simply woven through the stitches once the border is complete. For a ribbon accent with bows at the corners, cut a length of ribbon one-and-a-half times the length of each edge, weave the pieces through the edges as desired and leave the same amount of excess at each corner. After weaving is complete, tie the remaining ends in bows and trim ends. To secure the bows, use sewing thread to tack each bow together at the "knot" so they don't come untied.

When you've worked hard to crochet a great-looking afghan, don't forget to use a great-looking edging to complete it!❧

Afghan
Index

Like frosting on a cake, even the most simple of edgings makes your handcrafted afghan just a little more special.

Page 55

Page 50

Page 130

Page 166

Page 46

Arkadia Mock Ripple by Kathleen Garen

TECHNIQUES
Fringe-As-You-Go Embellishment, Ripple

FINISHED SIZE
45 inches x 51 inches, including fringe

MATERIALS
❑ Worsted yarn:
  16 oz. cream
  10 oz. lt. green
  7 oz. teal
  3 oz. rust
❑ H hook or size hook needed to
  obtain gauge

GAUGE
In ripple pattern, 13 sts = 3 inches,
6 rows = 3 inches.

BASIC STITCHES
Ch, sl st, sc, hdc

INSTRUCTIONS

Row 1: With teal, ch 198, sc in second ch from hook, ch 20, sc in same ch as last sc made, skip next ch, hdc in next 5 chs, 3 hdc in next ch, hdc in next 5 chs, (skip next 2 chs, hdc in next 5 chs, 3 hdc in next ch, hdc in next 5 chs) across to last 2 chs, skip next ch, (sc, ch 20, sc) in last ch. Fasten off. **Do not turn.** *(195 hdc, 2 ch-20 loops made)*

NOTE: *Ch-20 loops form* **fringe.**

Row 2: Join teal with sc in first sc, ch 20, sc in same st as last sc made, skip next st;

working in **back bar of hdc** *(see illustration),* hdc in next 5 sts, 3 hdc in next st, hdc in next 5 sts, (skip next 2 sts, hdc in next 5 sts, 3 hdc in next st, hdc in next 5 sts) across to last 2 sts, skip next st, (sc, ch 20, sc) in last st. Fasten off.

Rows 3–8: With lt. green, repeat row 2.

Rows 9–10: With teal, repeat row 2.

Rows 11–16: With cream, repeat row 2.

Row 17: With rust, repeat row 2.

Row 18: With cream, repeat row 2.

Row 19: With rust, repeat row 2.

Rows 20–25: With cream, repeat row 2.

Rows 26–27: With teal, repeat row 2.

Rows 28–85: Working in color sequence as established in rows 3–27, repeat row 2, ending with teal.

Row 86: Join teal with sc in first st, ch 20, sc in same st as last sc made, skip next st; working in back bars of hdc sts, sc in next 5 sts, 3 sc in next st, sc in next 5 sts, (skip next 2 sts, sc in next 5 sts, 3 sc in next st, sc in next 5 sts) across to last 2 sts, skip next st, (sc, ch 20, sc) in last st. Fasten off.

Row 87: Working on opposite side of starting ch on row 1, join teal with sl st in first ch, sl st in each ch across. Fasten off. ❦

Fun With Fringe & Tassels by Jennifer McClain

If a simple tailored edging is too ho-hum for you, then fringe and tassels are just the thing to spice up your next afghan. From elegant single-strand fringe to fun, chunky tassels, it's easy to breathe new life into a less-than-adventurous design by adding these versatile trims.

The most common fringing method is **separate fringe** where long strands are cut and attached to the edges of the afghan (see Fringe on page 12 for basic instructions). You can easily change the look of the fringe by varying the length, number and color of strands used. Mixing colors is common for patterns that use several shades, but you may wish to use only one for a totally different look. You can also alternate shades every third, fourth or fifth fringe to suit your personal preference. Try different fringe on just one corner of the afghan to get a feel for how they will look; they can easily be removed if you change your mind.

For decorative projects, adding a specialty yarn such as lamé or a mohair-type will lend sparkle and elegance. To incorporate different yarns, simply cut a strand or two the same length as the regular yarn and hold together with the other strands. To really make a statement, you may wish to use more strands of the specialty yarn, or, use yarn that is in complete contrast to the design for even more drama.

The finished length of the fringe and how it is trimmed is just as important as the color and texture. Fringe that is the wrong length or color will take away from the overall look of your afghan. Always start with fringe strands that are longer than needed to allow plenty of room for trimming. However, if you want a more casual look for your afghan or throw, you might consider not trimming the fringe at all. If you want super straight ends, a cutting mat (like the kind quilters use) and rotary cutter work great!

For a really dramatic edging, **Knotted Fringe** fits the bill. As shown in the steps below, using strands at least twice as long as for basic fringe, start Knotted Fringe just as you would regular fringe.

For the second row of knots, beginning at one edge, divide the strands of the first and second fringe knots in half. Using the divided strands, tie another knot 1–2 inches below the first knots, then divide and tie the third fringe with the remaining strands of the second fringe; continue in this manner across the row.

For the third row of knots, tie the remaining strand at end of the previous row with half of the strands from the next knot, then continue across the row as before. Several rows of knots can be added in this manner, depending on the look you wish to achieve. When all rows of knots are finished, leaving ends at least one and a half times as long as the knotted portion, trim all fringe ends even across the row.

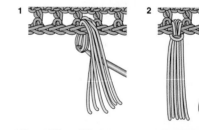

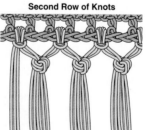
Second Row of Knots

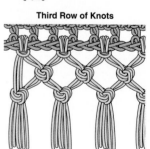
Third Row of Knots

If cutting all those strands sounds a little tedious, then try the fringe-as-you-go method of crocheting the fringe as you work. In "Guatemalan Tapestry" on page 88, you will see that the fringe is stitched on the last round using alternate colors, but a single color can also be used. For a straight edged or panel style afghan, at the ends of the rows, simply chain out the length needed (double the length you want the fringe) and then turn and continue back across the row as shown in "Arkadia Mock Ripple" on page 170.

Tassels are used in much the same way as fringe and will create an entirely different visual effect with only minor changes *(see Tassel instructions on page 31 for basics).* Unlike fringe, tassels are made separate and "sewn" onto the afghan; but if done correctly, they will hold up with time and use just as well. While making the tassel, the single piece of yarn used to tie the tassel strands together at the top should be left at least eight inches long. This allows enough length to sew the tassel to the afghan.

To attach the tassel, thread one of the strands at the top into a tapestry needle and then through the edge of the afghan. Run the needle back through the top of the tassel, going through the "bulb" portion and under the strand used to tie it together. Repeat this process again. Finally, run the needle back through the afghan; take a small tacking stitch on the wrong side of the afghan; then insert the needle down through the center of the tassel and slide it off the strand to hide the end inside the tassel. Trim if needed; then repeat this whole process with the second strand going in the opposite direction as the first. Tassels attached securely will help keep your project looking lovely years longer.

As with fringe, tassels can be changed to suit personal preference simply by varying the color and texture of the yarn. Experiment with different sizes or shades before making all that are needed for the afghan. To add another dimension, use a contrasting color or texture of yarn to make the wraps.

The finishing touches added to your afghan are what make it something special. Don't be afraid to try something out of the ordinary. You may be surprised at the difference the right tassel will make for the look of your project!✿

Afghan
Index

Whether you're feeling frilly or funky, there's a fringe or tassel style to suit your every mood.

Page 12

Page 88

Page 170

Page 24

Page 94

General Information

Yarn and Hooks

Always use the weight of yarn specified in the pattern so you can be assured of achieving the proper gauge. It is best to purchase extra of each color needed to allow for differences in tension and dyes.

The hook size stated in the pattern is to be used as a guide. Always work a swatch of the stitch pattern with the suggested hook size. If you find your gauge is smaller or larger than what is specified, choose a different size hook.

Gauge

Gauge is measured by counting the number of rows or stitches per inch. Each of the patterns featured in this book will have a gauge listed. Gauge for some small motifs or flowers is given as an overall measurement. Proper gauge must be attained for the project to come out the size stated and to prevent ruffling and puckering.

Make a swatch in the stitch indicated in the gauge section of the instructions. Lay the swatch flat and measure the stitches. If you have more stitches per inch than specified in the pattern, your gauge is too tight and you need a larger hook. Fewer stitches per inch indicates a gauge that is too loose. In this case, choose a smaller hook size. Next, check the number of rows. If necessary, adjust your row gauge slightly by pulling the loops down a little tighter on your hook, or by pulling the loops up slightly to extend them.

Once you've attained the proper gauge, you're ready to start your project. Remember to check your gauge periodically to avoid problems later.

Pattern Repeat Symbols

Written crochet instructions typically include symbols such as parentheses, asterisks and brackets. In some patterns a diamond or bullet (dot) may be added.

( ) Parentheses enclose instructions which are to be worked again later or the number of times indicated after the parentheses. For example, "(2 dc in next st, skip next st) 5 times" means to follow the instructions within the parentheses a total of five times. If no number appears after the parentheses, you will be instructed when to repeat further into the pattern. Parentheses may also be used to enclose a group of stitches which should be worked in one space or stitch. For example, "(2 dc, ch 2, 2 dc) in next st" means to work all the stitches within the parentheses in the next stitch.

* Asterisks may be used alone or in pairs, usually in combination with parentheses. If used in pairs, the instructions enclosed within asterisks will be followed by instructions for repeating. These repeat instructions may appear later in the pattern or immediately after the last asterisk. For example, "*Dc in next 4 sts, (2 dc, ch 2, 2 dc) in corner sp*, dc in next 4 sts; repeat between ** 2 more times" means to work through the instructions up to the word "repeat," then repeat only the instructions that are enclosed within the asterisks twice.

If used alone, an asterisk marks the beginning of instructions which are to be repeated. Work through the instructions from the beginning, then repeat only the portion after the * up to the word "repeat"; then follow any remaining instructions. If a number of times is given, work through the instructions one time, repeat the number of times stated, then follow the remainder of the instructions.

[ ] Brackets, ◊ diamonds and • bullets are used in the same manner as asterisks. Follow the specific instructions given when repeating.

Finishing

Patterns that require assembly will suggest a tapestry needle in the materials. This should be a No. 16, No. 18 or No. 26 blunt-tipped tapestry needle. When stitching pieces together, be careful to keep the seams flat so pieces do not pucker.

Hiding loose ends is never a fun task, but if done correctly, may mean the difference between an item looking great for years or one that quickly shows signs of wear. Always leave 6–8 inches of yarn when beginning or ending. Thread the loose end into your tapestry needle and carefully weave through the back of several stitches. Then, weave in the opposite direction, going through different strands. Gently pull the end and clip, allowing the end to pull up under the stitches.

If your project needs blocking, a light steam pressing works well. Lay your project on a large table or on the floor, depending on the size, shaping and smoothing by hand as much as possible. Adjust your steam iron to the permanent press setting, then hold slightly above the stitches, allowing the steam to penetrate the thread. Do not rest the iron on the item. Gently pull and smooth the stitches into shape, spray lightly with starch and allow to dry completely.

Supplier Listing

Stitch Guide

Chain (ch)
Yo, draw hook through lp.

Slip Stitch (sl st)
Insert hook in st, yo, draw through st and lp on hook.

Single Crochet (sc)
Insert hook in st, yo, draw lp through, yo, draw through both lps on hook.

Half Double Crochet (hdc)
Yo, insert hook in st, yo, draw lp through, yo, draw through all 3 lps on hook.

Double Crochet (dc)
Yo, insert hook in st, yo, draw lp through, (yo, draw through 2 lps on hook) 2 times.

Treble Crochet (tr)
Yo 2 times, insert hook in st, yo, draw lp through, (yo, draw through 2 lps on hook) 3 times.

Front Loop/Back Loop (front lp/back lp)

Single Crochet Color Change (sc color change)
Drop first color; yo with 2nd color, draw through last 2 lps of st.

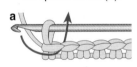

Reverse Single Crochet (reverse sc)
Working from left to right, insert hook in next st to the right (a), yo, draw through st, complete as sc (b).

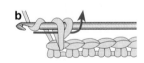

Front Post/Back Post Stitches (fp/bp)
Yo, insert hook from front to back or back to front around post of st on indicated row; complete as stated in pattern.

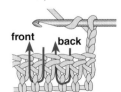

Single Crochet next 2 stitches together (sc next 2 sts tog)
Draw up lp in each of next 2 sts, yo, draw through all 3 lps on hook.

Half Double Crochet next 2 stitches together (hdc next 2 sts tog)
(Yo, insert hook in next st, yo, draw lp through) 2 times, yo, draw through all 5 lps on hook.

Double Crochet next 2 stitches together (dc next 2 sts tog)
(Yo, insert hook in next st, yo, draw lp through, yo, draw through 2 lps on hook) 2 times, yo, draw through all 3 lps on hook.

Standard Stitch Abbreviations

ch(s)	chain(s)
dc	double crochet
dtr	double treble crochet
hdc	half double crochet
lp(s)	loop(s)
rnd(s)	round(s)
sc	single crochet
sl st	slip stitch
sp(s)	space(s)
st(s)	stitch(es)
tog	together
tr	treble crochet
tr tr/ttr	triple treble crochet
yo	yarn over

The patterns in this book are written using American crochet stitch terminology. For our international customers, hook sizes, stitches and yarn definitions should be converted as follows:

US = UK

US		UK
sl st (slip stitch)	=	sc (single crochet)
sc (single crochet)	=	dc (double crochet)
hdc (half double crochet)	=	htr (half treble crochet)
dc (double crochet)	=	tr (treble crochet)
tr (treble crochet)	=	dtr (double treble crochet)
dtr (double treble crochet)	=	ttr (triple treble crochet)
skip	=	miss

Thread/Yarns

Bedspread Weight	=	No. 10 Cotton or Virtuoso
Sport Weight	=	4 Ply or thin DK
Worsted Weight	=	Thick DK or Aran

Measurements

1 inch	=	2.54 cm
1 yd.	=	.9144 m
1 oz.	=	28.35 g

But, as with all patterns, test your gauge (tension) to be sure.

Crochet Hooks

Metric	US	Metric	US
.60mm	14	3.00mm	D/3
.75mm	12	3.50mm	E/4
1.00mm	10	4.00mm	F/5
1.50mm	6	4.50mm	G/6
1.75mm	5	5.00mm	H/8
2.00mm	B/1	5.50mm	I/9
2.50mm	C/2	6.00mm	J/10

Technique Index

Special Stitches & Stitch Patterns Index